5"

D0990924

Oc235 C

12 56C

P. 120-1   Lib.

THE
DESTRUCTION AND
RESURRECTION
OF POMPEII
AND HERCULANEUM

R1134-1

EGON CAESAR CONTE CORTI

THE

DESTRUCTION AND RESURRECTION OF POMPEII AND HERCULANEUM

ROUTLEDGE & KEGAN PAUL

UNTERGANG UND AUFERSTEHUNG VON
POMPEJI UND HERCULANEUM
First published in Germany 1940

THE DESTRUCTION AND RESURRECTION
OF POMPEII AND HERCULANEUM
Translated by K. AND R. GREGOR SMITH

First published by
ROUTLEDGE & KEGAN PAUL LTD
Broadway House, 68–74 Carter Lane
London, E.C.4
1951

Printed and bound in Great Britain by William Clowes and Sons, Limited,
London and Beccles

CONTENTS

SH 93X.7 C82QuE

Rel 24554

SH-A 20 Sep 51 Wittenborn 4.50 (Arch)

v

423725

ILLUSTRATIONS

vii

FOREWORD

HISTORICAL research is in a sense comparable with a kind of chase, in which the game — in this case the documents — has to be tracked down in the paper forests of archives both at home and abroad. In the course of this chase through the archives of many towns I came to Naples, to which I had till then paid only one fleeting visit as a tourist. The secrets of the buried towns of Pompeii and Herculaneum have always fascinated me, but the explanations of the guide-books and my own too superficial visit to the cities did not satisfy me. So I looked for a book which, without going into too much detail, could provide me with a readily understandable and clear survey not only of the historic eruption of Vesuvius in A.D. 79, but also of the re-discovery and resurrection of the classical sites buried by that eruption. Though there is an enormous number of praise-worthy and penetrating monographs on the subject, both archaeological and historical, there is no short summary which is both popular and comprehensive. So I resolved, in order that I might teach myself, to attempt this task, with the help of the available literature and of my own investigations.

Fully conscious of my archaeological and other imperfections, I should not have dared to approach such a task if I had not been assured of the support and the co-operation, both in testing and improving my work, of the outstanding living expert on the conditions of Pompeii and Herculaneum. His Excellency Professor Dr Amedeo Maiuri, member of the Roman Academy and Superintendent of classical remains in the provinces of Naples, Avellino and Benevento, has helped me in the kindest way in my work in Naples, Pompeii and Herculaneum, has given me access to museums and archives, and finally has read and improved my work. He has also given the greatest help in the matter of the illustrations. I have therefore to thank my distinguished colleague most profoundly.

ix

My hearty thanks are also due to His Excellency Benedetto Croce, to Professor Matteo della Corte, famed for his out-standing work in Pompeii and for innumerable excellent monographs which he put at my disposal, to the Director of the National Archives in Naples, Count Ricardo Filangieri di Candida Gonzaga, and his kind assistant Dr Onofrio Pasanisi, and to the ladies and gentlemen of the National Museum in Naples. In Rome I am especially obliged to the helpful librarian of the Archaeological Institute, Dr Jan W. Crous.

If in spite of all my care errors have crept into my book, I should like to emphasise that it is particularly difficult always to find the right way through material that is both much debated and remote in time, where so much is still unex-plained and at the mercy of conflicting opinions. But taken as a whole, this book will, I believe, give the reader, in the illus-trations and in the text, an idea of those memorable cities, resurrected from classical times, which will stir him to visit them. With its help the cities will be able to make their effect on a much better-stored understanding than that of the many thousands of tourists who have never been able to work through the whole immense literature of the subject.

So I hope that my book will awaken in wide circles both interest in and understanding of the great cultural achieve-ment in Pompeii and Herculaneum, or, where that interest exists already, will further and deepen it. In this way I hope to increase the delight in the recovery of those incomparable mirrors of classical life.

Summer 1940   THE AUTHOR.

1

PRE-HISTORY AND ORIGIN OF POMPEII AND HERCULANEUM

TILL 80 *B.C.*

" I cannot easily think of anything more interesting. . . ."
Goethe about Pompeii, 13 March, 1787.

THE primitive history of life in the fertile Apennine peninsula, which divides the Mediterranean into two parts, is to this day not clear. We have long had firm historical dates, established by scientific research, for many other peoples settled on the shores of this enormous basin, but the early history of the peninsula is still sunk in the darkness and mist of legend. Who the first settlers of modern Italy were and what was the provenance of its Stone Age dwellers are still conjectural questions. It is certain only that the original tribes settled partly in those regions whose heights offered greater security against enemies and partly where they were attracted by the special fertility of the district. In the mountain country men lived mostly on scattered country farms (for each could easily defend himself); while in the flat fertile districts, which were more difficult to defend, several families joined in a communal life and surrounded their camp with ditches and stockades as a protection against enemies from without. Soon settled homes arose, and thus the nucleus of settlements which flourished and gradually became villages and towns.

In the latter districts was included the land round the richly blessed gulf of modern Naples, which even in the earliest ages was called "the crater" on account of its circular form. On the northern edge of this circle lying open to the sea

1

and also on the heights east of Naples were signs, such as the shape of the hills, warm sulphur springs, and the like, which bore witness to the volcanic character of large parts of the land bordering the gulf. Earthquakes, too, were frequent in this district, afflicting both the mainland and the islands north and south of the gulf, such as Ischia and Capri. So, too, the upper part of the bay of Naples was later given the name, which may still be heard, of the "phlogistic" or "burning" fields. On the other hand — and on account of this volcanic character — the soil round the gulf was extremely fertile. It produced everything almost of itself without cultivation. Apples and pears, cherries and figs, melons, almonds, quince, chestnuts and pomegranates, wheat and millet, barley and vegetables of every kind, and above all vines—all grew there in first-rate quality, and friendly Nature often permitted two or even three harvests of grain in the year.

Above the gulf towered a mountain, now called Vesuvius, which was one of the volcanically active formations of the district, and in remote times in terrible eruptions poured streams of molten lava over the surrounding countryside. On one such occasion a particularly powerful stream of lava poured out from Vesuvius in a south-easterly direction, and finally, about a quarter of a mile before it reached the sea, not far from the mouth of a river (the Sarno), came to an abrupt halt and cooled. So there arose in the plain near the sea an extended, isolated hill, about a hundred feet in height. It ended in the direction of the sea at the point where the lava had suddenly broken into two tongues and piled up. During that eruption, of which there is no tradition, the earliest inhabitants of these regions probably died or fled; but as the settlements would be sparse at first and the loss of life consequently slight, memory of the event completely disappeared in the course of time.

Vesuvius remained inactive for many centuries, perhaps millennia, the crater completely closed up, and the mountainside was covered with vines and trees to a great height; the danger was in course of time completely forgotten, and only a faint echo of it survived in legend. There was no more than idle talk of a battle of giants with the gods. The victorious lords of heaven, armed with thunder and lightning, were said to have forced the defeated giants down into the earth, where

2

they lay beneath the weight of the mountains, and now and then shook themselves in a wild effort to win free of their graves; this was felt by the mannikins above as earthquakes. So runs the legend, which is told especially of the extinct volcano on the island of Ischia.

The great stream of lava which sprang from that eruption of a dim early age was slowly covered with a layer of humus and fresh greenery. To an incoming tribe it offered a welcome possibility, amid the marshy land of the river Sarno, of establishing a settlement in a position which was both dry and, owing to its slight elevation, somewhat protected. Meanwhile, Vesuvius itself was completely quiescent. Where the great crater must once have been there was now only a flat, bare and unproductive plain, which, with its smoky pumice-stone and ash-coloured cinders, still gave the impression that something had once burnt there.[1] But in the course of centuries this sign alone remained to show that Vesuvius contained something uncanny, and even this sign was only noticed by clever and observant men. The people who dwelt there in their succeeding generations had not the remotest notion of any danger threatening them from the mountain; they peacefully built their homes on the cold lava, and thus there gradually arose the little place later called Pompeii, a name whose origin is still in dispute and not definitively explained.

The communities which arose in this way were, however, still weak in defence. They could defend themselves only against wild animals or scattered groups, and were defence-less against heavy attack by a more civilised and therefore better armed people. The earliest settlers, who bore the tribal name of the Osci, were too immersed in the struggle for their daily bread and for personal security against dangers of every kind to take much notice of nature round about them, and considered the land on which they lived and built and slept as completely unchanging, solid and secure.

This was the state of affairs when, about 1100 B.C., a stream of tribes from the north, seeking new homes — the so-called Dorian wandering — made its way towards Greece. This little peninsula was soon not able to contain its original inhabitants plus the Dorian and other immigrants. As a result

[1] See Strabo, *Description of the Earth*, V, 4, viii.

of the battles and troubles which ensued, many of the best men of the old Greek stock, such as the Aeolians and the Ionians, were forced to leave their home and seek a new one on the coasts of the Aegean and the Black Sea, and soon, indeed, on most of the shores of the Mediterranean basin. In this way Ionian ships were the first to reach the southern edges of the boot-shaped peninsula, which at that time still had no name as a whole, and the Ionians established themselves first of all where natural harbours offered protection and accommodation for their ships. As early as approximately 800 B.c. they founded a trading settlement, called Cumae, on the northern side of the gulf of Naples, and coming from Sicily settled the southern tip of the peninsula as well as the gulf of Tarentum. The immigrants were charmed by the fertility of the land, and above all praised its wealth of cattle. It was at this time that the name (V)Italy, supposed to be derived from the Oscan word *viteliú* = *vitulus* = calf, gradually began to spread over the whole peninsula, which was thus described as "rich in calves".

The Greek immigrants, who came from the very adaptable Ionian merchant people, easily came to terms with the native inhabitants, and mixed with them without any significant struggles. The one side learned from the other, the Oscans naturally learning more from the more highly cultured Greeks. So in course of time the whole area round the gulf of Naples, from the foothills of Misenum to Cumae, Pozzuoli and Parthenope, and soon Pompeii and Nuceria to the east as well, was settled by Greeks, who remained, however, principally on the coast. The settlement in the area of modern Naples was still called Parthenope, after the dangerous siren of that name. From remote times a road ran from there along the coast, as far as Pompeii at the foot of Vesuvius, and there branched in two, the one continuing on the peninsula of Sorrento which bounds the gulf to the south, the other heading by way of Nuceria (Salerno) to the southern tip of Italy, where Rhegion (Reggio) arose.

In the intellectual sphere the original inhabitants had almost nothing to give to the Greeks. They preserved their language, indeed, but for the rest they succumbed to the influences of the foreign conqueror. Soon there arose a garland of Greek settlements around the gulf, and at different times

1. The 'Ephebos' (Greek youth under military training) comes to light. The splendid bronze statue, after a Greek original of the fifth century B.C., emerges from the volcanic cinders (lapilli). It stood in the house of a wealthy merchant, P. Cornelius Tegetus. The right arm held an oil-lamp.

(See pages 76, 203)

Photo: Exclusive News Agency, Ltd.

2. Aerial View of Pompeii.

The upper road from left to right is the Nolan Way, the road leading off the market-place or forum to the right is the Street of Abundance.

(*See page* 210)

fortified coastal bases were built; it was as one of these that Herculaneum was established, between Pompeii and Parthenope (Naples), next the coast road at the foot of Vesuvius. But while Herculaneum was at first merely a transit point, pleasantly enough situated, it was soon evident that Pompeii, built somewhat farther off on the lava hill, adjacent to the mouth of the navigable Sarno, with its possibilities as a harbour, and at the crossing of important roads, was eminently suited to become an important commercial town. So the Greeks turned their attention to this place, erecting there buildings which faithfully reflected the unique cultural and religious qualities of their homeland.

In the rest of Italy the wandering of the tribes in the peninsula had gradually ceased. In modern Tuscany there dwelt the strongest race of the time, the Etruscans; to the east, beyond the Tiber and in the northern Apennines, dwelt the Umbrians and the Sabines; and south of the river the Latins and the Volscians. Beyond these, in the mountains fringing the fruitful gulf-land, dwelt the tough and warlike Samnites. Relations between these tribes, however, were still not completely stabilised. The Etruscans were the strongest of them; they had become great by sea commerce and piracy, and soon spread out northwards as far as the Po and southwards by Rome and the district of Latium as far as the gulf-land of Naples. There is no doubt that the Etruscans occupied Capua, and possibly extended their power much further to the south, so that Herculaneum and Pompeii might for a time have come under their rule. But this is by no means certain; it is not certain indeed that there was Etruscan influence even in religion and architecture. On this point scholars are at variance.

From the eighth century B.C. till the beginning of the fifth is the period of the great development of Etruscan power; thereafter it began to diminish. In a battle fought out near Cumae the Greeks of southern Italy brought to an end, after hard struggles, the dominion of that people in the southern part of the peninsula.

Meanwhile there had arisen in the plain of the Tiber, and in the most favourable position on hilly land, a settlement called Rome, which first rose and flourished under the rule of Etruscan kings. When the city succeeded, shortly before

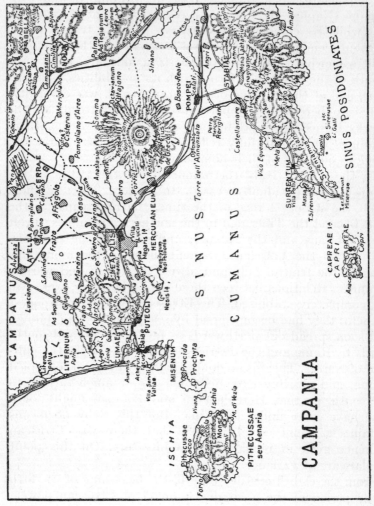

Map of the District round Vesuvius (Beloch, Campania).

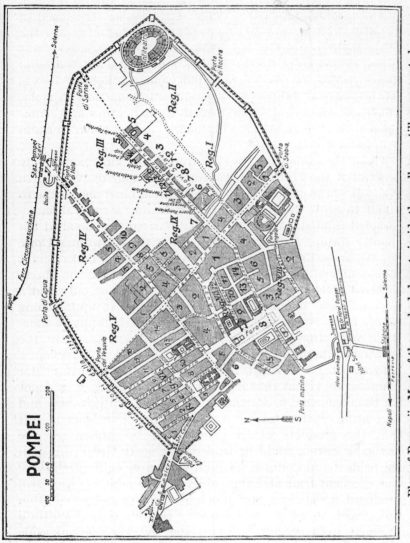

Plan of Pompeii. Most of the unshaded parts inside the walls are still unexcavated.

500 B.C., in breaking free from Etruscan domination, its expansion began, first through Latium and then gradually through all the neighbouring tribes. This expansion was the seed of the city's lordship not merely over all Italy but also over the whole Mediterranean world. This development, however, was at first slow; except for the Sabines none of the tribes around Rome yielded its freedom and independence lightly. It was this necessity of fighting for supremacy in tenacious struggles which exercised and strengthened Roman arms and, combined with their political skill, finally enabled them to claim the mastery of the world.

About the same time Greek culture had almost completely penetrated the Oscan regions round the gulf of Naples. In Pompeii, at the place where the lava stream had once come to a halt towards the south and west, raising a natural three-cornered rampart, there had already arisen the so-called triangular forum, a kind of Acropolis with a towering Doric temple, accessible through Propylaea, that is, a hall of eight Ionian pillars. It stood on the highest point of the three-cornered level space on the lava hill, which not only had a splendid view, but also made it possible for an approaching enemy to be espied in good time. For these buildings a limestone was often used, which, as wealth increased in the growing town, gradually replaced the old circles of stockades.

From 500 B.C. Pompeii became increasingly important, for it was soon evident that it could be used not only as a depot for the commerce of Parthenope (Naples), with Stabiae and Sorrentum on the Stabian Way, as well as with Nuceria, but that the products of the hinterland, brought down the navigable Sarno, could be loaded here on to Greek ships. In the fields round Pompeii splendid vines were cultivated, there was excellent fruit and vegetables, and in addition the town produced a delicious and much-liked sauce, prepared from fish, which found a wide market. Besides the agricultural products from nearby Vesuvius and the whole countryside there was pumice-stone in plenty which was exported in large quantities both as whetstone and cleansing material.

At first most of the houses of the growing town were built of limestone and in the old style: round about the "atrium", the chief room in the centre, were arranged the small bedrooms and dining-room. This atrium, so called from the smoke

8

of the fireplace, which blackened the walls (*ater* = black), had a roof which sloped down to the centre, leaving a square opening. This served to take away the smoke, as well as to let in the light, and the rain-water, which was collected in a shallow basin on the floor. Originally this sharply sloping roof was sustained by only two beams,[1] but in the Hellenic era the opening in the atrium was often supported by pillars at each corner.

Naturally such houses were small and cramped, and dark too, since light entered only from the opening in the roof. At first the atrium served as kitchen and as dining-room, so that in fact the whole life of the house was lived there. The only disadvantage was that from the roof uninvited guests could spy out the life of the people in the house, which happened only too frequently, and gave writers like Plautus material for their comedies. The very small adjacent rooms were used solely as bedrooms. Only as prosperity increased did the houses of Pompeii and Herculaneum become more richly appointed and more comfortable. Soon there were added to the atrium one or even several courts surrounded by pillars (peristyles), round which more living-rooms were built. Thus countless houses arose in the towns on the gulf which combined the Hellenic with the old Italian style of architecture.

Besides the little three-cornered forum there was another, square in form: at first intended only as a market-place, it later became the most fashionable meeting-place for the people. As a result, proud temples and stately civic buildings rose about this square. Around 400 B.C. the population can be reckoned at about three thousand, of which approximately two-thirds were the original native inhabitants.

By this time Pompeii was probably surrounded by a wall, but neither the colonising Greeks nor the indigenous Oscans were particularly warlike. The fine air, the warm climate, the fertility of the land as it were tossed everything into the laps of the inhabitants, and multiplied their wealth, but softened them, and drew to them, as they waxed in prosperity, the envy and covetousness of the much ruder and more warlike tribes of the Samnites dwelling in the mountains to the east.

---

[1] The oldest example of such a house is that of the "doctor" in Pompeii, so called because a great many surgical instruments from Roman times were found there.

The whole district, from the gulf to the foot of the Samnite mountains, acquired the name of Campania, and not only Pompeii but all the cities founded by the Greeks in this region attracted the Samnite lust for plunder. The original settlement, Parthenope (north of the modern Castell dell' Ovo in Naples), had extended and embraced the "old city", Palaeopolis; in the fifth century the new city, Neapolis, arose as a result of an influx from the Greek island of Euboea, and finally absorbed the two earlier settlements. The increasing wealth of this city, too, through its trade with Greece, and the slightness of its precautions against hostile raids, were contributory causes of the invasion finally launched by the Samnites. The Samnites stormed out of their mountain country westwards and southwards to the coast and in a short time the whole of Campania and the fine district on the gulf, and with it the oldest Greek colony of Cumae, were in their hands, and Herculaneum and Pompeii were soon added. Meanwhile the Hellenic people in far Greece were at grips with one another in the Peloponnesian civil war and could not help their colonies. This happened in the last third of the fifth century, about 420 B.C.

Physically and militarily the Samnites were the stronger, but in spirit the defeated Greeks and hellenised Oscans proved their superiors, and it was not long before the conquering mountain people adopted Greek culture and customs. The victors, too, grew accustomed to good living, to beauty in art, and to handsome and comfortable dwelling-houses and public buildings. In the time that followed, the destiny of the communities of Pompeii and Herculaneum, as well as of the whole of Campania, was determined by these influences, with the Samnite influence as the chief. Everything remained more or less as before the Samnite conquest: the Greek divinities, Zeus, Apollo and Athens, were worshipped as before, and business was continued, the only change being that greater attention was paid to the fortification of the towns, in particular of Pompeii. Between 400 and 300 the outer walls, which had not been touched by the Oscans, were reconstructed and much strengthened,[1] and this was indeed necessary, for Rome's growing power was reaching out to possess

[1] Amedeo Maiuri, *Studi e ricerche sulla fortificazione di Pompei*, Rome, 1930.

the lovely and fertile Campania, which the Samnites, hitherto friendly with the Romans, defended in three campaigns of varying fortunes.

In this period, in the year 302 B.C., Pompeii is mentioned for the first time in a historical context. During the second Samnite war the Roman admiral Publius Cornelius brought a number of galleys to the mouth of the Sarno, which was the harbour of Pompeii; the crews pushed on up the river, reached Nuceria, and plundered and robbed whatever they could lay hands on. Then the inhabitants of the neighbouring cities, fearing a like fate, rose up, banded together, attacked the Romans, who were heavy-laden with booty, tore their plunder from them, killed many of them, and chased the rest back to their ships, which put out to sea with all speed. But that was only an episode; the Romans finally succeeded, about 290 B.C., in defeating the Samnites completely and bending them beneath the Roman yoke.

Everything that was built remained, as before, under Hellenic influence. Everywhere, in the public squares, on the temples and in the houses of Pompeii there arose the slender picturesque pillars of various types. The building material, however, was not noble: since the limestone had long been exhausted, use was made of the hardened volcanic ash of the greyish-yellow tufa, which was broken up at Nuceria and could be readily worked — and it occurred to none to wonder how this material had come into existence. With peace the people again increased in prosperity, and to satisfy their growing desire for self-assertion they covered the walls of their houses with fine stucco, which was meant to look like marble and expensive stone. The square forum developed in grandeur. Beside it there arose, on the high crest, a proud temple to Apollo, girt with Corinthian pillars. In the holy of holies there was a picture of Apollo, and in front of the steps leading up to the temple stood the altar on which burnt offerings were presented to the deity.

As this forum, later paved with great flagstones, grew in size and importance, the triangular forum gradually became less important, and finally, when for some unexplained reason the old Greek temple, built on the spot where long ago the lava had halted in its tracks, fell into ruin, it was not built up again in the old form. In course of time the triangular

11

forum, while preserving the associations of a place dedicated to the gods, became a public pleasure resort. There the Pompeians were wont to take their ease and enjoy in peace the fine panorama of the gulf. The pillared arcades which gradually arose round the forum provided shelter in sudden bad weather, and there were seats and amenities of all kinds.

The desire for amusement and the higher cultural level of the people which had resulted from Greek influence soon gave the impulse to the building of a theatre near this old forum, now given over wholly to recreation. It was planned to hold an audience of about five thousand people, since Pompeii had now become a well-populated town. The building was provided first with two, later three, circles; and, nearby, a palaestra, a sports ground for the youth, was constructed, while south of the theatre arose a great building with huge pillared halls, which offered shelter in rainy weather to the audiences at the comedy, as well as accommodation for the actors and other theatre people. Thus in course of time the triangular forum became the centre of a pleasure city, which was soon to prove too small for the increasing population, the more so as inhabitants of nearby places attended the festivals.

It was probably in the second century B.C. and clearly under Roman influence that there arose an enormous bathing-place, the Stabian Thermae, so named because it stood at the corner of the main Stabian Way and the road leading to the harbour (the Street of Abundance). These baths grew in size and splendour in the years that followed, and to them was added a great pillared courtyard as a gymnastics exercise ground. Everything was there, from the individual room to the great communal swimming-pool, from the Turkish bath in dry air to the warm water baths at varying degrees of heat according to taste. Clothes were put away in special niches by slave attendants. Heating was ingeniously laid on beneath the floor and arranged to suit the varying temperatures of the water. Men and women were still separated. In the evening and at night too the baths were used, for in every room shallow earthenware oil-lamps were hung, either singly or in clusters on high candelabra. So the Thermae were fitted out in time with every comfort and adornment: a place of luxury, refreshment and pleasure where the day's burden and cares could be forgotten.

Contemporaneously with the development of public buildings in the Samnite-Greek era, when Roman influence had still not reached its height, there was progress in the building of private houses. At first the living premises were for the most part on one floor; their façades only were built of dressed stones, for the rest a mortar was used in which stone chips could be set. Most of the walls were built of this so-called *opus incertum*. In the interior of the houses the walls were painted in different colours, but not with pictures, for there was still no naturalistic painting. The walls were skilfully painted in bright yellow or red, in such a way as to give the impression that they consisted of dressed stone. This style, which dates back to the fourth or third century, has usually been termed the first style; its aim was to deceive, it achieved a counterfeit splendour.

In the second style, which made its appearance about the first century B.C., the walls displayed paintings of pillars and arches designed to give an illusion of space and grandeur to the rooms. This style, reflecting as it did the desire of the citizens of Pompeii to make an impression of luxury and wealth beyond their means, persisted until Roman influence alone became determinative, though some few great and lavishly decorated houses were in fact built by distinguished citizens who were rich by heritage or trade. There was one, for instance, on the street leading to the East Gate in the direction of Nola, the so-called House of the Faun. There were two atria, one of them showing the oldest form with mere supporting posts, the other the opening of the atrium in the roof, flanked by four columns. Beside the rain basin stood a beautiful statuette of a dancing faun. Around the atrium were the living-room, the dining-room and the reception-room, and narrow passages led to a magnificent adjoining peristyle, a hall, that is, with columns in the Greek fashion, surrounding decorative flower-beds. Behind this peristyle there was, in this house as in others belonging to rich people, a second large peristyle, which surrounded a garden. The inhabitant of this house had heard of the deeds of Alexander the Great with astonishment and admiration, and his wealth permitted him to have copied, in mosiac, a Hellenistic painting representing the personal encounter of that hero with King Darius of Persia at the battle of Issus in

333 B.C. This work of art decorated the floor of a spacious hall, the most splendid room in the house.[1]

It is evident that a rich and distinguished family of either Oscan or Samnite origin had united two or more houses here of different periods and supplied them with the latest achievements of Greek progress and luxury. Apart from the painted architecture there were no paintings adorning the walls, but the lovely mosaics on the floor made amends. At the entrance a (H)Ave, worked into the floor in coloured marble mosaic, greeted the visitor. Within the house itself there were other charming mosaics, fighting cocks, white doves drawing a string of pearls out of a small coloured box, little birds, fish, and shell creatures, all of them of a high technical and artistic standard. In this home of a rich and cultured Pompeian of Roman origin are to be found, because it had developed from the simplest to the richest dwelling-place, every feature characteristic of the houses of the period.

The political situation, however, was still troubled, so that in the second Samnite-Roman period of Pompeii, that is, about 300–180 B.C., there was added to the outer wall, which had surrounded the town from earlier times, an inner wall which greatly strengthened the town's defensive resources.

The smaller Herculaneum, situated halfway between Pompeii and Naples, and less than three miles distant from either, had shared in the Greek-Samnite influence, and the slowly following Roman influence. But on the whole the fortified port on the slopes of Vesuvius had not developed as had Pompeii, because from its inception it had been thought of as a place of transit. It was too near the great town of Naples to develop an independent activity of its own, nor had it any connexion with its hinterland, not being situated, like Pompeii, on a navigable river. Thus the main occupation of its inhabitants, besides agriculture, was fishing, and it was only slowly that one or two patrician houses arose, belonging to Neapolitans who had become rich and longed for more quiet, in pleasanter surroundings, away from the stir and bustle of the town. The port of the little town was, indeed, better developed, but the town itself remained small; the religious needs of the inhabitants were cared for by several beautiful temples.

[1] Called the *exedra*.

The unification of Italy under Roman leadership had meanwhile, in many struggles, made great progress. Rome had gradually become the strongest military power of the cultural world of the Mediterranean. After the defeat of the Italian seaports its economy had changed slowly from agriculture to world trade; and world trade meant mastery of the sea and engagement in world politics. But Carthage was not completely overthrown after the First Punic War. A provisional decision between the two western powers was reached only in the strife of the Second Punic War, when Hannibal overpoweringly defeated the Romans at Cannae and in their ears sounded the terrible cry: "Hannibal is at the gates!" Then the Samnites, and with them most of the Greek towns of Lower Italy, including the places subject to their influence, Herculaneum and Pompeii, thought that the hour had come to throw off the Roman yoke. The city of Capua joined forces with the Carthaginian victor, opened its gates to him, and thus hoped to win complete independence from Rome. But in the year 215 B.C. the Romans defeated Hannibal at Nola, and in order to save his army he was forced to leave the allied towns of Campania in the lurch. Capua was taken, and harshly punished. When the battle of Zama, which took place in 202 on African soil, brought about the complete defeat of Carthage, it was clear that this victory would result in the absolute domination by Rome of the whole western Mediterranean, together with the complete romanisation of Lower Italy and thus of all the towns round the bay of Naples. The only questions at issue concerned the extension of Roman citizenship and the limits to be set to the self-administration and self-government of the defeated tribes and towns.

None of them, however, willingly assumed the Roman yoke. The original Oscan inhabitants, like the later Greek colonists and the Samnites, still hoped for an opportunity to throw off the Roman tyranny. These expectations were nourished by the inner tensions in Rome, which were to be fought out now that the foreign struggles were over. Bitter strife convulsed the city about the form of the state, and social revolutions threatened the rule of the Senate. As Roman citizenship was denied to or withdrawn from several Italian tribes and towns at the same time, the Samnites took advantage of the consequent discontent to put themselves anew at the head of a coalition, which led to open battle in the so-called Confederates' War. The walls of the towns were speedily strengthened with towers, then Pompeii and Herculaneum, like other Italian towns, rose up in the year 91 B.C. in opposition to Lucius Cornelius Sulla, the commander on the Roman side, a man of unscrupulous brutality and decisive energy, who had restored the threatened rule of the Senate and had now undertaken to fight the rebellious tribes. At Stabiae, hardly two miles from Pompeii, he first encountered the enemy, who were commanded by the Samnite Pontius, on whose side many Pompeians were fighting. But this part of their army was beaten by the Romans, and Stabiae was terribly destroyed. Sulla had also sent to Herculaneum the legate Titus Tidius, who took the little town by storm, but was himself killed. After Herculaneum had submitted unconditionally, his legion rejoined Sulla's army, which marched upon Pompeii at the end of the spring of 89 B.C. The Romans attacked the town from the north, concentrating their heavy showers of stones on the sector of wall between the so-called Porta Vesuvio and Porta Ercolanense. The storming-party followed, but in vain. Twice the Romans were thrown back from the gates and walls of Pompeii with bleeding heads. From the summer of 89 till the winter of 88 the town maintained its resistance; to this day inscriptions in the Oscan-Samnite language on the walls bear witness to these fights. They indicate the positions of the defendants, and even the name of Sulla, the beleaguerer, is to be found inscribed on the inner wall of a tower. The names, too, of the commanders of several sections can be read there, for instance, that of Lucius Popidius, who commanded an important part, if not the whole, of the Pompeian force. This man belonged to one of the most distinguished families of Pompeii, which at all times helped to fill the most important civic offices. Though the houses lying outside the walls and the walls themselves suffered, the town itself escaped, at least for the time being, the bitter fate of Stabiae.

The town continued to resist; then the Confederates sent reinforcements under Lucius Cluentius, which threatened Sulla's troops without heeding the unfavourable nature of the territory. The Romans were able to attack them and overthrow them completely. They pursued Cluentius, who had withdrawn on Nola, and there once more defeated him, so thoroughly that Sulla was able to penetrate into the heart of Samnium and take its capital.

In this way Pompeii escaped direct capture and destruction. But the final victory had fallen to the Romans, who cleverly strengthened themselves by granting Roman citizenship to those of their allies who had remained loyal, as well as to the newly made allies. In this way the rebellion was deprived of its last supports, its expansion was prevented and the rising of Campania and Lower Italy was at an end.

The land and its cities were now wholly at the mercy of Rome. On the whole the victors treated the defeated mildly, leaving them more or less to govern themselves, only adjusting things to suit Roman forms and Roman law. Sulla, however, after his victory over Mithridatus in Greece, did not forget the resistance of Pompeii, which had never been properly overcome in the field. When the town, like all other places in the Campania, at last opened its gates to the Romans, the dictator gave orders, in 80 B.C., that a great many veterans should be settled in it under the leadership of his nephew Publius Sulla. These were intended to be a safeguard against any possible movements of independence. One third of the landed property of the town was requisitioned and handed over to these veterans, and thus Pompeii was sharply punished for its resistance. This led, of course, to some opposition and to violent strife; but as the event proved, this colonisation had its advantages for the town, for it provided a certain guarantee of safety and protection against dangers threatening from outside.

No such colony was settled in Herculaneum; but it was just as dependent on Rome. Henceforward the Roman Senate was responsible for the administration of the whole of Campania. Henceforward, too, Roman life and customs penetrated deeply into the life of Campania, and thus of Pompeii and Herculaneum. Pompeii received the name Colonia Veneria Cornelia Pompeianorum, after the goddess of the town, Venus Pompeiana, and the family name, Cornelius, of the dictator Sulla. He chose Venus, for she was his favourite goddess, even as she was of the Pompeians; to her protection he ascribed all the happy events of his life, among them the occupation of this town. The Samnite element lost its political power completely, the Oscan-Samnite language slowly gave way to Latin, and in outward appearance the towns were more and more adapted to the Roman model. But there were other influences too.

The lively sea-traffic with the Hellenistic east, especially with the Egyptian port of Alexandria, not only helped Alexandrine art to penetrate the coastal towns, including of course Pompeii and Herculaneum, but also paved the way, from 150 B.C., for religious influences. The inhabitants of Campania were very susceptible to those cults which contained mystical amd mysterious elements giving scope to the imagination. So alongside Zeus, Apollo and Venus, worship of the Egyptian Isis was practised, that goddess of heaven who, with her husband and brother Osiris, was one of the most popular Egyptian deities of the Nile. Sorcery and worship of the dead played a great part. Isis was above all the patron goddess of navigation, and as Pompeii's importance as a port and trading centre grew, a temple was erected near the great theatre in honour of this goddess — usually represented as a woman with cow's horns and a solar disc on her head.

The political revolution, the transition to full Roman influence, continued, meanwhile, relatively quickly and painlessly. The peoples of the towns of Campania soon recognised the advantages which came from their submission to a world-power, and appreciated the delight and enthusiasm of the Roman guests, who flocked to see the magic garden round the gulf of Naples and the beauty of its scenery. After all, they had not been wholly free in bygone times, and the new régime was certainly preferable to the rough one of the Samnites. Thus Pompeii and Herculaneum enter their purely Roman time.

2

UNDER ROMAN RULE. THE EARTH-QUAKE OF A.D. 63

80 *B.C.–A.D.* 64

POMPEII had got off cheaply from the troubles of the wars. It had merely been compelled to cede land and a share in the town's government to Sulla's Roman colonists — which led, indeed, to difficulties between the original inhabitants and the newcomers — but the town itself was intact. Its importance as a trading-place had even increased, since in the neighbouring town of Stabiae, which had formerly been a dangerous rival, people had their hands full with the reconstruction of the town. So a large part of the functions of Stabiae now fell to Pompeii. The romanisation of the town began above all, as in Herculaneum, with the replacement of the former rulers by Roman officials and the transformation of their offices into those of the Roman type. As the highest authority a town council was formed, which corresponded to the Roman Senate. The assembly of these town councillors (*decutiones*) was presided over by two men (*duumviri*) elected by the citizens, who summoned the council and administered justice. In addition they had to regulate the elections for the whole administrative body of the community. Next to them were the quaestor, as minister of finance, and two architects (*aediles*), whose duty was to survey the streets, buildings and markets, and administer the police and dispense justice in less important cases. Men who applied for such high offices had to prove that they were wealthy, for their position was honorary. In fact, not only were high salaries from the town's exchequer impossible, but the office-bearers were obliged to erect, out of their own means, splendid buildings for public use, and to provide for the entertainment of the populace by arranging games and theatrical performances. Thus there was no danger of those in high office enriching themselves at the expense of the community.

Besides these chief officials there was a considerable number of lesser ones, with minor responsibilities, who like the leading men were mostly chosen from among the Romans or from those Pompeians who were devoted heart and soul to the new régime. In consequence the two places, Pompeii and Herculaneum, were soon thoroughly permeated with the spirit of Rome; hence also the transformation, both outwardly and inwardly, of the town's appearance, in accordance with Roman architecture and customs. During this development the Latin language gradually began to replace the Oscan. Weights and measures were also changed, and at the gauging table on the forum the former Oscan measures had to give way to those used in Rome.

It was soon evident that the population of Pompeii offered little resistance to this development, and that of Herculaneum still less. The citizenship awarded to the inhabitants of the two cities reconciled them more easily to the new order. From this time they began to flourish, commercial activity increased, and as a result of their incomparable position on the gulf of Naples, both places, but especially Herculaneum, became towns of many villas and health resorts for distinguished Romans who wished to retire for a time, or for good, from the turmoil of the capital to a quiet, peaceful and beautiful district. They built villas and magnificent houses, they brought money among the people, and the public buildings and institutions and the fora began to profit from these new circumstances. This was particularly true of the main forum, which was the centre of political and economic life. Situated as it was not in the middle of the town but towards the sea, its architectural style could easily be developed and changed.

The Roman influence, now apparent everywhere, certainly lowered the artistic level, which had hitherto been determined by the Greeks; but the Roman technique of architecture and the use of materials represented decided progress. There was lively building activity everywhere, especially on the forum. With its glorious situation — the view of the bright bay of Stabiae and the island of Capri in the background, to the east

20

Photo: Anderson

3. View of the pillared court (peristyle) in the House of the Vettii in Pompeii. Reg. VI, Ins. 16, No. 1.

(See pages 33, 52, 195)

Photo: Anderson

4. View of Vesuvius from a surviving part of the Portico which once surrounded the forum, the chief marker-

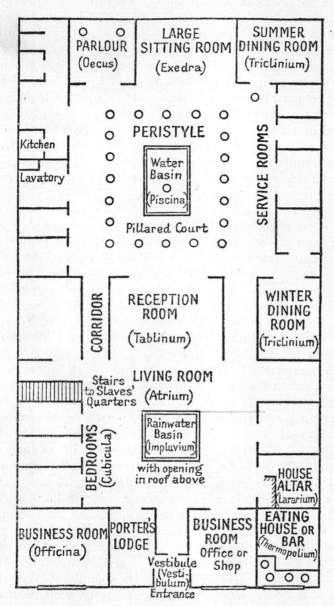

Plan of a large house in Pompeii.

the mountain range and in the north towering Vesuvius — the forum, which was surrounded on three sides by Doric columns (built by Vibius, of the highly esteemed family of the Popidi), presented a magnificent sight with its huge temples: the Temple of Jupiter on the north side, the Temple of Apollo nearby on the west side, and the basilica with its many columns in the south-west corner. Now the Romans set to work to pave it with travertine blocks; they added to the Doric columns a second row in the Ionian style; they decorated it with statues of gods and eminent citizens; and they planned quite new buildings. These were meant especially for the east side of the forum, where at that time some private houses were still standing.

The great temple on the north side, dedicated to the supreme deity, Jupiter, was given further prominence by the erection of gigantic triumphal arches on each side of it, which at the same time provided a splendid entrance to the forum. The approaches were closed to chariots and horses, so that the citizens might stroll quite undisturbed and the business of the market be carried on smoothly and easily. People went to the forum in order to visit the temples and sacrifice to the gods, they met their friends, talked business, went into the offices to pay their taxes. In the basilica, an enormous building which served the needs of trade and the business of the market, people looked up their business friends and advocates, sought justice — in short, here in one place was everything one could need or desire. Moreover, the foundation-stone of splendid baths had been laid next to the forum, so that that amenity too was near the focus of the whole life of the town. The public baths of Samnite-Oscan times, which were on the Stabian Way, no longer met the needs of the time.

The great open-air amphitheatre, which was built towards the Stabian Gate, served for amusements. In the forum too festivals and religious processions had been held from earliest times — and even bull-fights and other games, for which there was still no other theatre. The Romans loved these things, but they also knew that the populace everywhere seeks and needs distractions, and that by such means its favour may be won.

So before 80 B.C. people longed to see an enormous public building erected, which might accommodate almost the whole population of the town. If there was such a theatre, surely Maecenases would also emerge to arrange gladiatorial games and bull-fights in it at their own expense. It was not in vain that the people hoped. The enormously wealthy builders of the small theatre, Caius Quinctius Balbus and Maurus Porcius, after being elected to the highest offices of the town in fact decided upon the erection of such a huge theatre. In the days of Sulla's fight for power in Rome Balbus had acquired immense wealth by speculating in the properties of families who were banished or destroyed. With this wealth he had retired to Pompeii and this was his way of currying public favour. The amphitheatre was constructed to hold about sixteen thousand people, not less than thirteen thousand of them seated. As at that time Pompeii numbered at most fifteen thousand inhabitants, it is clear that an increase in the population had been reckoned with from the beginning of the plan, and also that the inhabitants of surrounding places were expected to stream in to the performances. Since the sun's strength is very great in those parts, provision was made for an enormous canvas roof to be stretched over the arena and the spectators. The amphitheatre was built in the extreme south-eastern corner of the town and somewhat sunk into the ground, and there it became the nucleus of a sports district, which gradually rose around it. It was admirably planned by the architects, and the entrances and exits were so constructed as to allow the whole place to be speedily filled or emptied. Pompeii could justly be proud of this immense "Round Theatre", the more so as not even Rome had its like at that time (80 B.C.). The cruel games, for which it was planned, where men fought against one another or against wild beasts till the fight ended in blood or in death, were, it is true, an inhuman aberration. The Pompeians were so obsessed by the games that one of them, Umbricius Scaurus, a man who had made his fortune by making and selling a popular fish-sauce, left orders in his will for a picture to be carved on his tombstone of the fights of gladiators against one another and against wild beasts. Beneath the picture was an inscription to the effect that the gladiator Bebrix, victorious fifteen times, was opposed to Nobilius, with only eleven victories. The fights which were depicted were those performed as the funeral rites for Scaurus. Lions and panthers

23

are also to be seen, as well as wild boars, bulls and gazelles, fighting or fleeing, with sometimes two animals, perhaps a panther and a bull, joined together by a long rope to incite them and to render their escape impossible. Such fights were also represented in paintings on the outer socle of the amphitheatre stage. Sometimes, however, there was a bloodless athletic combat, such as has become fashionable again in our time. But all this did not satisfy the growing craving for amusement. The open-air theatres could not always be used in the less favourable season, so that as early as 75 B.C. plans were made for a covered theatre next to the open-air one, capable of holding about fifteen hundred people. It was built near the big theatre because this was now the district for amusement and recreation.

While Pompeii was thus developing, and Herculaneum too was profiting greatly from Roman administration and the closer contact with Rome, the imperial city itself had not attained peace either at home or abroad. It was still involved in struggles for the supreme power. The Republic was nearing an end. Its expansion had enriched enormously the senatorial oligarchy; but the import from the provinces of captives and tribute had disastrously affected the position of both town and agricultural worker in Italy. Craftsmen and small-holders were thereby ruined and driven into abject poverty. It is impossible to give accurately the size of the population of Italy at that time. Oscar Jäger estimates the number at 20–22 million, of whom 13–14 million were slaves.[1] Such a disparity of numbers was a source of great danger, and in fact in 71 B.C. a great effort was made to stir up the slaves against their often cruel masters. The movement came to a head when a Thracian called Spartacus, a wrestler doomed in any case to die before long, persuaded about seventy of his fellows in a gladiators' school near Capua to break out and to kindle the hope of liberty in the hearts of the millions of slaves. The ever-increasing band first defeated a detachment of Roman troops sent against them from Capua, captured their arms and equipment, and then looked for a strategically favourable position from which to defend themselves against the Roman legions which would be sent out against them. They found this position on the precipitous slopes of Vesuvius, which with

[1] Oscar Jäger, *Geschichte des Altertums*, p. 432.

its scattered caves served as a kind of fortress, offering protection as well as a base for surprise attacks. The descriptions of the battle against the Roman consul Clodius Gabrus, who thought he had surrounded Spartacus, give a picture of the appearance of Vesuvius at this time which differs somewhat from other descriptions, for instance that of the Roman geographer Strabo. "With the aid of ropes made from vine branches the slaves flung themselves down the precipitous slopes of the mountain with its numerous caves," Lucius Aeneas Florus tells us; "and when they reached the foot they advanced on a route hitherto thought impassable and fell on the camp of the Roman commander, who was totally unprepared for the attack." The beleaguerers were completely routed. Spartacus occupied and sacked numerous unfortified places in the neighbourhood, and succeeded in ruling for some time over a great part of southern Italy, including Pompeii and Herculaneum. He even planned to march against Rome itself. But after two years Crassus succeeded in defeating the rebels, completely destroying the brave fighter Spartacus and his slave army of 60,000 men.

After those two anxious years Roman rule was completely restored, in Herculaneum and Pompeii as elsewhere. Pompeii resumed its daily occupations. On the main streets running through the towns there was a great development of traffic which left deep ruts and made the paving of the roads essential. Along the roads numerous shops were opened which sold the produce of the town, mainly household provisions. In the thermopolii, in a kind of bar open to the street, warm meals, and drinks from bronze vessels sunk into the counter, were sold to passers-by.

In Herculaneum, however, there was no such development. There was little wheeled traffic (no grooves were worn in the paving-stones), and only a limited number of shops; but everywhere there were signs of seafaring and fishing: nets and lines, ropes and other shipping paraphernalia indicated the chief occupation of the inhabitants. In addition, many villas sprang up, and the architects took full advantage of the beautiful situation by the sea and the lovely prospects.

Meanwhile, the political situation in Rome had advanced to the final struggle between the Republic and the men and forces favouring a monarchy. The mighty figure of Caesar went on his way: in the civil war he overcame his great antagonist Pompey, by 47 B.C. he was absolute monarch, and the power of the Senate in Rome seemed to be completely broken. But the assassination of Caesar at the ides of March, 44 B.C., put a sudden end to this concentration of power of supreme commander, judge and priest in one person. But the idea embodied in the struggle for the absolute power of an individual (as in the world monarchy of Alexander the Great) did not disappear with Caesar's death.

In 197 B.C. Rome defeated Philip V of Macedon; within sixty years Roman rule extended to all the Mediterranean lands. Compared with these countries, Roman civilisation was backward. Thus was completed the thoroughgoing hellenisation of Italy. Pompeii and Herculaneum, Greek in origin, now the resorts of the wealthy Roman governing classes, became typically luxurious and pleasure-loving. There the love adventures of the gods were the main subject for artistic representation.

Belief in the Roman gods, long since identified with those of Greece, had weakened. Scepticism was widespread in the upper classes, superstition in the lower. Imported gods of every kind were worshipped, including Isis, Bacchus and Mithras. These new cults were sensational and emotional; consequently the more orgiastic of the mystery religions, from Greece and the Orient, were favoured. Morality generally was in decline.

This development found an attentive observer in the famous Roman orator, lawyer, and adherent of Pompey, Marcus Tullius Cicero. He had an enormous influence on the political as well as the intellectual life of his time. After such stirring events as the discovery and overthrow of the Catiline conspiracy, which aimed at the consulate and the highest power in the State, Cicero felt the need for rest and refreshment far from the turmoil of the world. Among the many country mansions which offered him this refuge there was a "Pompeianum", as he himself called it, a peaceful villa, beautifully situated near Pompeii, to which he withdrew from time to time. But after Caesar's assassination Cicero's good fortune came to an end. A year later he too was murdered, and he did not live to see the rise of Octavianus, Caesar's grand-nephew and adopted son. After a decisive battle against Mark Antony, formerly his fellow-consul, in 31 B.C. this brilliant man won absolute power in Rome and over almost the whole known world. He was awarded the title of Augustus, which means the blessed and revered enlarger of the Empire, and the Senate gave him, besides the dignity of consul, the so-called imperium, the power of absolute rule with the official title of "imperator". It soon became apparent that Augustus was a capable, far-seeing, and industrious ruler. This appeared in the products of his government: magnificent buildings witnessed to his love of splendour, the plastic arts and painting in the Greek style were encouraged, and the conscious pride of every member of the empire was strengthened. In his *Aeneid* Virgil justly addressed the Emperor: "You are a Roman, let this be your profession. Rule the world, for you are its master."

Augustus, who often travelled through the land, was like everyone else delighted with the situation and the beautiful scenery of the gulf of Naples. He was careful to see that the wounds inflicted by the struggles for supreme power in Rome were gradually healed, while he pushed the imperial frontiers as far as the easily defended Danube, holding the line of the Rhine against the Teutons, and of the Euphrates in the east. Peace and order, the consequence of all wise measures, made internal consolidation possible in all regions. This could be felt at once in Campania, in Pompeii and Herculaneum. The population rapidly increased, Pompeii numbering about fifteen to sixteen thousand inhabitants, Herculaneum four to five thousand. These circumstances were further improved by the increasing imperial trade which passed through the gulf of Naples. The most precious goods, the products and delicacies of the whole world, flowed into Rome and its countryside. Millions of slaves toiled to serve the luxurious life of the Roman caste of lords and victors. Italy, which had attained to the mastery of the world, took from the Greeks the fruits of art and beauty, copied them and adapted them, and adorned her homes and cities with them. More and more Roman visitors came to the towns and villages of the gulf of Naples, with their gardens of myrtles and roses. Many beautiful houses were built for their accommodation. The technique of architecture had undergone great changes. Freestone was now used for the façades alone, and for the rest it was fashionable to connect square-hewn stones together with mortar, to form a kind of stone network. But a new type of flat, oblong tile, well known to all visitors to Rome, was already coming into fashion. Pillars were more frequent, with stucco to cover them and the walls, and even expensive marble came into common use. The fora and their great public buildings were adorned with a forest of statues. Many small houses were bought by rich Pompeians or wealthy Romans who came to settle there, and great mansions with marvellous pillared courtyards were raised on their sites. A second storey was often added, mainly for servants' quarters. In all this new building could be seen the desire to introduce beauty into the houses.

Just as the real life of the house was moved from the simpler atrium to the grander portico or pillared hall, so there was an increasing tendency to decorate the walls with paintings and representations of the gods, instead of with counterfeit architectural grandeur. Thus in the second and third styles, from Greek models, there developed an art of fresco work of which three-quarters treated mythological religious subjects, especially the love affairs of the gods. Gaston Boissier is not far from the mark when he jokingly says: "Jupiter seems entirely taken up with seducing Danae, Io or Leda, or with raping Europa. In twelve pictures Daphne is pursued by Apollo, Venus is represented fifteen times in the arms of Mars and sixteen times in those of beautiful Adonis. The amorous intrigues of the gods are the most popular motives."[1]

Portraits were seldom painted, people preferring the busts and Hermes heads of the sculptors. In painting, romantic landscapes vied with graceful representations of winged genii, creatures somewhat like the dwarfs of our fairy-tales, who are cooks and joiners, shoemakers and smiths, fullers and vine-workers, and thus convey to us a faithful picture of the daily occupations of the Pompeians.

In general, the frescoes of the cities of Campania show the desire of the people for erotic pleasures and for quiet good living. The whole planning of the houses shows the desire for seclusion and for keeping trouble at a distance, and emphasises the complete independence of personal life. Hence the almost repellently simple and unadorned aspect of the house

[1] *Promenades archéologiques Rome et Pompéi*. Paris, 1901.

towards the street and the wonderful, often luxurious interior. But material things had to be thought of too, so rooms and shops were let in Pompeii and Herculaneum, or to increase their incomes people had their own produce, such as wine from their country estates, sold in the streets, or their slaves did some business for them in their houses. Returning from public life in the forum, the theatre, the temple or the baths, people retired as rulers into their little kingdoms, their own quiet houses. There, with the help of various comforts, especially, as wealth increased, those of good eating and drinking, they tried to make life as pleasant as possible. Meals were taken in the triclinia, rooms in which cushioned and upholstered sofas standing on bronze pedestals ran round three sides, or in which the seats were built of stone and ranged round a small table. On each of such couches up to three people could be accommodated, the Romans holding that a dinner-party to be lively and animated should not exceed the number of the Muses or be less than the number of the Graces. The fourth side, to the front, was empty, so that the slaves could serve the guests from the service-table, where the food was divided, across the small table in the middle. For the Romans did not use forks, but only spoons, and the servants prepared the courses beforehand with knives. The places of the different members of the family, especially that of the master of the house, were often marked on the backs with their names. People reclined on the couches, propped on their left elbows; the middle couch was the place of honour, where the host and the most honoured guest took their places. These rooms too were adorned with charming frescoes representing either the different dishes or such a picture as the one of women playing with peacocks. The children ate at a small table which stood at the foot of their parents' couches.

The very varied dishes, composed of fish, oysters and other sea-fare, as well as chicken, venison and pork, were prepared in quite small kitchens, which were, however, lavishly equipped with crockery and with moulds, in the shape of hares, piglets, fish, etc., for special occasions. Asparagus was known, and mushrooms such as the orange-agaric were a common delicacy. Besides the grape, the favourite fruit was the fig, introduced into southern Italy by the Greek colonists.

The quince, consecrated to Venus as a symbol of love and happiness, took the place of the orange, which was not known at that time. There were also apples and pears, but they were not as well known as they are nowadays. The cherry-tree too was much rarer, whereas the date, though not growing in Campania, was to be found, as it is today, in many lands round the Mediterranean. Bread was baked of wheat and barley in big round loaves, marked almost exactly as our small dinner roll. The other kinds of corn, such as oats and rye, were not known. With the meals wine was served, excellent qualities of which were available everywhere, but especially from the slopes of Vesuvius. It tasted best in magnificently adorned drinking vessels, which were sometimes of silver or of wonderfully iridescent glass.

If one of the guests over-ate or if someone was ill, there were few experienced doctors, and these few were naturally highly esteemed. Surgery especially enjoyed a comparatively high standard, as may be deduced from the instruments used by the Pompeian doctors. There were all kinds of spatulas, lancets, tongs, scissors, midwifery instruments, and so on, of outstanding technical excellence. Richly equipped pharmacies sold the medicines prescribed by the doctors, in tablets, pills or liquids.

When dusk fell, the lighting of the houses was adequately cared for. The little flat, round earthenware lamps, with wicks for oil, stood everywhere. To give a brighter light, all that could be done was to increase the number of the lamps, and these were hung up on branched candelabra.

The other furniture in the houses, such as tables and beds, was mostly made of wood with beautifully worked bronze feet. For the rest, the daily utensils showed a remarkable likeness to those we use today. Instead of our heavy iron safes with their locks and keys, there often stood in the atria enormous money-chests, which were either made wholly of iron or bronze or at least braced with it, and were often decorated with reliefs of the finest craftsmanship. Even the simplest utensils of daily life were embellished in some way — the hair-pins, perfume-bottles, little spoons and scissors used by the ladies, as well as the razors, daggers and knives of the men. Only the agricultural implements, which had almost the same shapes as now, were of simple and practical design.

When the question of supreme power in Rome had been settled and a time of peace and quiet for Italy followed, it was clear that wealthy people who wanted to build a big and well-situated mansion need no longer be restricted to the area within the town walls. People now dared to build outside, chiefly near the shore, on account of the lovelier views. It was at that time that there arose, some distance from the so-called Gate of Herculaneum, outside the north-west corner of Pompeii, a luxury villa, square in form, on land falling so steeply away to the sea that one side of the building had to be supported by strong cross-vaulting. It was decidedly a patrician house, containing wonderful wall-paintings of the second style. A large atrium, an enormous peristyle, magnificent public rooms, even a semi-circular verandah, were built. But the masterpiece of the house was a salon in which a Campanian painter, in approximately the first years of Augustus's reign, represented in no less than twenty-nine figures, greater than life-size, the dramatic process of initiation into the Dionysian mysteries — the work evidently being carried out by order of his mistress, who was herself a priestess. The villa was splendidly planned and comprised nearly ninety rooms with private bathrooms.

In those wonderful frescoes the new Roman owner, who did so much to adorn the house, connecting the luxurious salon direct with two alcoves for himself and the lady of the house, had reproduced the secret ceremonies of the mystery, which at that time, in spite of the Senate's prohibitions, had spread through the length and breadth of Italy. The rites of flagellation and purification, the unveiling of the phallus before the trembling young girl, and the licentious dances of a naked Bacchante, are dramatically represented in this luxurious ante-room of the nuptial chambers.

Proceeding from this house towards the Gate of Herculaneum, you come upon another large villa built at approximately the same time; it was the country-house of a rich patrician and was for a long time falsely ascribed to a wine-dealer named Arius Diomedes. The house had several storeys, though there was space enough for extension, of which, indeed, good use had been made. Through a three-cornered ante-room you came at once into a magnificent peristyle with elegant Doric columns. Here too there were charming frescoes of the second style, a separate bath building, and — a great rarity in Pompeii — small round windows of thick glass, precursors of the glass windows which are taken as a matter of course today. An enormous vault contained innumerable huge wine pitchers, the so-called amphoras, proving that in this splendid establishment an extensive wine business was carried on.

The villa adjoined the Street of Tombs, along which the most distinguished Pompeians were buried and monuments erected in their honour. From there the way into the city was through the Gate of Herculaneum, which spanned the broad carriage-way in a wide arch and left passages for pedestrians to right and left. The passage for wheeled traffic could be closed by means of a kind of drop-shutter, the side passages by means of gates. There was a lively traffic of porters, labourers, carters and muleteers, who transported the goods between the town and the harbour. These men immortalised themselves by inscriptions in the numerous taverns and thermopolii near the gate, where warm meals and drinks were sold. The traffic from Naples and Herculaneum also flowed into the town through this gate.

At first, in Greek and Samnite times, the dead had been buried, not cremated, in stone coffins, and in practically all such coffins a coin was found, the fare for Charon, whose task was to ship the dead across the river of Hades into the kingdom of the dead. Later, in Roman times, the custom of cremation prevailed. The relatives of the dead person attended in mourning clothes beside the pyre where the body was ceremonially burnt. Then the ashes and bones were collected, wine and milk were poured over them, and they were laid in an urn with fragrant spices and a mixture of water, wine and oil. This urn was then put in a niche in the family vault, which looked like a dovecote, for which reason these sepulchres were called *columbaria*. Many vaults had a beautifully painted triclinium where the funeral repast was eaten. Here the monuments of members of the greatest families of Pompeii could be admired, for example, those of the Istacidians; and the inscriptions recorded which of the departed deserved so well of the town that they received their memorial with special honours at state expense. Examples of these are the memorial to the priestess Mamia, the founder of a temple on the forum, and to the duumvir Aulus Umbricius Scaurus.

The houses in the north-west, in the streets just behind the Gate of Herculaneum, gave evidence of another great stream of traffic, whose requirements had to be met in every possible way. Thus the house of Sallust at the corner of two large streets (the *Strada Consolare* and the *Strada di Mercurio*) was provided with a bar and an inn. This building had also four shops, in one of which the slaves sold wine and oil, while a mill and a bakery were established in the others. The building dated from Samnite times and possessed paintings of all the three styles so far known. Caius Sallustius, the owner, had grown rich in this business, and began to adorn his house with beautiful works of art. In the atrium he set up a fine bronze statue of Hercules with the hind which the demi-god, according to legend, took alive to Mycene. A whole year he pursued it, till at last he lamed it with an arrow and thus captured it. Sallust also decorated his house with frescoes, one of them many yards broad and high, representing the legend of Actaeon, who surprised Artemis bathing, and was metamorphosed into a stag and torn to pieces by hounds.

Following up the Street of Mercury you came through a side-street (*vicolo dei Vettii*) to a house of the Vettii, a notable Pompeian family whose members often held the highest civic offices. The builder of this house must have been a man of fine artistic taste and culture, for the walls were not covered with the kind of paintings found in most houses, but with works by true artists. Here you may discern the taste of a person of nice artistic judgment. A similar house can be found further down, on the Stabian Way, belonging to a freedman, Caius Iucundus, who made a large fortune as a banker, by arranging purchases for a fee of one per cent. of the price, and administering his own property and that of other people — transactions which were very profitable for him. His house was richly, indeed, luxuriously furnished: in the atrium, besides the altar to the household gods, there were magnificent treasure-chests and a bronze bust of himself dedicated by one of his freedmen to the banker's "genius". The moneylender, who had also rented a large fuller's workshop opposite his house, seems to have been, with all his keen sense of business, also an artist in living, for beneath a beautiful fresco he had

had Ovid's words inscribed: "Long live the lover! Perish the one who does not know how to love! And accursed be he who will forbid us to love!"

The banker's office was on the first floor of the house, and it was there, in a large bronze-bound chest, that he kept the accounts, receipts, and the like of the auctions which he arranged for his clients. These were preserved on wooden tablets covered with wax, in which the banker scratched his figures with a fine stylo. His business had many ramifications and reached as far as Egypt, whose popular linen he imported into southern Italy. One of his best clients was the wealthy Roman Gnaeus Alleius Nigidus, who lived in a very large house with a splendid garden peristyle, which covered the area of a whole block between the Streets of Mercury and *della fortuna*. Nigidus had a large bakery with three mills and a large furnace installed to the left of the atrium. Above the place where the corn was ground was a lucky sign: "Here happiness resides". Nigidus divided up his house and let out parts of it in order to increase his income. On the threshold a mosaic of the word "Salve" greeted you, and made you feel at home. Such inscriptions were to be found at the entrance to many houses, for example these words: "My door is closed to thieves, wide open to honest people"; or beneath the mosaic of a dog the words, "Cave canem". At the door of the house of a certain Siricus, who must have been a business man, the words "Salve lucrum" — "Welcome profits" — left no doubt in the visitor's mind about the owner's profession and interests, and similarly in another house the frank assurance that "Profits mean joy".

The rich of Pompeii, especially when they were elected to high office, also contributed generously to the development of public buildings. Special attention was now paid to the forum, and about 10 B.C. its west side was bordered with an arcade, the pavement was improved and the temple given by the priestess Mamia in honour of the tutelary genius of Augustus was begun. This was on the north-east side of the forum; immediately to the south the priestess Eumachia, in her own name and that of her son Marcus Numistrius Fronto, substantially enlarged a big building (which was apparently a business house as well as a meeting-place for the fullers' guild), providing it with a great ante-room opening on the forum. This building was dedicated to the reigning emperor and contained, amongst other statues, those of Romulus and Aeneas. On the south-east corner the comitium or election-chamber was erected, so that the whole forum was now surrounded by buildings and porticos, and gave the impression of a splendid hall, perhaps not unlike the piazza of San Marco in Venice. At the beginning of our era another temple, that of the *Fortuna Augusta,* was built outside the forum, in the Nolan Way.

In the reign of Augustus the fortifications of Pompeii on the side towards the sea were abandoned. The walls were partly demolished, so that there was now no obstacle to the extension of the town in this direction. This was the more important as the population was increasing, and the emperor himself had sent new colonists who settled outside the walls. At the same time the water-supply was carefully reorganised, the water being collected in a water-tower and then conducted through an ingenious network of lead pipes to the individual streets and houses. This supplemented the service of the innumerable public fountains with their little shrines built into nearby houses or niches. Pictures of the gods were painted on the façades of the houses, on one wall being depicted the twelve deities worshipped in Pompeii at that time — Jupiter, Apollo, Mars, Vulcan, Mercury, Hercules, along with the goddesses Juno, Minerva, Venus Pompeiana, Proserpina, Diana and Ceres.

Under the emperors who succeeded Augustus — Tiberius, Caligula and Claudius, who reigned from A.D. 14 to 54, when Nero ascended the throne — Pompeii's material prosperity continued to increase, and those in business and industry especially became very wealthy. The textile industry increased by leaps and bounds. Fruit, wine and vegetables, as well as the excellent fish-sauce, which is perhaps to be identified with the favourite modern Italian tunny-sauce, were produced in great quantities. Thus it became necessary to construct a market-hall on the forum. This had marble forecourts, surrounded by pillars, and was capped by a central dome; there were rooms used as slaughter-houses, and meat and fish halls decorated with fine paintings. There were also many shops opening on to the forum, in which fruit, dates, figs, cakes and bread were sold. Close by was a magnificent temple, probably dedicated to the patron gods of the town.

Good living and luxury still increased. Monuments were everywhere; marble, though still very costly, was liberally used. The forum baths were extravagantly equipped, having a portico, baths for women, and ingeniously planned air heating. Besides the aristocracy who filled the public offices and donated most of these buildings, there arose a moneyed aristocracy, who bought up houses, transforming their old-fashioned forms with pillars and other additions, using the new narrow tiles, and covering the buildings with stucco and ornaments. The demand for more and more comfortable houses continued to increase; the public water-supply was now led into the houses, so that the peristyles, the atria and the gardens could be provided with large basins and fountains.

The wealth and business life were most in evidence in the Street of Abundance, which led to the forum, crossing the Stabian Way. In this street there lived at one time a certain Holconius Rufus, who enjoyed successively all the dignities of the town and had even been priest to Augustus. He renovated and enlarged the theatres and built a splendid house for himself, remarkable for its colonnaded peristyle, with its ingenious playing fountains and wonderful frescoes. This building too had numerous shops. The owner had a dyeing business, which, thanks to his business versatility, yielded enormous profits.

These houses were mostly places of quiet, happy family life. The children were the centre of this life; they often left marks on the walls, scratches a few feet above the floor or childish drawings.

A highly respected duumvir, Publius Paquius Proculus, who had already held several public offices, possessed a large house somewhat more to the east in the same street. In the middle of its lovely peristyle there was an arbour laced in vines, and in its shade a summer dining-room with three wooden couches. Paquius was perhaps a relative of that Terentius Proculus who owned an extensive bakery in the Stabian Way, and had a fresco of himself and his wife painted in his house. He was represented with a book-roll in his hand, she with a threefold wax tablet, as if he wanted to divert attention from his real business of baker and point out to posterity that he was a cultured and learned man.

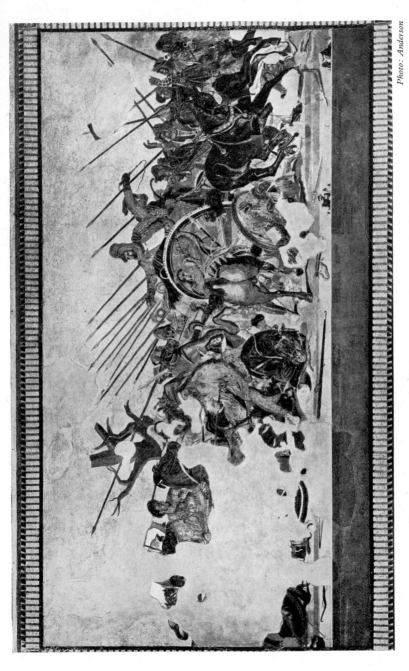

Photo: Anderson

5. The Clash between Alexander the Great and Darius in the Battle of Issus, 333 B.C.
A splendid mosaic, from a Greek painting, which adorned the floor of the house of a rich Pompeian citizen, the House of
the Faun. Reg. VI, Ins. 12, Nos. 2–5.

(See pages 13–14, 45, 182–183)

Photo: Alinari

6. Mosaic with the inscription 'beware of the dog', in the house of a wealthy merchant in Pompeii. The house is the original of the house of Glaucus in Lord Lytton's novel *The Last Days of Pompeii*. Reg. VI, Ins. 8, No. 3.

(*See page* 34)

Photo: Alinari

7. Cock-fight in front of a table with a wand of Mercury, a purse, and an olive-branch. Perhaps symbolises business rivalry. Mosaic from Pompeii.

(*See page* 14)

Not far from this was the home of the priest Amandus, a modest house quite surrounded by businesses and shops, which sheltered a numerous family on its two floors. Part of the house was let to a maker of those wooden tablets which, when covered with wax, could be written on with a metal pencil.

In the same district there was a splendid house belonging to the family of the Poppaii, another of the Pompeian families which provided candidates for the highest offices. It was a fine building, with splendid reception rooms as well as spacious accommodation for slaves and their overseers, who obviously worked in the fields. Over them was a steward (*procurator*), who had the care of the whole household. The owners, very wealthy people, possessed other properties outside Pompeii, dividing their time between them, so that the town house was often in charge of the steward for many months.

The increasing number of rich people in Pompeii was due not only to commercial prosperity but also to the fact that the town, like Herculaneum, was attractive to wealthy Romans who longed for beauty and peace. It had the additional attraction of having been from time to time a place of sojourn for various members of the imperial family. On one occasion there was a sad mishap: in A.D. 21 Drusus, son of Claudius (who was later to be emperor) a boy thirteen years of age, was playing with a pear. He threw it up and then tried to catch it in his mouth. The fruit went down his throat and the lad was suffocated before a doctor's help could be obtained.

While Pompeii was developing mainly as a commercial centre, and gradually losing its military importance, Herculaneum retained its character as a fortified post; and in the time of Augustus a beginning was made with re-establishing the walls — which, however, did not prevent luxury villas rising up outside the walls. For a town possessing at most only one-third of the population of Pompeii, Herculaneum had by now remarkably fine public buildings. Above all, there was a lavishly appointed amphitheatre, made to hold about 2,500 spectators. On the wall which surrounded the highest seats there were large bronze statues of members of the imperial house and of high officials of the town. The scenic wall, which ran along the back of the stage, was a splendid work of art, richly decorated with rare coloured marble. Marble and bronze statues were grouped in niches round about the main entrance and the two side entrances by which the actors reached the stage. This stage wall was by far the most costly and richly decorated part of the open-air theatre. It was built in the time of Augustus, statues of later emperors and of outstanding men being gradually added.

Paved streets crossed one another at right angles through the regularly laid out town. In one of them there was a large building, perhaps a basilica, whose walls were crowned with a great bronze quadriga. This building too was adorned with so much statuary of bronze and of marble that, like the theatre, it resembled a very forest of statues. Most of them represented members of one of the first families of the town, that of the Balbi, whose outstanding representative was Marcus Nonius Balbus, Proconsul of Crete and Cyrenaica. At the entrance, beneath the pillars of the forecourt, stood the equestrian figures of this man and his son, and within the building there were statues of his mother, his wife, and his daughters. It was he who built this basilica and restored the walls and gates of the town. The statues displayed the serious and refined features of one of the most highly cultivated Roman patrician families.

Not far from the basilica there stood the Temple of Cybele, mother of the gods, embodiment of the fertility of nature, to whom the Romans had erected a temple on the Palatine as early as 200 B.C. Venus and Hercules, along with Isis, were, after Jupiter, the gods most worshipped in Herculaneum. It is a remarkable fact that the inhabitants of the little town used magnificent transparent alabaster for the pillars of their temples.

About 30–20 B.C. public baths were built in Herculaneum on a particularly clear plan, though still with separate baths for men and women. They were not far from the forum, which was the focus of private and public life, though more modestly planned than that of Pompeii. Yet there were splendid buildings, such as the *albergo* (as it is called today) or hotel, which with its wonderful mosaic floors and frescoes of the second and third styles, its magnificent portico and its blossoming gardens, must have been most impressive, though little of all this has survived to our time. Besides the houses of the rich there were a great many smaller and more modest dwellings, but these too showed their owners' desire to make their homes as artistic and pleasing as possible. Most of the owners of these houses were fishers, as is proved by the discovery of rods, nets and the like.

The proximity of Naples preserved the authentic Greek element in Herculaneum much more purely than in Pompeii. The beauty of the neighbourhood encouraged the rich to build villas and to cultivate the arts and their favourite pursuits away from the all-too-busy life in the nearby cities of Naples and Pompeii. Thus there arose, for instance, the villa of a highly cultured patrician, on the outskirts of the town to the west, beyond the walls on the slopes of Vesuvius, with a glorious view of the sea. The villa was set in an extensive garden, with a small and a large portico, and in the latter a great water basin. The house was luxuriously furnished. Protected by Vesuvius from the cold winds and situated halfway between mountain and sea, it lay apart without being isolated, its terraces looking across the picturesque gulf of Naples.

The villa probably belonged at one time to Lucius Calpurnius Piso, son-in-law of Julius Caesar and opponent of Cicero, and in the imperial era remained at first in his family. Lucius Calpurnius was a disciple of Epicurus, the Greek philosopher, who taught at Athens in the fourth and third centuries B.C., and sought happiness in the joys of the intellect. But whereas Epicurus thought happiness impossible without self-discipline, self-control and justice, that is, without virtue, his teaching had been much coarsened during the centuries. Numerous followers, for example the philosopher Philodemos, had transformed and developed his teaching so as to justify the desire for a comfortable and gay life. This Philodemos, a friend of Lucius Calpurnius Piso, probably lived and died in the beautiful villa at Herculaneum as Piso's guest, giving into the care of his host and friend his large library and all his own works, which consisted of numerous papyrus rolls neatly and carefully preserved in containers. Most of these works were written in Greek, and only a few in Latin. The highly cultured host of Philodemos was not only a philosopher and author, but also a great art connoisseur. He collected bronzes and statues, turning his house into a veritable museum in which not only excellent Roman imitations but also some first-rate Greek originals were to be found. Marble and bronze busts of outstanding men, such as Scipio Africanus, the conqueror of Hannibal and Carthage, and of thinkers and poets, filled the rooms, peristyles and gardens of the villa. The whole place was a jewel, which bore witness to the assimilation of Greek by Roman culture. After the death of the philosopher and his hospitable master, who had lived together there for at least thirty years, the splendid villa remained in the possession of the Pisos.

In quiet Herculaneum such a home could be enjoyed in greater tranquillity than in Pompeii, with its streams of lively traffic. But in both places the inhabitants were able to follow their chosen occupations and inclinations; the turmoil of the struggle for the imperial power in Rome reached them only in a muffled form. The peace of the empire and the ridding of the Mediterranean of pirates caused a steady increase in trade, including that in wheat, metals, pottery and many luxury goods. In this trade Naples, with its excellent harbour, together with the neighbouring towns, had a large share.

Commerce was no longer confined to the Mediterranean. Roman merchant ships, accompanied by warships, were now to be met with in the Red Sea, and with goods from tropical India there arrived now and then a picture of a god, or some other object which introduced Indian religion to the Roman people. At this time, too, news may have reached Pompeii, by means of Jews or travellers from the lands to the east of the Mediterranean, of the Man who was to bring salvation to the world and had been crucified. But Christian teaching was certainly not widespread in Pompeii, nor did it have any importance there. If it was known at all, it was only to a few individuals. There is scarcely a trace in Pompeii of actual adherents of Christianity. Only a so-called cryptogram of the Lord's Prayer or a magic square of letters which, read from any side, always produces the same mysterious words, could perhaps be interpreted as a secret confession of Christian faith and its main teaching, the incarnation and resurrection of Christ.[1]

[1] See Della Corte, "Il Crittogramma del 'Pater Noster'," Naples, extract from vol. XVII of the *Rendiconti della Reale Accademia di Archeologia, Lettere ed Arti*, Società di Napoli, 1937.

It was different in Herculaneum. Here, especially among the slaves and poor people, there lived adherents of the new teaching, at first probably individuals whose conversion can be traced to the preaching of the Apostle Paul in nearby Pozzuoli in the year 60. There was, however, a sort of private praying-place, with a wooden cross set in the wall, which could be concealed from the uninvited by means of a box with wooden doors. In front of it was a piece of furniture which probably served not only as a receptacle for holy objects, but also as an altar: its design betrayed its derivation from customary pagan forms. But the persecution of Christians under Nero in the year 64, or the interference of the priests and believers of the old gods, caused even this trace of the glorification of the sign of the Cross, as preached by the Apostle Paul, to be destroyed, and the wooden emblem forcibly removed, certainly before the year 79, from that modest room, perhaps a slave's room in the upper storey of a patrician house.[1]

Besides religious interests and daily work for obtaining the necessities of life, the games in the amphitheatre continued to engage the hearts and minds of the citizens of Pompeii and Herculaneum. Officials vied with one another in preparing this pleasure as often as possible for the people. Pompeii, with its enormous amphitheatre, such as the surrounding towns, Stabiae or Nuceria or Sorrento, did not have, drew the people of these places to its games, eager trade rivals though they were. Opposition of trade interests, envy and jealousy, especially on the part of the Stabians and Nucerians, whose towns had suffered so terribly in earlier wars, had stirred up a great deal of enmity. But the temptation to attend the games in Pompeii, which were greatly developed in imperial times, proved stronger than any other impulse.

The gladiators were trained in special schools and then hired to the promoters of the games. They had to undergo iron discipline, for since the rebellion of Spartacus and because, by the nature of their calling, they had to risk their lives at any moment, one could never be quite sure of them. On the other hand the populace would become enthusiastic about specially heroic fighters, the women above all singling

[1] See Amedeo Maiuri, "Sulla scoperta della Croce ad Ercolano," in *Le arti*, 1940, p. 187.

out their favourites. Frescoes in private houses depicted their fights, and the names of gladiators were scrawled on many walls and pillars, for example, that of the great Thracian favourite Celadus, who was called "the desire of women and the master and physician of maidens".

The murderous human combats, which were in such striking contrast with the Greek theatre, were perhaps a vestige of Etruscan influence and life, but the people were passionately fond of them. They derived from an act of the cultus, in which, after a victory, as expiation and glorification of the fallen, captured enemies were paired against one another in mortal struggle. The gladiators themselves, who had often to be urged and forced to their crude work, thought quite differently about their destiny. Thus one of them wrote on the dining-room wall of the barracks these bitter words: "The philosopher Annaeus Seneca is the only Roman writer to condemn the bloody games."[1] When such games were arranged, they were advertised beforehand on the walls of the houses. Then at every street corner in Pompeii something like the following could be read: "Twenty pairs of gladiators, offered for as long as they live by Lucretius Satrius Valens, priest of Nero, and ten pairs given by his son, will compete against one another in Pompeii on the fourth of April. There will also be a fight between men and wild beasts. The canvas roof will be used to protect spectators from the sun."

An advertisement of this kind, which could also be read in Nuceria and Stabiae, summoned the theatregoers in A.D. 59 to a gladiatorial contest and bull-fight in the amphitheatre. A wealthy Roman senator, banished from Rome to the provinces on political grounds, had arranged games there in order to curry favour with the people in his new home. A great concourse of spectators had streamed in from all quarters, including the neighbouring towns and villages, especially Nuceria, which had suffered from Pompeii's rise to prosperity.

On that day the combatants, in their richly ornamented helmets, armour and cuirasses, emerged pair by pair from what had formerly been the portico of the great theatre and was now the gladiatorial barracks. To the strains of martial

[1] See Hieronymus Geist, *Pompejanische Wandinschriften*, p. 29. Munich, 1936.

music they entered ceremoniously, mounted and on foot, through the wide doors into the arena of the amphitheatre, every place of which was occupied. The combats began. The spectators followed the fights with passionate interest. It was they who by a sign, the turning of the thumb upwards or downwards, decided mercy or death for a wounded gladiator who was unable to continue the fight. On this day it happened that the spectators disagreed about the fate of such a one. In a flash the Pompeians were for one decision, the Nucerians for the opposite. At first the division was confined to jeers and harsh words, but it soon turned into execrations and stone-throwing. Finally the opposing parties stormed into the arena. A Pompeian weighed in, a Nucerian struck back, and in the twinkling of an eye what had been a show by specially trained fighters turned into a bloodthirsty struggle which soon overflowed from the arena into the spectators' benches. The Pompeians were in a decided majority, and it was clear that the outsiders would have to pay. A great many of them were severely wounded, and many were left dead on the scene of battle; and many Nucerians were left to bewail the loss of parents or children. They took their complaint to Rome and, telling the tale of the dead and wounded, besought the Emperor to do justice and create order. Nero commanded the Senate to give judgement in the affair. In consequence the Pompeians were forbidden to hold such games in their amphitheatre for the next ten years. Luvenius Regulus, who had arranged the games, was forced to disappear from Pompeii, and any of the persons who had engineered the riot and who could be laid hold of were banished. The duumviri for that year were also dismissed; new elections were arranged and an imperial commissar was made responsible for the restoration of order.

This bloodthirsty struggle, however, was only an episode; the excitement died down, and soon the citizens of the rival towns went about their business again undisturbed. To be sure, they keenly regretted that as a result of this incident they had to go without the entertainment of the fights for many years, but it appears that this prohibition fell into abeyance after a short time.

The struggles among members of the imperial family and leading men in the state did not affect Pompeii, and its inhabitants and those of Herculaneum could therefore peacefully order their lives as they pleased. They rejoiced in the surroundings of their towns, looking without the slightest mistrust on Vesuvius, "set in the green shade of grapes", and enjoying their possessions and the profits of the fruitful plains, which were bespangled, as it were, with country houses and gardens.

So midday of 5th February, A.D. 63, drew near, in the tenth year of the reign of the Emperor Nero. Most of the people of Pompeii and Herculaneum were just preparing to have their meal when suddenly a terrible earthquake shook the whole district. The shocks came in waves from east to west, that is, from Vesuvius towards the sea. A great number of public buildings collapsed, those, in fact, which towered highest above their surroundings and were most richly and beautifully adorned with pillars. But the ordinary houses also suffered severely. The devastation was worst of all on the forum. The great Temple of Jupiter, with its towering portico, completely collapsed; and the nearby Temple of Apollo, one of the loveliest buildings in the town, as well as a great many of the pillars of the arcades round the forum, were razed to the ground. The basilica too was very badly damaged, and the Temple of Isis became a ruin. A priest at table in the room of an adjacent house was killed, as were children playing in the arcades of the forum. The two theatres, the covered and the open, suffered such damage that they could not be used. The Gate of Vesuvius collapsed, as did the nearby water-tower; and the lead pipes of the water system were so damaged that recourse had to be made, as formerly, to the fountains, though some of these had dried up.

The house of the banker Caecilius Iucundus, near the Gate of Vesuvius, was badly damaged: the upper storey fell in and buried the chest containing the banker's receipts, which dated from A.D. 15 to 62. When the earthquake struck the town, he happened to be on business at the forum. He saw the mighty Temple of Jupiter break up, its surrounding porticos sink down, and heard the cries of someone buried by the falling ruins. In the fear of his heart he hurriedly vowed that he would make a costly sacrifice to his household gods, the *lares*, if he reached his home again safe and sound. Though he found his house almost a heap of rubble, he himself was untouched. So in the work of restoration he commissioned an artist to set a relief in the atrium, which by depicting the collapse of the buildings in the forum would show the peril in which he had been placed, and at the same time would show his gratitude for his escape.

The consequences of the earthquake were terrible; there was scarcely a building in all Pompeii which was undamaged. In the so-called House of the Faun, for example, the wonderful mosaic of the encounter of Alexander the Great with Darius in the battle of Issus in 333 B.C., which adorned the main room, was severely damaged in that part of the design which shows the Macedonians pressing on behind their captain. Truly the destruction in the town was frightful. A comprehensive view of it could scarcely be obtained, for many small streets, especially those lying between the Street of Fortuna and the Street of Abundance, had suffered severely. The Temple of Venus also lay in ruins.

At first the inhabitants fled terror-stricken from the town, in order to save at least their lives, to the open countryside. But the earthquake lasted only a very short time, and when the shocks were not renewed the fugitives gradually returned to their devastated dwellings. The country houses near the town, in particular those on the slopes of Vesuvius, suffered terribly. Among them was the great villa at the south-east foot of the mountain, whose owner, passionately attached to music and the games, had adorned it with paintings of gladiators, athletes and musicians. This house was so badly damaged that it had to be completely abandoned.

In Herculaneum things were not much better. All buildings, public and private, suffered severe damage, the Temple of Cybele collapsed, and the inhabitants were faced with terrible devastation. There was, naturally, great loss of life. The survivors were the more shattered by the catastrophe because it happened in winter, while previous earthquakes had occurred in summer. So on account of the season they had thought themselves safe from such disasters. Nuceria and Naples were less severely hit, the private houses on the slopes suffering more than the public buildings in the plain. But there was misfortune enough there too, for instance a flock of six hundred sheep being engulfed in a chasm which suddenly opened in the earth.

45

Many people in the district were severely injured or even killed in their houses by falling ruins; others were crazed by terror, and wandered about the streets screaming and moaning and execrating the gods. Some families left Pompeii never to return; others left it for a time until their homes could be rebuilt.

But that was the great question. The extent of the destruction in both Pompeii and Herculaneum was so enormous, and the cost in material and money for their reconstruction was so great, that it had to be decided whether or not the towns should be abandoned and the inhabitants settled elsewhere. But the citizens were with one accord against abandonment; scarcely had the shocks subsided than they forgot all danger and fear of recurrences and thought only of how to repair the damage as speedily as possible. Naturally this could not be done by their own unaided powers, and they had to turn for help to the Emperor and the Roman Senate. These hesitated for a time in view of the enormous expense involved. Finally, however, following the importunate pleas of the high officials who were sent to Rome, the reconstruction of Pompeii and Herculaneum was decided upon. Since as a matter of course everything was rebuilt in the Roman style, this meant not only modernisation but also the complete disappearance of Oscan and Samnite characteristics.

No one was much troubled about the causes of the earthquake. Such shocks were frequent in southern Italy; this time the shock happened to be sharper than usual and its centre had unfortunately lain near Pompeii and Herculaneum. But no one had the remotest idea that subterranean volcanic events had played a part in this. In undisturbed, majestic peace Vesuvius lay there, surrounded by vines and olives, and no one connected the mountain with the disaster which had just been experienced.

3

FROM THE RECONSTRUCTION TO THE CATASTROPHE OF A.D. 79

A.D. 64–79

THE earthquake, which had afflicted not only the two towns near Vesuvius but the whole region of Nuceria and Naples, was of about the "ninth degree" in Pompeii and Herculaneum, that is, "devastating", while in the surrounding district it was of only the "sixth degree", that is, "destructive to very severe". In Naples some houses collapsed, among them the gymnasium. In Nuceria the buildings suffered some damage, but not one collapsed. The centre of the shock lay in Vesuvius; it was a volcanic event, the steam and gases which had gathered inside the mountain seeking an outlet. In fact, the earthquake was an abortive attempt on the part of Vesuvius to create an open vent for itself such as it now possesses. Although such natural events were a frequent phenomenon in those volcanic regions, there was at that time, of course, nothing resembling the modern system of seismic observation. People ascribed these events to supernatural influences, that is, to the gods, to the conflict of Titans, and the like. Sacrifices to appease the almighty were doubled, and prayers were offered at the altars of the temples that the lords of heaven and earth might in future avert such a disaster.

Immediately after the decision of the Roman Senate to rebuild the ruined towns, the people zealously set to work to make good the damage and to restore their homes. But not everyone returned to the stricken towns; there were some far-sighted people who did not trust the future, who feared a repetition of such events and preferred therefore not to return.

These were, of course, mostly persons and families who possessed estates elsewhere or people who were economically independent and not absolutely bound to the land. But those who could not be separated from their homes — and they were the great majority — remained behind and devoted all their strength to the reconstruction of the towns.

Above all, the approaches had to be restored, especially the Gate of Vesuvius, which had completely collapsed, for through this gate flowed the whole of the traffic for Stabiae. This was also true of the seriously damaged Gate of Herculaneum. The work on these began at once. Not less urgent was the restoration of the water system. The ruined tower at the Gate of Vesuvius was rebuilt, but in spite of this the system did not function. The subterranean lead pipes had been burst at many points and the breaks were not discovered, so that the water system could serve neither the houses nor the baths which it had formerly fed, such as the Stabian Baths. Water had to be drawn from the fountains and cisterns, while a completely new system was planned which was to be laid down on Roman principles. In the meantime the most essential work was begun on individual houses to make them habitable again.

The Roman Senate did everything possible to further these efforts. Things went slowly, however, for the extent of the damage was so great that work needed to be done everywhere at the same time, and there was especially a lack of technicians to meet the sudden great demand. The Emperor Nero, too, eager to show a remarkable side of his nature to the people, did a great deal for the stricken towns. Not content with his high office, he was filled with a passionate desire to be accounted a divinely inspired artist. So he resolved, in disregard of the imperial dignity, which forbade him to make a public appearance on the stage, to sing in the theatre at Naples, in the annual music festival, in the year A.D. 64. Filled with feverish excitement, he had just taken his place in the crammed theatre (in which many soldiers were present to provide professional applause), when an earthquake lasting several seconds shook the building. There was a rush to the stage to warn Nero, but he went on with the song which he had already begun as though nothing had happened, and won more applause from the public for this proof of courage than for his songs. But scarcely was the recital over and the audience departed, than the theatre, shaken to its foundations by the earthquake, collapsed; the rest of the city was more or less undamaged. It had been only a small shock, with its centre somewhere in the sea near the island of Ischia. In Pompeii and Herculaneum it was felt only slightly; but the news from Naples roused great terror and fear of a repetition of the recent disaster.

But when as the years passed this earthquake in Naples was not followed by others, people settled down again and eagerly continued the restoration of the town. After the main streets of Pompeii had been cleared, work was begun on public buildings. The forum especially, with the ruined temples and porticos, bore a desolate appearance. Since the places of worship had suffered most severely, and they could not all be rebuilt at once, the sacred rites had to be carried on temporarily in other less stricken places. Thus the worship of Jupiter and Juno, hitherto conducted in the largest temple in the forum, as well as the worship of Minerva, were transferred to the little Greek-Samnite temple of Zeus, which had suffered only slight damage. The basilica, too, was completely unserviceable and the Temple of Venus Pompeiana behind it lay in ruins. It was impossible to think of a speedy reconstruction of these three enormous buildings; the work had to be spread out over a considerable period of time.

A beginning was made with the Temple of Apollo, the oldest on the forum, including its porticos. In the rebuilding the pure and simple lines of Hellenic architecture were abandoned, and everything was restored, in accordance with the taste of the time, in a fantastic style resembling the Corinthian yet diverging widely from it. Great use was made of stucco painted in loud colours. This was completely in accord with the general tendency, which was to use the reconstruction as a political weapon to blot out all recollection of the earlier time. It was in the nature of things that this should be done with greater splendour, but not always in better taste.

As a result of this new order enjoined by the Roman officials, many shafts and capitals of the columns had to be altered, stucco and countless ornaments and figures had everywhere to replace the old styles, and all this slowed down the work of restoration. This was also true of the second storey of the arcading round the forum, which had just been begun in the time of Augustus, and which was naturally one of the first things to collapse in the earthquake. For more than a decade, therefore, the once magnificent forum was a desolate confusion of columns, cornices, enormous blocks of travertine (with which the forum was to be repaved), and marble of all kinds. This marble was to decorate the buildings and to cover the socles for the statues of famous persons, which were to be erected between the pillars of the arcades. For the immediate future the forum could be used only to a very limited extent for its proper purposes, and looked more like a great workshop and building site. But how was the rebuilding of all those buildings and temples, once so grand and now in ruins, to be financed? The reconstruction was far beyond the financial resources of the community. Wealthy private individuals had to be approached and the suggestion made that they might bear the expense of restoring a building — as, for example, the duumvir Marcus Tullius did with the Temple of Fortuna Augusta. It was a sign of the popularity of the mystery cult of Isis that a rich freedman, of the distinguished house of the Popidii in Pompeii, was at once found ready to build this temple, which he did in the name of his six-year-old son. For this the son was elected by the Senate of the town to be one of themselves, an honour which the child could actually enter upon only when he was thirty years of age. The father did this for his son and not for himself, because he himself as a freedman could not receive such an honour. Thus it was possible for the worship of the Egyptian goddess to be resumed at once; this cult was popular because it promised not only eternal blessedness hereafter but also a happy life in this world and, besides, offered a ritual which was both mysterious and magnificent, with processions and festivals. Isis was the patron goddess of seafaring, which was avoided as far as possible in the winter and fully resumed only in the spring. And this resumption was a festival occasion, the so-called "Boat of Isis" in March, when after a brilliant procession to the harbour the ships put out to sea once more.

The magistrates, as well as the rest of the Pompeians, whose taste increasingly favoured Roman culture and customs, had specially at heart, after the places of worship, the fate of their great baths and thermae. For a long time these had been not merely places for physical cleanliness, but also places of amusement and of social rendezvous after the day's work was done. Now the public baths had been hard hit, not only by the damage to their water-supplies but also in themselves. Thus the men's bath in the Stabian Thermae had been seriously damaged by the collapse of the lukewarm room and by the destruction of the warm-water bath itself. The same was true of the baths next to the forum, and since Roman imperial taste particularly favoured magnificent and luxuriously equipped baths, with their opportunities for physical culture and games, it was resolved to build a large, entirely new bathing-place, the so-called Central Bath. This was erected at the junction of the Nolan and the Stabian Ways, and its plan was so grandiose that it took more than ten years to complete.

Simultaneously the reconstruction of the theatres was taken in hand. The large theatre, and apparently also the amphitheatre, could not be used. The roof of the small theatre had fallen in; it was not renewed, but the building was restored just sufficiently to serve as a temporary roofless venue for the modest performances which were given in the years after the earthquake. Since the amphitheatre too was in course of being rebuilt, no big gladiatorial games were arranged for the time being.

Work on those large public buildings took a long time, of course, since many architects and builders were required for the reconstruction of hundreds of private houses. Besides, many of those houses had changed hands, and the new owners restored the houses to their own taste, often completely transforming them.

This happened also to the mansion beyond the Gate of Herculaneum, the lovely rectangular villa with the semicircular verandah looking to the sea, the cool vaulted hall, and the incomparable frescoes of the mysteries in the great salon. Its wealthy and cultured Roman owner sold it to people who had no understanding of beauty, but were only interested in farming. The mistress of the house, the priestess of the mysteries, had very likely died or been killed in the earthquake. On one wall of the villa there was a delightful drawing of a bald man, crowned with a laurel wreath, and with the inscription "Rufus" (see p. 107); perhaps it represented the man who now became the owner. The new master set to work at once to transform the lovely patrician villa into a dairy farm. He had no interest at all in the beautiful paintings of the second style which covered the walls. Everything was covered over with the new, fantastic paintings of the so-called fourth style, whose unnatural architecture, with its excessive ornaments, witnesses to the change of taste and the departure from the noble and simple lines of Greek art. Yet somehow the new owner did have the feeling that the room containing the paintings of the mysteries was something quite special, and this room at least he left untouched. At first the great villa, with its ninety rooms, was only partly used, obviously by farm-workers and the men who were carrying out the reconstruction.

In the town itself the new building and the changes in the private houses went forward more speedily than the restoration of the great public buildings. During this work the Roman officials saw to the removal of all signs of independence, especially of Oscan and Samnite inscriptions, so that the memory of that time might be completely extinguished. This policy was particularly supported by the Romans who took possession of houses whose former owners had been of the old aristocracy. Thus two brothers, Aulus Vettius Restitutus and Aulus Vettius Conviva, freedmen of the new-rich family of the Vettii, had bought a noble patrician house, and in the manner of parvenues who wish to display their wealth to all the world had remodelled and refurnished it. They had taken over a house of pre-imperial times which had suffered severely from the earthquake, and had rebuilt it and decorated it with paintings of the fourth style, whose loud colours and sharp contrasts compared badly with the beauty and harmony of the pictures of the second and third styles.[1] Most of the pictures had garlands of flowers painted round the borders, chiefly myrtles, ivy, vines, oleanders, laurel and narcissi. Myrtle was much used because it was sacred to Venus. According to the legend the goddess was born in the sea, and when she rose out of it in her nakedness, she hid herself for shame among the myrtle bushes which grew along the shore. The oleander too was often depicted and the Damascene rose,

[1] For example in the great triclinium of the house of the Vettii.

Photo: Alinari

8.   A Menu in Mosaic. Pompeii.
(*See pages* 14, 29)

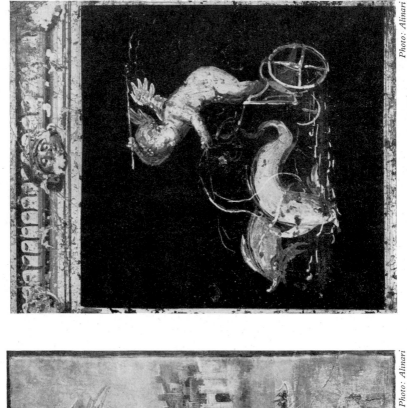

Photo: Alinari

10. Dolphins harnessed by Eros. Fresco in the House of the Vettii, Pompeii.

Photo: Alinari

9. Wall-painting from Pompeii, representing the fall of Icarus, who according to the legend flew with wings of wax until they melted in the sun, when he fell to his death. A fatal attempt to fly in a kind of glider probably lies behind

which as a symbol alike of love and of beauty was dedicated to Venus. The legend tells that its petals, which used to be white, were changed to crimson by the blood of the goddess, who had been pricked by its thorns.[1]

It became fashionable to decorate the walls with paintings expressing the purpose of the various rooms. In public rooms there were mainly mythological scenes, while in the atria and porticos and peristyles, which often surrounded a small garden, there were landscapes and country scenes containing the characteristic pine-tree of the district. The dining-rooms, or triclinia, had mostly paintings of fruits and vegetables. But in spite of the exaggerated paintings of the last period the house of the Vettii, with its atria, peristyle and pillars, and its marble and bronze statues scattered among the flowers and shrubs, was an enviably pleasant retreat, set in perpetual sunshine beneath a blue sky. The two freedmen who dwelt there were unashamed hedonists. One little room proved this beyond all doubt, being obviously dedicated to the joys of Venus, for its walls were covered with pictures which were highly suitable for exciting lovers to the utmost.

So in the course of the fifteen quiet years which followed the great earthquake, Pompeii was slowly transformed, losing the last signs of its former individuality and preserving no fear of new convulsions. It became a Roman country town with a great many wealthy guests from the capital on the Tiber, who enjoyed the countryside, in peaceful meditation eating the delicious food and fruits of Pompeii and drinking the delicate wines from the slopes of Vesuvius.

In Herculaneum matters developed in much the same way. This little place, lying as it did nearer the centre of the earthquake of Vesuvius, had suffered correspondingly greater damage than Pompeii. But its inhabitants were for the most part rich settlers who could contribute more to its speedy reconstruction. In general, in the fifteen years following the earthquake there was, in spite of the greater damage, much greater progress than in Pompeii in rebuilding private houses as well as the theatres and other public buildings. All the same, here too much remained to be done, even though there was substantial financial help from the Emperor, for example

---

[1] " Illustrazione delle piante rappresentate nei dipinti pompeiani " (article by Dr Comes).

in the building of the new temple to Cybele. Here too the memory of the terror of the shock grew dim, people looked to the future gaily and joyfully, and rejoiced in life.

With the progress of the rebuilding, which brought money to the people, numbers and wealth increased in both towns, and the love of art and the desire to beautify things in public and private life also became more widespread. In the cellars the great two-armed wine-jugs, the amphoras, with their delicious contents, accumulated steadily; the age of the wines could be told from a note on the jugs naming the consuls of the vintage year. In the shops goods and provisions, which met with a ready sale, were heaped up. There was a general revival of prosperity, and people began to take an interest in purely eastern events, as well as in the world politics of imperial Rome. In A.D. 68 Nero had been murdered after an exciting political struggle. The Emperor had yielded too much to his artistic inclinations. The vanity which took him to Greece to seek laurels as a singer and a charioteer kept him away too long from Rome, and blinded him to the decline of the imperial prestige among his neglected legions. Their disaffection was the cause of his end. But the rebellious troops who summoned the seventy-three-year-old Galba to be emperor were no better pleased with him and he was assassinated. Then one of Nero's favourites, called Otho, was raised to the throne, but in less than a hundred days the legions of the Rhine Army had made one of their own men, Vitellius, emperor. He crossed the Alps and defeated the troops of Otho, and Otho committed suicide. Now the legions in the east had something to say. They were fighting the Jews, and their commander, Vespasian, the son of a simple customs official, and a brave, reliable, and hard-working man, seemed to them to be the right person for the imperial dignity. Although Vespasian himself remained in the east, the battles between his adherents and those of Vitellius were decided in favour of the leader in the Jewish war.

By the end of A.D. 69 the conflict was over, and the Senate entrusted the government in Rome to Titus Flavius Vespasian; the house of Caesar was set aside and the *petit bourgeois* house of the Flavii had gained the mastery. Vespasian entrusted his son Titus with the final defeat of the Jews, and entered Rome in the year 70. He at once threw himself into the task of restoring the peace which had been so sadly disturbed in the previous year, with its four emperors. So far as peace and quiet were restored and trade and the arts flourished again within the area of Roman rule, the towns of Campania were encouraged in the work of reconstruction and in the development of their trade by Vespasian's policy. Incoming Romans of good family did not, of course, condescend to undertake any kind of trade. A Roman patrician was ready to take up the pursuit of agriculture, but he left the despised trade of the merchant to freedmen and foreigners, Jews and slaves. Roman officials, however, recognised its importance and were far-sighted enough to allow it the greatest freedom. There were regular market-days in Pompeii and Herculaneum, and advertisements urging attendance were painted on the walls of the houses, both in these towns and in neighbouring places. On those market-days there was lively activity in the parts of the fora which had been restored. Cobblers and tailors, bankers, vendors of fruits and wines and fish, and merchants of every kind offered their wares, while numerous eating-houses, open to the street, provided speedy meals for the great numbers who streamed into the town.

This life was so picturesque and animated that one Pompeian had it depicted in frescoes in his house. There the potters and other craftsmen exhibit their work; a young slave girl is for sale, and the seller makes her hold up a sheet of papyrus describing all her qualities. School scenes, too — the whipping of a small miscreant, and so on — were represented in the porticos of the forum; and on market-days the forum was further decorated with garlands hanging between the pillars. There were advertisements of all kinds, either painted in great coloured letters in the public squares or scratched with a pointed instrument on the outside walls of the houses. And indeed the whole rich and busy life of the town, both public and private, was reflected in those revealing inscriptions. The election notices which could be seen everywhere on the walls of Pompeii played a very large part. These invited support for this or that candidate for public office, and it was quite common to write on the walls of your own house somewhat as follows: "Paquius recommends Lucius Popidius Ampliatus as aedile"; or someone else would paint on the house of an influential man: "O Trebius, bestir yourself and make that excellent young man Lollius Fuscus an aedile." It could be seen from such writings that in the one instance the house belonged to Paquius, in the other to Trebius Valens. It appears that not only individuals but also the corporations, such as the boilermen, the fullers, the felt-makers, the dyers, the goldsmiths, the muleteers, the barbers, the vintners, the confectioners, the worshippers of Isis, even the ball-players, supported one or the other candidate as a group — that is, they combined to advertise their views on public buildings, espousing the cause of one of the candidates, naming him as duumvir or aedile, as being fit and worthy, as one who would give splendid games, see that the bread was of good quality, and so on.

Women too, such as the mistress of a tavern or a bar, and even the individual maids in the place, of more or less good repute, would take a hand in the elections. Jokers were not lacking: rogues and vagabonds recommended the lazy Vatia as aedile, and the sweetheart of Claudius wanted people to make her beloved a duumvir. There were also threats: "If anyone does not vote for Quinctius may he be carried through the city on a donkey's back to be mocked at." Boastful tips about how to solve economic problems could also be read: "Just share out the public money, that's what I favour — for the public coffers have plenty of money."

The election notices clearly gave the names of the most important people in the town. A man usually had three names, a first name, for example Marcus, a family (*gens*) name, such as Holconius, and an additional name, such as Priscus. The first name varied, but the eldest son was always given his father's name. The first and the family name were passed from father to son, the additional name very often came from the mother's family, but could also come from elsewhere. For example, freed slaves, who as slaves had only one name, added the *gens* of their former masters as well as a third name, such as Januarius, Apollonius or Iucundus — these names, in fact, being so popular among freed slaves that they were sufficient to indicate the man's origin. A collection of the names on the houses of Pompeii would produce almost a complete list of the most important citizens and even of the owners of the various houses on which the election appeals were to be found.

The elected officials had to be of responsible age and to be known as honourable citizens. The electors were all adult citizens. The period of office was only one year, from the first of July, and the elections took place every March. When the elections were over, the appeals on the walls were obliterated by the candidates' own "painters", and thus space was made till the next elections for new announcements of every kind.

In Pompeii, with its busy and active life and the great influence of the authorities on trade and commerce, interest in the elections was very strong. The election struggles and political strife were keen, and the great interest taken by the people was shown in these writings. It was quite different in Herculaneum: there was a lack of opposition because trade rivalries among the inhabitants were not very strong. The elections took a quieter course. The people took less interest in them and there were fewer appeals to vote for or against the candidates; the struggle was not so coloured by personal sympathies as in trade-loving Pompeii. It is useless to look in Herculaneum for inscriptions which heap every virtue on this or that candidate, call down curses on an opponent, simply call an opposing voter an ass, or even solemnly declare that Venus herself wishes this or that one to be aedile. Even the beggars in Pompeii proposed certain people as aediles, no doubt in the hope that once in office they would better the lot of the poor. The writings on the walls in both towns, however, showed in general what great value the inhabitants set on people being able to read their names again and again. Hundreds upon hundreds of names were scratched on the walls of the basilica, on the forum at Pompeii, in the theatre and the amphitheatre — wherever the people were in the habit of gathering together in great numbers: an abuse still practised today on monuments and outlook towers and the like. The painters had a hard job. But they too did not fail to give their names. "Sosius wrote this", "Onesimus has whitened the stone again", one can read at one place. This was mostly done at night, by the light of the moon or of a lantern, and the lantern-bearer had also to hold the ladder. But the walls were not only used for election appeals, advertisements of games and the like, but also for direct written correspondence among the citizens—for praise and blame, for rendezvous and congratulation, for philosophical and ironical remarks, as well as for the affixing of emotional effusions and quotations from the best-known poets whose truth was felt by this one or that in his own body. Thus on a wall next to the house of Caius Julius Polybius could be read the verses:

> Nothing can last for ever:
> Though the sun shines gold
> It must plunge into the sea.
> The moon has also disappeared
> Which but now so brightly gleamed.
> If one day thy fair one storms
> In wildest fury
> Hold fast, this storm will soon yield
> To the soft zephyr.[1]

While most of the public notices, such as election appeals, were painted in black or red-brown, the more private notes, the jeers or jokes, the greetings, the sighs of the lover, maledictions and the like, were mostly scratched on the wall. Along with countless friendly words, such as "Greetings, brother Emilius Fortunatus", there are some which do not sound in the least friendly, such as "Samius wishes Cornelius would hang himself". Warnings too are not lacking. "The smallest evil, if neglected, becomes the greatest" is one man's opinion. And on the walls of Pompeii there is even the advice that if you have no idea what to do with your time, you can scatter millet and gather it up again. The small sorrows and joys of life are mirrored there. A win at dice, and moreover an "honourable" win, as is significantly added, is triumphantly proclaimed.

Drinking was not peculiar to the ancient Germanic tribes, it was at least as much a habit of the Romans. One inscription on the basilica betrays a limitless thirst: "Suavis craves for full wine-jars, please, and his thirst is enormous." Another has assuaged his thirst: "Good day to you. We are as full as wine-skins." But it is not always the best Falernian which is set before the drinkers of Pompeii. "May you be laid low yourself one day by your tricks" is one man's curse on the landlord, "You sell us this watery liquid and drink pure wine yourself." But often the money was lacking for food and drink, and many a one looked enviously on the rich man with

[1] Della Corte, *Pompei, I nuovi scavi e l'anfiteatrfo*, p. 37. Pompeii, 1930.

his groaning table and ample supplies of wine. "May the man prosper who bids me to his table," could be read on one wall. "Lucius Istazidius, who doesn't invite me, is just a barbarian."

Far the greatest amount of space in these personal writings was taken up by love. Everything revolved round love; it was the beginning and the end. "One must enjoy life, for there is nothing better in the world" was the fundamental principle of the pagan philosophy of the time, and everyone strove to live according to it. It was quite in vain, men thought, to try to ward off love, for "he who tries to separate lovers would bind the winds and forbid the murmuring streams to flow".[1] One man was impatient to reach his beloved as quickly as possible, and while the muleteer took time for relaxation and a drink, the lover, on tenterhooks, scratched these verses on the wall: "Oh, if you too felt how love burns, you would bring me much quicker to my love. Now on, drive on the animals, drink up, hurry, take the reins and use your whip. On to Pompeii, for my love is there." There are innumerable compliments paid to loved persons. There is one enraptured and graceful piece of writing on a wall: "If you have not seen the Venus painted by Apelles, look at my beloved — she is as charming as that." And one who is far from his beloved writes with sighs: "Victoria, I greet you, and wherever you are may your sneeze bring you luck." Amor dictated to another writer and Cupid guided his hand: "Oh, I should rather die than be a god without you!"

But not everyone found that his affection was requited, and the attention of the beloved was often sought by a note written on a wall, since the lover did not dare to confess his secret direct: "Marcus loves Spendusa and Rufus loves Cornelia Helena. I must away!" "Farewell, my Sava, and love me just a little. Oh, if you know the meaning of love and if you have any human feelings, have pity on me, and permit me, flower of Venus, to come to you." But many fair ones were prudish and would have nothing to do with the adoring lover, and even gave him a rather unloving rebuff: "Virgula to her friend Tertius: my dear man, you are too ugly for me." Serna cannot endure Isidorus, and Livia says to Alexander: "I'm not interested in your welfare. On the contrary, I should rejoice in your failure." One rejected suitor went off with

[1] On the door-post of a house in the Vico dei Soprastanti.

scorn: "One loves, another is loved; I don't care a hang." Another hand made the biting addition: "The man who doesn't care a hang is in love." Another rejected suitor took a mean revenge: "Lucilla makes money from her body." Another disillusioned lover wrote on the wall: "What is the use of a Venus when she's made of marble?"

The various feelings of the people of Pompeii and Herculaneum could be followed in these writings. The less ideal side of love also took up much space. Hate and fury against rivals who are in pursuit of the beloved filled many a heart and guided the hands of the writers: "May the man who seduces my girl be devoured by a cruel bear of the wild mountains." Filled with rage, a husband who had surprised his unfaithful wife in a tavern of ill repute wrote: "I've got you, I've got you! There is no doubt that Romula is here with this rascal."

Sometimes a man longed for his wife, and such a one wrote sadly on the wall of the inn: "Vivius Restitus slept here alone, and thought with longing of his Urbana." In such cases there was nothing left but to betake oneself to the house of joy, the little lupanar lying hidden in a side-street, where the guests were not ashamed to write on the wall their own name and that of their mistress for an hour, and praise her qualities. It was not surprising, in all this obsession of writing, that one man ill-temperedly cursed all the scribbling: "Wall, I am amazed that you haven't collapsed long ago, you are condemned to carry so much idle chatter."

The loosening of morals was accompanied by some weakening of faith and of worship of the gods. There were even many who despised the gods, and one Pompeian did not hesitate to write abusive words about Venus, the goddess of his city, because she had afflicted him with an unrequited love. "I will knock Venus's ribs to pieces with rods, and I will whip her till she's lame. If she is able to pierce my tender heart, why should I not be able to smash her skull with a cudgel?"

But these were isolated instances. The majority of the people lived in fear of the gods. Wherever one went there were altars; no house was without its little chapel for the household gods; pictures of the chief gods were painted everywhere and shrines stood at the cross-roads and beside the fountains. The worship of Isis was very flourishing. There was probably only meagre information about Christianity. So the sun shone on just and unjust alike.

Meanwhile there was another decisive change of government in Rome. Vespasian, under whose rule the complete subjugation of the Jews (in A.D. 70), the destruction of Jerusalem, and conquests in the island of Britain had been achieved, died on 24th June in the year 79. He was succeeded by his son Titus, proved in war and peace. An orderly inherited succession such as this was unusual. Although the new ruler had been unpopular, with a reputation for cruelty, he proved himself immediately after he ascended the throne so well-meaning, noble and circumspect that his contemporaries soon described him as the joy and delight of mankind.

In Pompeii preparations were being made to adorn the Temple of Augustus with the statue of Titus and to complete the unfinished sanctuary. The new buildings on the forum had progressed slowly. The Temple of Jupiter still lay in ruins, and looked like a great mason's yard. Nor was the two-storied portico completely finished, the statues being still lacking; and the basilica likewise awaited reconstruction. On the site where the Temple of Venus Pompeiana had been before the earthquake, a wooden building seems to have served as temporary accommodation for the worship of the goddess. The Temples of Fortuna Augusta and of Isis, on the other hand, were in use again, and the theatres were almost wholly restored.

In July the new councillors and officials, who had been elected in March, had entered on office. The election appeals had not yet been removed from the walls, and it was possible to read that for the duumvirate, that is for the two presidents in the city council, Marcus Holconius Priscus, Gaius Gavius Rufus and Publius Paquius Proculus were the most favoured names. For the office of aedile Marcus Casellius Marcellus was the most often named ("one whom even Venus would have chosen to be her lover"), and after him Marcus Cerinius Vatia and Lucius Popidius Secundus. It is highly probable that among these names are those of the four men who held office in the fateful days that lay ahead.

Quiet, peaceful and solemn, Vesuvius towered proudly over the life of all these towns, villages and country houses lying in a gay semicircle round the gulf of Naples, with its picturesque islands rising up out of the sea. The whole scene was one of peaceful progress and well-being in a charming countryside. But fate was waiting in the depths of the earth, hidden from the unsuspecting inhabitants. While Vesuvius, covered almost to its summit with splendid vines, did not exhibit the least sign of anything unusual, a mighty disturbance was being prepared in its heart. Nobody looked much at the mountain: in the countless pastoral frescoes Vesuvius was seldom depicted. And it looked very different in a fresco at Pompeii and one at Herculaneum. The picture at Herculaneum showed the broken-off peak, today called Somma, which fell away to the east, but to the west passed into a flattened plateau of a crater inactive for countless years and hence unrecognisable for what it was. The picture at Pompeii, on the other hand, depicted the mountain in much more rugged form, and gave most prominence to the vines covering the slopes and to the vine-clad figure of Bacchus, to whom Vesuvius was sacred. These were no great works of art and not true to nature, but one thing is clear: neither picture gives the least hint that the mountain was a volcano and was gathering in its depths a mighty conglomeration of fiery streams and gaseous masses. And this ignorance was general, despite Strabo's observations that the flat summit of Vesuvius was quite unfruitful, resembling a field of ashes, with cavities of soot-coloured stones which seemed as though they had been consumed by fire. Like most volcanoes, Vesuvius lies near the sea, and seawater penetrates the folds of the earth's crust and is changed into steam in the high temperature of the glowing centre of the mountain. Vesuvius at that time had no open crater, and the gases in their effort to find an outlet exerted pressure on the molten or solid stone which barred their way. If enough force is concentrated these great masses are raised in order to make a vent. The fluid masses of hot lava thus carried to the surface are molten, and flow slowly like a thick gruel. The gases break through this material, which is torn asunder and erupted in great lumps called clinkers; in small, almost featherweight pumice-stone, about the size of a ping-pong ball, called *lapilli*; and in fine, dust-like, sand-like material called volcanic ash — though strictly speaking it is not ash at all.

Volcanic activity had been greatly intensified in the sixteen years which had elapsed since the abortive eruption of the year 63, experienced as an earthquake. The pressure inside Vesuvius had enormously increased, and about the middle of the month of August, A.D. 79, about six weeks after Titus had become emperor, fresh earth tremors were felt. But they did not as yet constitute a real threat: in the houses and villages around Vesuvius here and there some object fell to the ground, a crack appeared in the wall, a fountain ran dry; for the time being that was all. These slight incidents seemed at first to offer no ground for unrest. But about 20th August the shocks became more severe. They were accompanied by a subdued rumble as of distant thunder. Fear began to spread, and anxious spirits whispered that the giants were stirring again; there was uproar now in the mountains, now in the plains, and even in the sea, which in spite of the serene and sunny sky was strangely stirred and threw wild and foaming waves on the shore. On 22nd and 23rd August the earth settled down in most places, except in the mountainous valley running towards Vesuvius. The countryside lay at peace, the garland of houses and cities, resting in a splendour of flowers about the lovely bay, was bathed in the blue of sky and sea and the luscious and exuberant green of ripening nature. The birds, which usually filled the gardens with their song, were strangely quiet, and fluttered uneasily hither and thither; dogs barked without any apparent reason; the cattle in the stalls began to low, straining at their chains despite the quietness which lay upon the land. There was something in the air, and the farmers looked anxiously at the skies, fearing a gathering hail-storm which could destroy their crops in a moment. But no, there was nothing of that kind in sight. The vault of heaven was blue and cloudless over the earth, and on the morning of 24th August the sun's scorching rays beat on the little towns and villas, on Pompeii and Herculaneum and the city of Naples shimmering white in the distance through the haze.

All at once a new shock convulsed the earth. It was more terrible than all that had preceded it. And now thousands thought they saw the superhuman mighty ones clearly moving about among the mountains and hovering in the air from the direction of the sea. Suddenly, in the forenoon of 24th August, there followed a fearful clap of thunder. The ear-splitting detonation came from the direction of Vesuvius, to which all eyes turned, terror-filled. And lo, the mountain-top had split open, and amid the crash of thunder fire seemed to be breaking from its heart. But no, the glow disappeared, an immense black smoke-cloud rose to heaven, deafening crashes followed one another in quick succession, dark pillars of stone disintegrated high in the air and sank down in heaps. And suddenly, no one knew how and from where, there was tearing rain everywhere, and with it showers of stones, fragments of earth, tiny pieces of light pumice-stone interspersed with great lumps like bombs, and all so thick and continuous that the sun was darkened. All at once it was night in the midst of day, while intermittent lightning-flashes lit up the dreadful scene. Killed or stunned, the birds fell from the air, and dead fish were cast on the shores by the raging sea.

What was it? What was happening to the world? Filled with fear man and beast plunged hither and thither, in aimless confusion, seeking only to flee, to save what could be saved. Surely the gods had come down from heaven, the immortals were punishing men and driving the whole world to chaos and destruction. Then there was no escape; for whither shall one flee when everything is crashing down in ruins, the sun is falling to the earth and the earth is heaving itself to heaven with fearful turmoil? There could be no doubt that was what was happening; it could be nothing else. And worse followed. Mixed with the rain of stones and ash which came from above, and spread out far and wide, burying everything beneath it, there came streams of water like the Great Flood. And no one knew whether the water came from the sky or the earth.

What had happened? The immense pressure of the steam and gases in the caverns of the volcano had become so great that it raised the enormous masses of stone, and these masses in their turn had with a mighty detonation torn a hole in the peak of the mountain. This hole became an enormous, threatening, circular fire-crater. The lighter pumice-stone and the finer ash-like sand were borne into the air by the violence of the eruption and carried away by the winds. They covered everything to a distance of ten miles in layers fifteen to twenty feet deep. Sixteen miles from the scene of the eruption, in the foothills of Misenum, at the Roman naval base, commanded by the famous naturalist and imperial dignitary the Elder Pliny, the ashes and stones which rained down out of the darkness had to be continually cleared away, lest the men should suffocate.

Meanwhile round the crater of Vesuvius a great mass of stones and erupted fragments had gathered. Mixed with the pumice-stone and the ash-like sand these formed, in the streaming rain, a fearful avalanche of mud, which began to flow down from the mountain towards the coast. For it was towards the sea that the crater leaned and on this side that the wall of the crater had collapsed. This mass of mud swallowed first the houses and villas on the slopes of the mountain, and then the stream poured straight into the peaceful, proud and lovely little town of Herculaneum, lying only two miles from the summit of Vesuvius, with its splendid houses and temples, its buildings and fountains and altars. For a moment the stream halted against the walls, then branched down the streets, which were filled in a flash. And new masses streamed behind, the rolling wall of mud reaching at places a height of thirty to forty feet, flooding over everything, burying houses and temples and filling the cellars. The mud flowed into the semicircle of the wonderful theatre as into a great bowl, first shattering in a fearful impact the lovely scenic wall with its marble statues and engulfing it in its stream. Here and there the statues were torn from their pedestals, and an enormous bronze quadriga crowning a public building was smashed into a hundred pieces in its irresistible course.

The mortally terrified inhabitants at once grasped the full significance of the catastrophe. In face of the ocean of mud and flowing stone, which swept on its way swallowing and filling everything, the continuous earthquakes, the rain of stones and the total darkness, there was only one thing to do — to flee, to flee as quickly as possible. The very children saw that there could be no remaining there. Those who had horses and wagons swung themselves up, whipped the horses, tried to hold up burning torches, and so took flight. Away, away towards the sea or towards Naples. The rest fled hastily on foot, grasping flickering oil-lanterns. Only some of the sick and aged, who could not move, and some unlucky ones imprisoned by the sudden collapse of walls, met a miserable end.

But there were only a few of these, for in Herculaneum everyone thought only of flight, and no one tried to take shelter in cellars or the like. This was prevented by the inexorable stream, which penetrated everywhere, even through the caved-in roofs of the houses. This was lucky for the Herculaneans, for in this way most of them escaped with their lives. It is true that many wagons of the fleeing people (who had tied cushions or heaped clothes on their heads to protect themselves from falling stones) overturned, the drivers having lost their way in the dark, which was relieved only by feeble torches, or met insuperable obstacles in the clefts opened in the ground by the earthquakes. And everywhere there was the suffocating air and the penetrating smell of sulphur. The flight was a terrible scene: wailing women, howling children, everyone crying for his family, many praying to the gods, others seeing in the terrible events the destruction of their gods as well. Heaven and earth were collapsing.

And now the stream of mud had rolled over Herculaneum and beyond. It reached the sea and pushed two hundred yards out into the waters. The flourishing town had disappeared from the earth. Gone for ever the glorious Temple to Cybele, mother of the gods, restored by Vespasian after the earthquake at such cost; buried the splendid villa on the outskirts with its wonderful collection of statues and bronzes and the library of the philosopher Philodemous. The forum too was buried, with its lovely buildings, and the basilica in which the family of the Balbi had been immortalised in statues. The inhabitants fled homeless, many crazed with terror, in the direction of Naples. There fear and anxiety also reigned, for the earth tremors and the rain of ashes caused heavy damage there too. And still the eruption of Vesuvius continued; ever new fountains of stone, gleaming fiery in the reflection from the molten masses, were hurled forth from the crater, and an immense pine-shaped cloud of black smoke, lit by fearsome lightning-flashes, hung over the mountain. But otherwise there was a terrible darkness, "not as in a moonless and cloudy night, but as in a completely sealed room".[1] But Herculaneum had ceased to be a town; it was a tomb, in which everything lay buried beneath at least forty feet of slowly hardening mud.

[1] Pliny the Younger in his letter to the historian Tacitus.

In the more distant regions and places, too, the eruption of Vesuvius had caused tremendous alarm. In Misenum, for example, the chief naval port for the Roman fleet entrusted with the security of the Tyrrhenian Sea, the explosion, it is true, was not heard, but the enormous cloud, now black, now white, rising out of Vesuvius was watched with great anxiety. The fleet commander, Caius Plinius, set out to see the dreadful sight from nearer at hand, using a light and speedy ship. In amazement he watched the dark cloud over Vesuvius rising up as on a long, slender stem and then dividing under the influence of the winds into many branches, its colour changing as lapilli, earth or ashes were thrown up.

Just as Pliny left his house to go to the ship, a letter was handed to him from a certain Rectina, the wife of his friend Cascus, in which she wrote to him in haste of the terrible danger in which she was placed in her house on the slopes of Vesuvius, and begged him to save her. Pliny at once had a great number of four-banked galleys made ready, for he wanted to help not only this lady but as many people as possible. So he gave orders that the ships should make direct for the neighbourhood of Vesuvius, where the danger to people and places was greatest. The nearer he came to the coast between Herculaneum and Pompeii, the hotter and thicker fell the white, light pumice-stone on the ships as well as black and fire-stained fragments of rock and white volcanic ash. The sea too was greatly agitated, and the pilots were of the opinion that great chasms had been formed in its bed which rendered impossible a nearer approach or a landing. The crews were in fear of their lives and the steersman besought Pliny to turn back. The experienced commander was at first unwilling to heed this plea, but he soon saw that it was really impossible to hold his course, and he therefore decided to make for the house of a friend, Pomponianus, which lay not far from the coast near Stabiae, four miles south of Pompeii. But there was no peace there either: ash and lapilli were falling upon Stabiae, driven by the north-west wind. It was in this direction that numerous villas lay (on the site of modern Boscoreale), as well as the town of Pompeii, and on these the rain of stone and ashes now poured in full force.

The splendid house on the slopes of the mountain, belonging

to the music-loving Lucius Herennius Florus, was speedily overwhelmed. In the earthquake of the year 63 the villa, and in particular the great peristyle, with its twenty Corinthian pillars, had been severely damaged. Now it was being rebuilt, so that the dwelling part was quite empty and only the rooms needed for the working of the land and especially the culture of the vine were inhabited. On this 24th August the wine-vats were empty, the wine of the previous year having been sold or transferred to amphoras. The mistress of the house was there to superintend the progress of the work on the bathrooms and bedrooms.

Here too, when the ash and stones rained down, terror took hold. Earthquakes convulsed the house to its foundations; the inmates tried to flee, but in the darkness and the suffocating, sulphurous fumes the mistress of the house, her steward and a slave turned back into the house, in the hope of finding shelter. All the treasures—the fine *objets d'art*, the silver plate and no fewer than a thousand glittering gold coins — were quickly gathered together. The slave was commanded to take them all to safety somewhere in the cellars of the house. Fearfully he looked for a place to make them secure, and so he reached the wine-vats. Here the air was already sulphurous and stifling, the wretched man could not breathe, and fell face downwards on his hands and knees, and so suffocated amid all the treasures; up above in the court-yard where the winepresses stood the mistress of the house and her companion tried in vain to protect their faces with cloths, and, falling one upon the other, likewise met death by suffocation.

The horrible calamity continued throughout the district. Pompeii too, which was much farther away from the summit of Vesuvius than Herculaneum, now lay under fierce torrents of stone and ash. Here the catastrophe took a quite different turn. There was no stream of mud to make clear to everybody that the only possible salvation lay in flight. The tremendous explosion, the eruption of fire and stone from the peak of the mountain, and the terrible convulsions of the earth had indeed been experienced with horror. But for too long the hope remained that all this would pass. Thus precious time was lost; but when the north-west wind drove the white pumice-stones in enormous masses towards the town, many sought

Photo: Alinari

11. A Loaf of Bread, Figs, Nuts and Wheat, as often found in Pompeian
houses. The bread, once golden and crisp, as seen in many paintings, is now
completely carbonised.

(*See pages* 29–30, 190)

Photo: Alinari

12. Money chest, as found in the atrium of many well-to-do citizens' houses in Pompeii, more or less artistically decorated. Naples Museum.

(See pages 34, 44, 192, 196)

safety in flight. For the lapilli were piling up in great heaps, the small light pebbles forcing their way in everywhere; while now and then the wind deflected boulders weighing as much as 14 lb. over the town. In no time everything was engulfed, and many roofs collapsed under the weight.

How was escape possible? Those possessing horses and wagons made off as quickly as they could, while many others sought safety in vaults, in solid corridors and cellars, sheltering from the rain of stones until the uproar of the elements subsided. But all who sought shelter thus were suffocated by the poisonous sulphur fumes generated in Vesuvius and wafted across by the wind. The majority, however, hastily snatched up all the valuables and money they could lay hands on and fled with cloak or cloth or pillow over their head. Oil-lanterns and torches cast a feeble light over the melancholy scene. While the fugitives struggled through the nine- or ten-foot-high heaps of lapilli, the white ash mingled with rain fell remorselessly, hindering the general flight; and countless Pompeians were suffocated even in the open street by the terrible sulphurous fumes. The damp ash clung to their hands and feet, and those who had not taken to flight immediately after the eruption suffered a terrible death.

Countless were the tragedies enacted in house and temple, in the rooms and streets of the once flourishing town, which had been transformed in the twinkling of an eye into a place of horror. In fear of death the Pompeians besought the gods for death. Gods? Yes, gods! But don't you see, they don't exist!

The catastrophe had broken so suddenly that the midday meal was in active preparation: a crisp sucking pig was still roasting in the bronze pot, the bread was turning golden-yellow in the oven, and everywhere people were at work as usual in the house, the outbuildings, and in the fields outside the town. But everything had to be left just as it was. The tragic hand of destructive fate had suddenly stretched over this flourishing life. There were no more distinctions — master and slave, husband and wife, all alike were stricken down. The beasts, like the men, were completely distraught: they tore furiously at their chains, and if they succeeded in freeing themselves they rushed out; but if not, they perished miserably in their sheds; the chained watch-dogs suffered the most miserable fate of all.

The rain of stones came from the direction of Vesuvius, that is, from the north-east, so that at first everyone took flight towards the west and the sea, and afterwards the south as well. The fugitives thronged along the three main streets leading to the Herculaneum Gate and the Porta Marina.[1] With pitiful shouts and cries they sought to keep in touch with one another, the husband trying to help the wife, the parents their children, amid the dreadful rain of stones. Many were crazed with terror, and raced blindly hither and thither. It was as in the Bible story of the two proud towns of Palestine. One man, perhaps a Jew, who had taken refuge in the room of a house, scratched the words "Sodom and Gomorrah" on the wall.[2] But as the air got worse he too ventured out into the horrible storm to save his life if he could.

The lovely houses and splendid mansions as well as the simplest huts and taverns all threatened to become tombs for their inhabitants. The hot lapilli and ash rained pitilessly down on the town. A fiery red reflection could be seen rising up from Vesuvius, as though mighty flames were leaping out of its peak. But apart from this glow everything was enveloped in intolerable thick darkness and sulphurous fumes — a hell upon earth. Terror-stricken, two sons of the banker Caecilius Iucundus, Quintus and Sextus, abandoned everything and fled across to the house of Vesonius, in order to reach the Street of Fortune. Their friend was already in flight with his family, and only the poor watch-dog had been forgotten. The stones rained in through the opening of the atrium, and the poor beast jumped as high as the chain attached by a bronze ring to his collar would let him, straining to get free. In the end he was miserably throttled, and lay with his four legs stretched out in the agony of death.

The numerous workers who had been employed on the building of the great central baths fled in terror. What availed riches to the proud owner of that splendid house with the great atrium in whose centre stood the bronze statue of the faun? Or what availed to that great lord his house with its many rooms and the peristyle with its flower-garden surrounded by twenty-four Ionic pillars? The inmates could not

[1] Vico di Mercurio, Strada della Fortuna and di Nola, and the main business street Strada dell' Abbondanza.
[2] In the house Regio IX, 1, 26.

make up their minds to take the only way to safety — in flight. Fearfully they saw the stones raining down through the opening of the atrium upon the bronze statue, and most of them sought shelter in the rooms of the house. The mistress of the house had hastily gathered together her most valuable possessions — massive golden bracelets in the form of snakes, rings, hair-pins and ear-rings, a silver mirror, a bag of coins— and attempted to flee. But when the stones and ash rained down upon her, she turned back in fear, and took refuge in the tablinum, the great room of state. Scarcely had she reached it when the ceiling collapsed beneath the burden, and buried the unhappy woman with her precious possessions beneath the ruins. Other inhabitants of the splendid house, who had not ventured out, were miserably suffocated in the rooms. Mighty duumvir, rich banker, or poor slave, they fled or died, sinking down one upon the other. The attempt to save his earthly goods cost many a one his life.

In one house in the same main street, at whose entrance was a mosaic with the picture of a dog and the warning "Cave canem", two young girls, hastily trying to snatch together at least their jewellery, wasted precious time, and sank down suffocated beside their valuables.

In the house of Pansa the inhabitants had quickly wrapped in linen some of their finest things, for example a little bronze group of Bacchus and a satyr, in order to take them with them. But they had not gone beyond the garden before they realised that such things could not be taken with them in their flight, and they threw the bronze group into a copper kettle that happened to be standing in the garden. While the owners were able to make for safety, four tenants, women of gentle birth, with golden ear-pendants and precious rings, thought they might survive by sheltering in a room of the house, and in the midst of their precious ornaments and silver coins all four met death by suffocation.

The great mass of fugitives poured along the street leading to the Gate of Herculaneum. Those who lived at the west end of the town, nearest the sea, were the first to reach safety, for example, Caius Sallustius, the owner of the lovely corner house at the end of the Street of Mercury. Only the mistress of the house seems to have lost too much time in the gathering of her valuables: she collapsed in the damp and sticky ash of the street, not far from her home; strewn around her were her jewellery, her money and her silver mirror, and nearby lay her three serving women.

It became increasingly difficult to flee. Now the lapilli piled as high as the roofs, engulfing every road. In the Street of Tombs before the Gate of Herculaneum there was chaos and confusion and a mad thronging. The bodies of the suffocated piled up near the Gate. For this was the shortest road for all who wanted to escape towards the sea. In fact, there was no safety on the coast either, for the earthquakes had been worst of all there, the waves were as high as houses, and the fugitives, seeing by the dim light of their torches the storm on the sea and the countless dead fish and animals strewing the shore, tried to return to the town for shelter. And all this went on while the rain of stones continued, forcing the people to turn up their clothes over their heads to gain at least some protection. So one after another sank down in the ocean of stone and ash; many went into eternity with a sack of gold and silver coins on their back.

In the Street of Tombs a funeral celebration had just begun when the catastrophe occurred, and those taking part had gathered for the funeral feast in the beautifully painted triclinium. There on the cushions of the dining-couches they perished, celebrating not only their kinsman's burial but their own as well. Close at hand a woman fled with a child on her arm into a pillared mausoleum, and scarcely had she entered it when the monument collapsed, to become a tomb for herself and her child.

Terror reigned in the house with the wine business, which lay in this Street of Tombs. This luxurious building possessed, besides the splendid peristyle, a great pillared hall surrounding the garden to the rear, beneath which a vault ran round three sides, a cryptoporticus reached by steps, which obtained light and air through little open windows looking on to the garden. There the amphoras of wine stood in long rows, with their pointed bases for fixing into the ground. The master of the house thought this vault offered the greatest safety from the rain of stone, and quickly took his people down into it, or as many as he could find in the time. Among them was the mistress with her heavy collar and buckle of gold, a child on her arm, a boy by her side, and her daughter, a tender maiden, clad in finest linen and wearing costly gold jewellery. The husband quickly made the slaves bring down bread and fruits and other provisions. He himself hastily filled a bag with ten golden coins and eighty-eight of silver, struck in the reigns of Nero, Vespasian and Vitellius, and then hurried with the house-key to the gate at the end of the portico leading into the open country. Accompanying him was his trustiest slave, who had snatched together the most precious silver. His purpose was probably to see what the prospects of flight were in the direction of the sea, then to return for his family and household. But it was of no avail: at the door of his house fate overtook him and the slave, and they sank down, suffocated, in the deep layers of stone and ash.

Meanwhile all who had remained in the house, as well as the fugitives in the cryptoporticus, suffered the same fate: the fine ashes penetrated through the garden windows, and with them came the gases and poisonous fumes, more deadly in the closed rooms than in the open air. Desperately the young girl with the precious gold rings on her fingers tried to turn her fine garments up over her head as a protection, and desperately the unhappy people held handkerchiefs over nose and mouth. But none of this was of any avail, they were all suffocated, and only the ornaments and the fineness of the sandals distinguished master from slave. The unhappy creatures did not even touch the food, for the decision to take refuge down there meant a sure and speedy end. Thirty-four persons and a goat met death by suffocation in the rooms of this villa.

Not far from there, in the great villa which still housed the beautiful paintings of the mysteries, three women were surprised in an upper room by the storm of stone and ash. They could not flee, since the floors as well as the roofs had collapsed, and they fell through to the ground floor. There they lay with their lovely jewellery, their rings and chains of gold adorning their broken limbs, and were poisoned by the sulphurous fumes. One of them, a young girl, still clutched convulsively a little bronze mirror. Some workmen busy with the reconstruction of the house fled to the cryptoporticus, and perished miserably. When they breathed the poisonous air it was too late to escape, for the only staircase was a heap of ruins. One girl had reached the entrance of the villa, then

73

her strength left her. A man, perhaps the porter, first wandered through the many rooms of the great house, then took refuge in his little watch-room, there to perish in its darkest corner. Still in death he gazed, as though enchanted, on the little finger of his left hand, on which he wore an iron ring with a stone of chalcedony, with a tiny female figure engraved on it. There were few occupants in the house, and some of them succeeded in escaping, so that only eight people lost their lives there.

In the southern half of Pompeii events were much the same. The wide amphitheatre and the nearby palaestra, with its great swimming-pool ninety feet long, were filled in a very short time with the lapilli, which were quickly followed by a thick layer of ash. There was only a small staff in the amphitheatre, and there were at the time no wild beasts at all. In the palaestra, on the other hand, where the young people of Pompeii carried on their gymnastic training, there was a great crowd of people, and when the hail of stones suddenly poured down they fled for safety to the surrounding portico, whose roof offered protection. But very soon this collapsed, and only flight was left to them. Many won through to safety, but others met the fate of the man, obviously a servant of the goddess Isis, who tried to rescue two silver vessels with the sacred signs of Isis from a nearby altar. He was overcome in the arena, which was already quite filled with lapilli, and perished miserably. And all those who hurried to closed cellars and did not seek safety in flight perished likewise. Here too the majority took up the cry, "Away, away — as quick as possible away from the town!" And mostly towards the south, for the terrible calamity came from the north and the north-east. With the fear of death upon them the people streamed out of the houses on the Street of Abundance; but many did not succeed in escaping. In the house of the rich and highly respected Trebius Valens, on the walls of which countless election appeals could be read, four people tried to reach the open from the atrium when the roof suddenly fell in upon them and buried them all. Everywhere the same terrible scene: in a rich patrician house the owners seem to have been away in the country, while the slaves remained behind, under the orders of a steward who was also the door-keeper, the freedman Quintus Poppaeus Erotus, to work on the land outside the town. The house was divided into two distinct parts: the typical front part, where in the owner's absence only a few people remained, in the rooms round the atrium and peristyle, with numerous servants housed in the second storey; and the quarters at the back of the house, where the slave-workers lived with the steward and overseer. When the storm of stones began, those in the front part of the house fled past the magnificent frescoes of the Greek comedian Menander and the busts of other writers, which formed a little sanctuary of poetry, across to the great salon, the loveliest room in the house. Two old people and three younger ones sank down suffocated not far from the entrance. The slaves in the upper storey had at first not ventured to leave their rooms, but when the rain of stones thrashed down ever more violently and the lapilli were piled almost eight feet high in the atrium, they too decided to flee. One of them went ahead with a bronze hanging-lamp and the rest rushed after him down the wooden steps, seeking to cross the atrium into the open. But these ten people sank down, one after the other, between the steps and the door of the atrium. With expressions of utmost terror they struggled in their death agonies. Two women of the house had chosen the opposite way: when they saw that the ground was already piled deep in stone and ash, they fled up a ladder to the first storey, above the cattle-shed, till the roof fell in on them and killed them.

In the workers' house at the rear the steward at first forbade the slaves to leave. But when the stifling air made it difficult for him to breathe, he fled with his little daughter into his own room, sat down on his bed and pulled the pillows over his head, till he and the little girl were poisoned by the fumes. All his worldly goods — a leather purse on a silver chain, with a few coins of gold and other metal — fell from his stiffening hands. So the trusty guardian of the house died where he kept the seal of his masters and the tools for the workers, and where his duty commanded him to endure.

Publius Cornelius Tegetus, who had grown rich in trade, lived not far from there, and had some wonderful works of art in his house. His first aim, when the downpour of lapilli began, was to save those precious things. He hoped that the whole episode would not last long, so he quickly had a wonderful bronze statue brought from the garden into the atrium and covered with cloths. This statue was overlaid with gold, and represented an *ephebos*, that is, a Greek youth destined to be a soldier. But soon Cornelius Tegetus left everything, and fled with his household towards the south.

The inhabitants of the nearby little house of the priest Amandus were less fortunate. A part of this house had been let by the priest to a maker of those wax tablets which were used for writing. Here too the people had hoped that they could wait under the protection of the roof, so that they took to flight too late. The nine members of the priest's family were suffocated, huddled together in the ante-room, before they could reach the street, which was now piled high with ash and lapilli. Next door, in the house of Paquius Proculus, seven children had come together, obviously to play. The upper storey collapsed just over their heads, and buried them in its ruins in the room below.

Nearby there was a building with a great underground hall, which ran round three sides of a garden, from which light entered through several openings. There too the strong vaults seemed to the inhabitants to be the safest place in the house, and they first sheltered there and wasted valuable time. When suffocation threatened them—for the ash penetrated there too—they had to force their way painfully out into the garden, holding linen sheets over their heads. But the layer of lapilli and ash was now too deep: they sank down in it and were suffocated. A young girl, who sought safety with her mother, desperately tried to nestle into her bosom as both were seized by the last agony of death.

Not far from there, in a great fuller's works where clothes were cleaned, the owner of the house and some wealthy customers who had business to transact, met their death. But even in the street, especially in the district round the old thermae, from where the fugitives mostly tried to reach the forum, many sank into the deep layers of stone and ash. Many decided on flight too late or were ill or otherwise impeded — thus a pregnant woman lost time not only through her condition but because she stayed to collect her jewellery and silver vessels and more than a hundred silver coins, along with the keys of her house, which she had obviously carefully locked behind her. She sank down into the damp ash in tortured posture. Behind her perished a woman and her daughter, a fourteen-year-old girl, who fell face downwards; resigned to her hard fate the girl drew her dress over her head, resting it on her arm in the sleep of death. Beside her was a giant of a man, a true athlete, who had probably gone with the women to protect them, and whose strength and courage were of no avail. He fell suddenly and was suffocated as he lay on his back, and was able to help his mistresses no more.

Those who lived in the temples and public buildings were also taken completely unawares by the sudden calamity. Thus in the Temple of Isis the priests were reclining round the table of their triclinium, which was laid with bread, wine, chicken, fish and eggs. Their first action was to implore help of the goddess by sacrificing on the altar. But as the storm of stones rattled down, threatening the whole structure of the temple, the priests decided to load one of their number with their most valuable possessions and to send him away. A great sum of money, including some quite new gold coins of the Emperor Titus, statuettes used in the temple services, silver sacrificial vessels and other sacred objects were stowed into a heavy linen sack. But they had taken too long, losing too much time in the amassing of the precious things. The priest thought that he could escape best across the forum, but he only reached the corner of the Street of Abundance. He could not fight his way through the stones, but fell to the ground, and the precious contents of the linen bag were scattered around him. Two more priests tried to escape across the triangular forum, from which there was a direct road to the Temple of Isis. But just as they reached it, an earthquake destroyed a part of the portico and the ruins engulfed the two unfortunate men. They lay dead, at their side a silver plate engraved with the figures of Isis and Bacchus, and other precious objects. The rest of the priests planned to remain in the temple until the storm of stones was over, and their fate was that of all who stayed behind in closed rooms. Some of them collapsed beside the steps behind the kitchen, one was imprisoned as though in a dungeon by falling walls — with an axe which happened to be lying there he attempted to force an exit for himself. He had broken through two walls when he fell down before the third and last, dead.

There were only a few people in the theatres at the time,

but in the great ante-room and its annexes to the south, which was now used as barracks for the gladiators and governed with stern discipline, it was a long time before the real seriousness of the situation was realised and the cry of "each man for himself" was raised. Then a dreadful flight began, past the pillars and walls with their records of gladiators and their heroic deeds. Two men incarcerated in a dark punishment-cell were forgotten, and perished miserably. But it was too late for most of the other inhabitants of the building who had fled out from the sixty-six little rooms, each of which accommodated two people. The lapilli and the ash were spread too deep, and in the fear of death the men crowded together in a few rooms, in one room no fewer than thirty-four, in another, where the armour and helmets were stored, eighteen persons — among them a richly adorned woman, perhaps the admirer of one of the heroes of the arena. In this building no fewer than sixty-three persons met their death. Several slaves, too, who had loaded a horse with valuables, stuffs and garments, did not get away: they sank down dead beside the beast with his precious burden.

Not far from the gladiatorial barracks, which had thus become one enormous tomb, there was a house on the Stabian Way the opening of whose atrium in the roof could be closed by an iron shutter. The twelve inhabitants hastily closed the roof and thought they were safe. All twelve were suffocated in the atrium.

The stream of fugitives, seeking an escape towards the sea, poured across the great forum, where work had been going on busily to transform it into a dazzling monument of Roman greatness. The workmen who were reconstructing the Eumachia building, the temples and the basilica fled headlong. The last of the columns of the Jupiter temple which had survived the earthquake collapsed, killing wretched fugitives as it fell. The restored portions of the portico round the forum collapsed once more, and the Pompeians made away at all speed over the ruins of this place of meeting and worship, which had once been their pride.

So 24th August drew towards its close, and still the downfall of stone and ash continued. The lapilli fell in smaller quantities, but the ash increased. The activity of the volcano and the downfall of ash continued during the night and covered the whole Sarno plain and the region south-east and east of Vesuvius. Not a living being was to be found in the immediate neighbourhood of the mountain. All had either fled or been suffocated on the first day. But the places further removed from Vesuvius, such as Stabiae, had also suffered heavily. The layer of stone and ash was, indeed, not as deep as in Pompeii, but it was deep enough, and was accompanied by sulphurous fumes, so that there were many losses to be mourned. The darkness was from time to time horribly illuminated by the reflection of the flames that leapt out of the heart of Vesuvius. Pliny, who sought to console his trembling friend Pomponianus in Stabiae, advised him not to flee, but to remain quietly at home and await the end of the calamity, but the stones and fine ashes began to fall again, the earth shook, and becoming anxious he hastened to Pomponianus and consulted with him whether to remain indoors or make for the open. Finally they decided on flight towards the coast, to discover whether there was any escape by sea. Everyone was hurrying towards the coast, cushions tied over their heads; but there were no ships. The waves were raging as high as a house, the air was growing more and more stifling, and breathing was made difficult by the sulphurous fumes and the thick smoke from a nearby burning building. At last everyone fled pell-mell, but Pliny was left behind, dazed by poisonous gases, and suffocated.

On the following day, 25th August, Vesuvius continued to scatter ashes far and wide in ever fresh eruptions. Again and again the pine-shaped pillar of smoke rose up with a thunderous crash out of the crater. Gradually, however, this activity became noticeably weaker, even though on this second day utter darkness, brought on by the great pall of ash and smoke, still reigned over the whole district and hid the islands of Capri and Ischia from sight. It was only on the morning of the third day that the wind began to tear the terrible black cloud into long strips, and then scattered it. The sun came through, at first weak and uncertain, like the red reflection of a nearby fire, till at last, conquering the dark clouds, it touched the gulf of Naples once more with its golden beams.

But what did the sun's rays show? Great areas south and east of Vesuvius were covered with white ash as with snow.

as though a great shroud lay over the whole land. Herculaneum had disappeared from the earth, Pompeii was almost completely covered; only those parts of the houses and buildings which were more than twenty feet high rose here and there out of the ashes as reminders of the once rich and happy town. Houses and villas had been obliterated from the slopes of Vesuvius and the neighbouring plain. It was vain to seek for numerous small places, such as ancient Oplontis and Taurania.[1] Over all there lay the thick covering of fine pumice-stone and ash, extinguishing every trace of the former surface of the land. Stabiae had also suffered severely, but less than other places; stones and ashes lay there only to a depth of nine feet. Most of the houses rose up out of this with their roofs intact, and where the earthquake had not destroyed them they could be repaired. In a circle of about twelve miles in radius from Vesuvius the land was more or less severely struck. The wind carried fine ash over Rome and the coasts of Africa, and even as far as Syria and Egypt.

The surviving fugitives went in their thousands to Naples, to Nola, to Sorrento, even to Capua, spreading the infection of their dreadful terror. When the sun returned and Vesuvius, quite changed in shape, had grown quiet, and only a light cloud of white smoke rose from an entirely new peak, the survivors were gradually able to construct a picture of the terrible calamity, which in the brief space of forty-eight hours had transformed a flourishing area into a bleak heap of stone and ashes, the grave of countless men and women till then accounted happy and prosperous.

[1] There were also places called Tora, Sora, Cossa and Leucopetra.

4

SUNK IN OBLIVION FOR MORE THAN 1,600 YEARS

A.D. 80–1735

THE inhabitants of the more or less unscathed towns into which the fugitives poured from the desolated places looked fearfully up to Vesuvius, lest it should break into fresh eruptions and again cast death and destruction over the land. The loss of life was heavy: in Pompeii alone two thousand people must have perished, and though in Herculaneum there was little loss of life, countless refugees from the towns and from the surrounding countryside were overwhelmed in the open fields.

The inhabitants of Herculaneum had fled towards Naples, while the Pompeians went in the direction of Stabiae and beyond. All eyes were on the terrible volcano. But was it the same mountain as of old? Instead of one there were now two! Vesuvius had become a walled volcano, whose higher rim to the north[1] now towered in solitude to heaven, for the western segment of the enormous crater (hitherto scarcely recognisable as such, because of its extent) had fallen in. But out of this crater a peak, which had not been there at all before the eruption, rose to a fair height.

Although the ground still shook here and there, there was no fresh eruption. The mountain became completely quiescent, and it was possible to appreciate the extent of the calamity which had overtaken the district. Detailed reports were sent by express messenger to the Emperor and Senate in Rome, with urgent requests for advice and help, money and food. How right had been that minority of the senators who had

[1] The modern Somma.

advised, after the earthquake, against the reconstruction of Pompeii and Herculaneum. Now, scarcely sixteen years later, what they feared had happened and a much more terrible disaster had destroyed everything in one blow, including what had been restored in the interval.

In Rome men could not understand at first where the ashes and dust were coming from, until finally the news of the eruption of Vesuvius arrived. The Emperor gave immediate instructions for a delegation of senators to proceed to the stricken areas and discover the extent of the catastrophe. When their report had been received the Emperor appointed two high officials to devote themselves to the restoration of the destroyed areas. But they soon discovered that their task resolved itself into helping only those places which had suffered minor damage. Herculaneum had disappeared from the face of the earth, and most of Pompeii lay buried to a depth of fifteen to twenty-five feet. The two officials had to be content to better the lot of the refugees and to save what could be saved from the ruined places.

The forum of Pompeii, lying towards the sea, with its tall buildings, was less deeply covered by ashes than the rest of the town. Its pillars and marble statues and triumphal arches towered up out of the lapilli. The order was at once given that a careful search should first be made for the pictures of the gods from the temples. This search was not wholly successful; the picture of Jupiter from the great temple could not be found, but most of the pictures were salvaged from the other great temples on the forum. Then came the order to remove the many statues which adorned the forum and to cut away the marble draperies, the pillars and capitals for use elsewhere. And this was done with such care that only a negligible amount of anything of value was left on the forum. The marble Temple of Fortuna Augusta, lying a little to the north, was also investigated, and its finest objects, together with great quantities of costly marble, were salvaged. Thus everything which appeared above the ashes was gradually removed.

When it was realised that reconstruction was impossible, the town was used for a time as a quarry, so that the tops of the walls, most of which were still visible, were reduced to the new ground level, about twenty-four feet above the old.

But it was not only official action which led to the salvaging of what could be salvaged. Many Pompeians now returned and sought out the approximate site of their buried homes. Without much effort they were able to dig away some of the ashes and light lapilli and let themselves into one of the rooms, where they first searched for those who had been entombed. Then naturally they took away everything moveable. Thus it often happened that the finders took possession of things which had never belonged to them. When one room had been cleared in this way, the next room was reached by breaking a hole in the wall, and the process was repeated. But often the wall would collapse, burying the salvaging party beneath it. When the most accessible places had been emptied, the search became so difficult and success, with the scanty means available, so slight, that the work was abandoned as soon as the most important things had been salvaged: Relatively few houses in Pompeii, however, were untouched by the searches of the survivors.

Weeds began to grow rank over the buried town; in time the ashes and earth covering the buildings were cultivated, and everything disappeared beneath rows of vines and greenery. A new deposit of fruitful earth, added to both by cultivation and by the wind, was slowly formed above the layers of lapilli and ashes, and the town was buried still deeper. Here and there single walls and stumps of pillars still rose up, but that was all, and in time even these last vestiges disappeared. The site could scarcely be distinguished from the surrounding countryside, and only an oval dip in the region of the amphitheatre could have informed experts that this was the site of the arena of the once beloved games of Pompeii.

In Herculaneum, on the other hand, the forty-five-foot deep layer of mud, which had buried everything, hardened into solid stone, and with the means then available it was impossible to reach the treasures of the town. Here nothing could be saved, everything remained where it was when the stream of misfortune had embraced it, filled it up or borne it away. Individual attempts to dig shafts in the hard stone were soon abandoned; the resistance of the stony mass was so great that after inexpressibly troublesome toil the workers succeeded in penetrating only a few yards. To this day the greater part of Herculaneum still lies untouched at a great depth, undoubtedly preserving invaluable treasures for the future.

The Herculaneans who had fled to Naples were settled in a district of the city set apart for them, which received the name of the Regio Herculanensis. The Pompeians, who had fled more to the south in the direction of Stabiae, did not settle as a compact group, but were taken in and cared for by the surrounding villages. Great numbers had perished without leaving any heirs for their properties in Rome and elsewhere. These were now taken over by the State and the money used to support the refugees. The places which took a leading share in the work of relief were given all sorts of special privileges by Rome, among them Naples, which had long borne the honorary title of "Roman colony".

After some months, when normal conditions had been restored in Campania, the delegates of the Senate completed their survey and made a final report to the Emperor Titus. Its peroration was to the effect that everything possible must be done both for the survivors and for the reconstruction of the damaged places. Only Pompeii and Herculaneum would have to be abandoned. The following year the Emperor himself went to Campania in order to be convinced with his own eyes, but he could do nothing but agree with the judgment of the senators. Thus the fate of the two places was sealed.

The Emperor was still on his journey when he received the news that a terrible fire was raging in Rome, which lasted three days and destroyed half the city. He turned back at once. After the fire came the plague, to which thousands of people fell victims every day. This new disaster temporarily diverted attention from the catastrophe in the south, but only temporarily.

The impression made throughout the Empire by the tragedy of Pompeii and Herculaneum was very deep, and every poet of importance alluded to the disaster in one way or another. Thus Statius recalls the burial of the two towns in a characteristic way.[1] Jupiter had torn out the entrails of Vesuvius, removed them from the earth and lifted them to the stars in order to cast them down on the unhappy victim.

[1] See S. Herrlich, "The Ancient Tradition of the Eruption of Vesuvius in A.D. 79," in *Clio, Beiträge zur alten Geschichte*. Leipzig, 1904.

Photo: Alinari

13. The square country house, the Villa of the Mysteries outside Pompeii, in its present condition.

(See page 31)

Photo: Alinari

14. The state room, representing the initiation of a priestess into the cult of the mysteries. The brilliantly coloured frescoes are the best preserved in Pompeii, and perhaps of all antiquity. From the Villa of the

The poet also asked whether future generations would believe that whole towns with their populations lay buried there. Then he spoke prophetically of the time when green fields would cover the devastated region again. When the satirist Martial visited the gulf of Naples in the summer of the year 88, he recalled in a short epigram the devastation on the slopes of the mountain so loved by Bacchus: "This is Vesuvius, only a short time ago shaded with green vines, where the sparkling juice of the grape poured into the barrels. Bacchus himself preferred this mountain to the heights of his birthplace Nisa. It is not long since the satyrs danced their joyful dance here, and Venus had her habitation. . . . The other place rejoiced in the name of Hercules. But now everything has been swallowed up by the flames and is buried by the grey-green ash. The gods themselves could not have dared to do such a thing."[1]

As always in such cases, some people claimed that the catastrophe of the Campanian towns had been foretold long ago in the Sybilline sayings. In this instance the claim was made with special force, for the home of Sybilla was in Cumae, only a short distance from Naples, so that it was only to be expected that this foresight would be ascribed to her. In sayings which were by nature cryptic a prophecy could easily be read into them after the event. The Fourth Book of the Sybilline Oracles, which contain heathen, Jewish and Christian prophecies from the first century B.C. to the first century A.D., seems to have been written by a Jew shortly after the catastrophe. He saw in the eruption of Vesuvius a punishment brought on men by the God of heaven "for trying to destroy the *holy* people." For the wounds opened by the destruction of Jerusalem in A.D. 70 were still bleeding, and in all the disasters which befell Roman cities in the years 79 and 80 he saw a divine punishment upon the Emperor Titus, who had waged war against the Jews. When the Emperor died after scarcely three years' rule, this too was looked on as a divine punishment and proclaimed as such to the world. The destruction of the cities of Campania vividly reminded the Christians, as well as orthodox Jews, of the destruction of Sodom and Gomorrah. But of course they had no idea that during the catastrophe one of their number

[1] 44th Epigram of the Fourth Book of Martial.

had had the same thought and had even expressed it in writing.

The disaster was of course a mere episode in the history of the mighty Roman Empire. At the beginning of the second century, under the Emperors Trajan and Hadrian, the area ruled reached its greatest extent. Not only the whole of the Mediterranean area, but even Britain lay under the Roman imperium. But at the same time the maintenance of military security in the immense Empire was attended by ever greater difficulties.

During the period of these great rulers there arose historians who aimed at presenting as faithfully as possible the course of the stirring events of their time. Among them was Publius Cornelius Tacitus, who was twenty-four years old at the time of the disaster. It had made a very deep impression on him, and when he set about depicting that time in his History, he tried to obtain as many eye-witness accounts of the catastrophe as possible. For this purpose he turned, about the year 106, to his friend Caius Plinius Caecilius Secundus (the younger Pliny), a nephew of the great naturalist who had perished in Stabiae, and asked him to tell him everything he knew of the destruction of the towns of Campania and of the death of his uncle. He wanted to write about it in order to keep alive for posterity remembrance of the catastrophe and the end of the great scientist.

"Thank you," answered the younger Pliny; "I know that my uncle will be granted immortal fame if you describe his death. For though he met his end in the destruction of that glorious region, yet thanks to that strange coincidence he will live for ever, like the people and towns that have perished. Though my uncle has left many works which will live for ever, your immortal writings will contribute much to his fame. For my part I count those persons fortunate to whom it has been granted to perform deeds worthy of being described or to write works worthy of being read. Still more fortunate are those to whom both these things have been granted. My uncle, thanks to his own and to your works, is one of these."

Pliny then proceeded to describe the impression made on his uncle by the terrible events on Vesuvius, which he had watched from Misenum, and how he had tried to reach the

place of the disaster by sea, to find at last death by suffocation in Stabiae, like so many unfortunate Pompeians. Tacitus
was deeply moved by Pliny's account and begged his friend
to give also his own first-hand impressions of Misenum. This
Pliny attempted in a second letter, which recounted his own
and his mother's impressions, how they had prepared to flee,
and how the frail old woman, who could only walk slowly
and with difficulty, besought him, with prayers and exhorta-
tions, to save himself, for he was still so young, and leave her
to her fate. But Pliny answered that he would save himself
only with her, and this at last he succeeded in doing, Misenum
being so far from the scene of the disaster. Tacitus made use
of these letters in his History, and in his foreword mentioned,
among the horrors of the time to be treated, the destruction
of the towns of Campania. His account of the catastrophe
must have been clear and thorough, for his seeking of information from Pliny shows how much weight he attached to
securing exact contemporary reports. The extant portion of his
History, however, only goes as far as the year A.D. 70, and we can
only hope that some day discovery of the rest (which Pompeii
and Herculaneum, to be sure, cannot provide) will provide us
with his thorough account of the great eruption of Vesuvius.

The buried towns were left to their fate in the reigns of
Trajan and Hadrian. The one Emperor had much to do in
the extending of the great Empire; the other had enough to
contend with in the securing of the ancient three-rivers
frontier of the time of Augustus. Nor did Marcus Aurelius,
the philosopher-Emperor, who mentions the fate of the towns
of Campania in one of his works as an example of the transitoriness of all earthly things, think of excavating them, far
less of undertaking their reconstruction.

Vesuvius was probably moderately active throughout this
time, as it is today. At least, that is what we may infer from
a remark of the famous doctor of ancient times, Galen, in one
of his works on the *Method of Healing*, dated approximately
A.D. 172.

In the third century there was a series of soldier-emperors.
Growing dangers from without and constant confusion in the
internal problems of rule and succession left them no time at
all for such a work of peace as the investigation of the towns
of Campania. Alien tribes of Germanic origin were not only

knocking at the gates of the Empire, but were already pressing on over the Alps.

In such evil times soldiers counted for more and more. Only too often the imperial succession was determined by the imperial guard. In this way Septimius Severus, an African, attained the throne. In his reign the historian Cassius Dio composed an account of the catastrophe in Campania, which was perhaps especially detailed because at that time, in the first quarter of the third century, another violent eruption of Vesuvius took place. The historian speaks of the appearance of the volcano, which with the upright walls of the upper part of the crater looked like "an arena for fights of wild beasts, if one may compare small things with great"— that is, it looked like an amphitheatre. "Moreover", he goes on, "there are many trees and vines on its heights, but the crater is given over to fire — by day to smoke, by night to a flame — so that it seems as if incense of all kinds were being kindled in it. The intensity of this fire fluctuates. Often, too, the mountain casts forth ashes and stones; when it is overcome by steam it roars and rumbles, for it has no regular vents, but narrow hidden ones. That is the character of Vesuvius, and that is what goes on almost every year."[1]

Only one Emperor of the succession of military rulers, Severus Alexander, a lover of art and science, both by taste and training a man of great promise, made an effort to reintroduce order into the administration of justice and finance. He was interested, too, in the remains of the buried towns. He is credited with having ordered a search to be made in the region of Pompeii, which yielded many fragments of marble, pillars and statues. But after the commander of his guards had been murdered by his men, the Emperor himself was slain by mutinous troops, after scarcely thirteen years of rule. Then no one thought any more of the buried towns.

While the area above Herculaneum, lying beneath 45 feet of solid stone, was gradually settled again, at first with a little village, on the area above Pompeii only a few winegrowers settled, who put up their huts here and there, and from time to time came on a buried house in the course of their work. For the rest, the layer of humus and the covering of plants became thicker and thicker, till at last the mantle

[1] *Historia Romana*, Books 66 and 76.

cast over the once flourishing towns was complete and impenetrable.

So the two towns gradually passed into oblivion: their very names disappeared, and only a dim recollection survived among the peasants of the district, who called the place where Pompeii once stood Civitas, later Civita. But they thought little of this, the name was just another place-name. It was only on maps that the old names were given, and that because the road-maps of imperial Rome, giving the distances between the more important places in the Empire, were made before the catastrophe and naturally showed Pompeii and Herculaneum. These old Roman maps were used far into the Middle Ages, and when they were reproduced the names of the two towns were included without thought of their significance. It does not really matter whether the famous Peutinger chart of Vienna, which mentions the two places, was made in the time of Theodosius, that is, about the fourth century, or only in the thirteenth century. This chart is a parchment which belonged to the Augsburg humanist Konrad Peutinger, giving all the roads of the Roman Empire, the bases and their distances from one another. The maker of this map has never been identified, but there can be no doubt that it derives from the old maps of the Roman legions. Mention of the destroyed towns, however, is by no means a proof that settlements of the same name had arisen there.

The complete oblivion into which Pompeii and Herculaneum sank was hastened by the convulsions which overtook the Roman Empire. The great extent of the Empire could not be maintained. The efficiency of the Roman soldier had decreased, while the struggles for the throne, the incursions of foes, and the depreciation of money all weakened the Empire. About A.D. 330, under the Emperor Constantine, the motherland of Italy was even made a province and the capital was transferred to Byzantium; and in 395 the whole was divided into two empires, an eastern and a western. Then the storms of the tribal wanderings burst upon Italy, the swarms of Germanic tribes penetrating to the southernmost part of the land, and beyond it to Africa. About A.D. 476 the last puppet Emperor died in Naples.

Through all other changes southern Italy and Naples remained till about the year 1000 under Byzantine rule. The

Germanic tribes brought about the fall of the Roman Empire, but their military power did not long survive it. Thus the Ostrogoths under King Teja were defeated on the slopes of Vesuvius in battle with the Byzantine general Belisarius; and the Langobards in the north in course of time under the influences of the land settled and became peaceful.

While the German emperors struggled with the Popes, whose power had increased after the seat of the Empire had been transferred to Constantinople, Naples remained Byzantine till the beginning of the eleventh century. Then Norman adventurers landed in the region of Salerno, joined in the perpetual wars there, and finally founded a Norman dynasty. After the conquest of Naples under Roger II, who had also inherited Sicily from his father, the whole of southern Italy was united, in 1137, in one great power controlling the Mediterranean.

Meantime the two buried towns had disappeared so completely from the memory of mankind that it was as though they had never been. They were no longer searched for, even the people who lived in the district having no idea of their exact sites, and the spirit of the Middle Ages was not favourable to any revival of a special interest in their rediscovery. Moreover, before the year 1139 (when there was another violent eruption of Vesuvius) there were innumerable small eruptions, accompanied not only by downfalls of ash but also by lava; and these buried Herculaneum still deeper beneath solid lava, and spread fresh ashes over the humus which had gathered on top of the material cast up in 79.

In the first twelve centuries after the great catastrophe the mountain was only moderately active. There were about eleven eruptions, one on an average every hundred years.[1] After that Vesuvius became more and more quiescent. From the fourteenth century it seems to have practically ceased activity; the crater was completely closed, and a covering of plants began to spread across it. Only hot springs rising from it indicated the presence of a subterranean fire. So the hidden towns, with their secrets of ancient Roman life, as well as works of art and everyday utensils, were faithfully preserved —all of which would otherwise have disappeared in the

[1] C. B. Alfano and I. Friedlaender, *The History of Vesuvius*, p. 22. Berlin, 1929.

devastation of war. Two ancient Roman towns were packed away, as it were, and sealed and reserved for discovery and appreciation by an age more open to knowledge and culture. But to the superstitious Middle Ages Vesuvius was, throughout the period of its activity, "the mouth of hell".

The Norman kingdom lasted till the marriage of the son of the German emperor, Henry VI, to Constanza, the heiress of the Two Sicilies, as lower Italy and Sicily were called from this time — that is, it lasted not quite two hundred years. Then came the Hohenstaufen, with whose brilliant representative Frederick II German imperial glory in lower Italy reached its culmination. But the jealousy of the papal powers in Rome was roused. With papal support all the powers suppressed by Frederick II rose up against the imperial rule, which after Frederick's death in 1250 no longer had such a talented leader. Although Manfred, the youngest son of the great Hohenstaufe, was alive, Pope Urban IV gave the throne of Naples to the brother of the French king, Charles of Anjou, in order to strike a blow at the German imperial power in Italy, and Charles gained a decisive victory in the field over Manfred in the year 1266. The last of the Hohenstaufen, Conrad, was also defeated, delivered up to Charles of Anjou, and executed by him in Naples. That was the end of German influence in the southern half of the peninsula, and the Pope's man became master of Italy. The decisive political power in the land was now lodged in the King of Naples and Sicily, a Frenchman.

The family of Anjou, however, made themselves so heartily hated that in 1282 there occurred the famous Sicilian Vespers, that is, the massacre of the French occupation troops in one evening. In this way the son-in-law of Manfred, Peter of Aragon, succeeded in seizing power in the island of Sicily. Charles II of Anjou, who had succeeded his father in Naples, made peace with the Prince of Aragon and confirmed him in his possession of Sicily. Thus Sicily had a Spanish dynasty, Naples a French. There followed continual struggles between the two formerly united states. It was natural that under such conditions, with the classical writings lying hidden in the monasteries, no one should show interest in relics of the classical world, such as in those lost Campanian towns.

The Aragon dynasty ruled in Sicily and the Anjous in

Naples till the middle of the fifteenth century, when the last member of the house of Anjou, Johanna II, adopted King Alfonso of Aragon and Sicily. But first he had to fight a battle for Naples. Once again the French attempted to win the city and its territory as the inheritance of Anjou, but they had only temporary success. The grandson of King Alfonso, Ferdinand, who now reigned in Naples, sought the help of Spain, which had become a powerful united kingdom in 1492, after the conquest of Granada by the union of Aragon and Castile. A powerful league was formed against the King of France, Spain and Austria fighting against him, and Spanish troops reconquered Naples for Ferdinand of Aragon. Henceforward Naples was for centuries under Spanish influence.

When the Hapsburg emperor Charles V united Spain and Austria in a great empire, he ruled at the same time over many Italian states, from Milan to Naples and Sicily. The empire of the Hohenstaufen was restored in a fashion more brilliant and powerful than before, and the primacy in Italy, as in all Europe, was in the hands of Spain. From this time Spanish viceroys ruled in Naples and Sicily.

The invention of printing in 1445 led to an enormous change in the cultural development of the western world. Whereas every book, including the writings handed down from the ancient world, had hitherto been reproduced by laborious hand-copying, this was now suddenly changed. The art of setting and printing books by means of movable letters spread with great rapidity throughout the world. This art was the forerunner of the Renaissance, of the rebirth of the classical world at the end of the Middle Ages, and in contrast with the backward centuries preceding it this new epoch introduced immense changes and cast brilliant light on every branch of culture, architecture, poetry and painting. It was no accident that, with countless books being written, the buried towns of Pompeii and Herculaneum should again be thought of — though still no actual investigations were carried out on the spot. Thus in 1488 Niccolo Perotto mentions these places in his *Cornucopia*, and Sannazaro in his *Arcadia* (1502) gives a kind of poetic vision in which Pompeii is uncovered in the neighbourhood of the vine-decked hill now called Civita. This had in fact not yet taken place, only the hope was there; the site, however, was quite accurately described.

It was a gain for the topic even to be mentioned, and there was a further advance when Pliny's letters to Tacitus were printed and disseminated. On a map prepared by Ambrogio Leone in 1513 the name Herculaneum Oppidum was entered at the place where modern Portici lies, that is, with fair accuracy.

On the death of Charles V his brother Ferdinand succeeded to the German throne and the Austro-Hungarian lands, and his son Philip II inherited Spain and the Italian, Dutch and American possessions. The position in Naples was unchanged, the Spanish viceroys continuing in power. In a description of Italy published in 1561 Leandro Alberti recalled the buried towns of Herculaneum and Pompeii and also mentioned their supposed sites with fair accuracy.

Towards the close of the sixteenth century, about 1592, the Regent Mutius Tuttavilla, whose family had been given ducal rank by Alfonso of Aragon, ordered the construction of a conduit to carry a subterranean canal from the river Sarno to Torre d'Annunziata, a village which lacked a proper water-supply. For this he engaged the famous Roman architect Domenico Fontana, who planned to drive a tunnel through the hill of Civita, beneath which, all unknown to the architect, Pompeii lay buried. Since the town lay at a depth of fifteen to twenty-five feet, much deeper than the proposed conduit, its surface was only grazed here and there by the conduit. This ran from the river Sarno, past the amphitheatre, and straight through, or rather over, Pompeii — past the Temple of Isis, across the forum and the Street of Tombs, north-west to Torre d'Annunziata. Here and there, where the layer of ashes and lapilli was thin, marble fragments were encountered in the course of the work. Even coins of the Emperor Nero were discovered, and two marble tablets with inscriptions relating to a Marcus Lucrezius and a Decimus Rufus, and mentioning the "Venus Physica Pompeiana". The word "Pompeiana", however, was abbreviated in the inscription, the coins quickly disappeared into the pockets of the workmen, the tablets were broken and forgotten, and no immediate conclusions were drawn from the other discoveries, the marble and so on. For almost six years, till 1600, the construction of the "Duke's Conduit" was carried on just above the buried town, without its being discovered.

All the same, such isolated discoveries provided incentive

for further searches and awakened interest in the matter. The historian Capaccio speaks in his *Historia Napolitana*, which appeared in 1607, of the excavations which took place during the construction of this water-system. So it was at least established that the site of some ancient place lay in the neighbourhood of Civita. But this was again forgotten, and the more completely as a result of an event which struck terror into men's hearts and for the time being made further search in this district impossible and highly dangerous.

For Vesuvius, which for probably more than four hundred years and quite definitely for the whole of the previous century had shown no sign of activity, began to stir again. In the year 1619 Doctor Niccolo de Rubeo and a certain Salimbeni had climbed the volcano and had even penetrated into the crater. It was at that time thickly covered with oaks, holm-oaks, ash and other trees, and even wild boar were said to be hunted there. All in all, the possibility of a fresh eruption could be discounted. Everyone considered that the volcano was quite extinct. In the last decades of the sixteenth century, however, there had been several tremors, whose origin were estimated to be somewhere in the country surrounding Naples. At the end of 1631 there were particularly violent earthquakes. In the first days of December the water once more ceased to flow from the springs; the animals were very restless, but the sky remained serene and cloudless. Then on the morning of 16th December, about seven o'clock, the peasants going to their work saw a gigantic cloud of smoke suddenly rising up from the peak of Vesuvius. Soon there followed fearful explosions and thunderclaps. Immense black masses rose into the air and whirled up to a great height. Ashes and lapilli began to pour down, and black night covered the district, just as in the year 79. Once more there was headlong flight from the rain of ashes and the poisonous gases. But since the plague was raging in many parts of southern Italy at that time, the villages closed their doors against any inrush of strangers, seeking to prevent the entry of the fatal sickness. So a stream of more than 40,000 fugitives poured on to seek refuge in Naples. When they reached the gates, they found them closed, but they were unable to turn back, for the way was barred by a stream of mud like that which had poured over Herculaneum in the year 79. So the viceroy was compelled to have the gates opened, and the mass of fugitives poured into the city.

So far the eruption of Vesuvius had followed almost exactly the pattern of the eruption of ancient times. But on 17th December, 1631, when the activity of the volcano increased enormously, there was a decisive change in the course of events. Great masses of water suddenly streamed out of the volcano, mingled with the ashes and lapilli, and rushed down into the sea. Everything standing in the way, trees and walls, men and animals and furniture, even great pieces of rock, were torn along in the raging floods. Then on the forenoon of the same day the side and base of the mountain suddenly opened and molten streams of lava poured out, as they had never done in the year 79. These streams branched into many parts and poured over the buried town of Herculaneum, through Portici and Torre del Greco, and down to the sea, rushing over it so that the waves seemed to be on fire.

The people of Naples desperately held processions with the famous blood of St Januarius, martyred in the reign of the Emperor Diocletian, which was alternately fluid and congealed. On 18th December the eruption continued, but the clouds on the peak of the mountain gradually broke up, and when the wind mastered them and the sun came through it could be seen that the great cone of the mountain had been, as it were, decapitated. The destruction was enormous, about twice as many people perishing as in the destruction of Pompeii and Herculaneum — that is, about four thousand — over six thousand animals being killed, stones hurled as far as sixty miles, and even in Naples the ash spreading to the depth of a foot. This time numerous villages were destroyed by water and lava, especially to the south and west of Vesuvius. The district round Resina, which lies forty feet above Herculaneum, was buried another fifteen feet beneath the lava. The district to the east and south of Vesuvius, that is, the district round Pompeii, was much less affected, on account of the direction of the wind as well as of the eruption; but it did not by any means escape. Before the eruption the circumference of the crater was somewhat more than a mile, but after the eruption it was about three miles.[1]

[1] See the representation of the eruption, also the proclamation (reproduced below) in Alfano and Friedlaender, *op. cit.*, p. 27 f.

Far and wide the land seemed to be smouldering or on fire; sand and ashes and devastation were everywhere. In order to warn posterity the viceroy of Naples, Emmanuele Fonseca, had a memorial tablet set up in Portici, which is there to this day.

"Children and children's children" (it runs), "this is for you. One day illuminates the next, and tomorrow learns from yesterday. Hear! Twenty times since the sun first shone, if history relates truly, has Vesuvius burned. It has always pitilessly destroyed those who were slow to flee. I warn you now, after this last catastrophe, that you may not be caught unawares. In the heart of this mountain is stored much evil, alum, sulphur, iron, gold, silver, saltpetre and springs of water. Sooner or later this mountain takes fire. But before this happens there are mutterings and roarings and earthquakes. Smoke and flames and lightning are spewed forth, the air trembles, and rumbles, and howls, and the population is driven away. Flee so long as you can. For soon the mountain will burst apart and spew out a stream of fire, which will rush down and bar the way for those who are slow to flee. If this overtakes you, you are finished. If you despise it, if goods and chattels are dearer to you than life, it will punish your recklessness or greed. If you are sensible you will listen to the voice of this marble which speaks to you. Do not trouble about your hearth and home, but flee without hesitation. Anno Domini 1632, in the reign of Philip IV: Emmanuele Fonseca, Viceroy."

The consequences of the earthquake were terrible. The sea had first withdrawn three times its normal distance, then returned to far beyond its old limits, increasing the destruction. Before the eruption the cone of Vesuvius had been about 120 feet higher than the northern rim of the crater, the so-called Somma, but now the cone lay many hundreds of feet below the level of this edge of the crater. Vesuvius continued to be slightly active; but, naturally enough, hardly a soul gave a thought to Pompeii.

There was one, however, who did think of it — the Hamburg scholar Luc Holstenius, who was living in Rome. Six years after the great eruption, that is, in 1637, he visited Naples and the districts east and south-east of Vesuvius, and turned his attention to the ancient towns. He also went to the hill called Somma, through which ran the water-system of Torre d'Annunziata. This hill had to some extent recovered from the light shower of ash and was again covered with vines. The scholar, who had been busy for many years with excavations in Rome, spent a long time in the district, pondering and investigating, and before he left he was convinced that Pompeii lay beneath Civita. He expressed his conclusions in his *Adnotationes*. There was immediate opposition to his view by those who held that Stabiae, not Pompeii, lay beneath Civita. This claim was more in harmony with the Peutinger Chart, though of course it was impossible to determine the exact site of a place from such an unreliable and merely schematic road-map.

Another scholar, Camillo Pellegrino, a historian, treated of discoveries of ancient remains in Campania in his book published in Naples in 1651.[1] He believed that Herculaneum lay beneath the village of Torre del Greco, and held quite erroneous views about the site of Pompeii. In his index, however, he says of Pompeii that "one may believe that it stood in the district called Civita today". There were many false suppositions about the location of the two places, especially of Herculaneum, over which the stream of lava had recently flowed. In 1688 Francesco Balzano explained in his book, *Ancient Herculaneum or Torre del Greco raised from Oblivion*, that these two places were on the same site.

In 1689 excavations were undertaken, at some distance from Vesuvius, in a search for water. The workers noticed several layers of different kinds of stone, very clearly separated and imposed horizontally on one another. These layers consisted, after the humus, of a narrow layer of lapilli, a deep layer of ashes, and finally an even deeper layer of lapilli from the eruption of 79. When the fourth layer had been penetrated, some stones with inscriptions were found, among them one with the name Pompeii on it. It was clear that the finds were genuine ancient memorials, and when the owner of the land was informed he gave instructions for the digging to be continued, so long as this could be done without interference from water. At the same time this man gave news of the

---

[1] Camillo Pellegrino, *Apparato alla Antichità di Capua ovvero discorsi della Campania felice*. Naples, 1651.

discovery to the famous architect Francesco Picchetti of Naples, who was also an amateur naturalist, and along with him made a more detailed examination of the different layers which had been uncovered. In the course of this examination some other objects were discovered, for example, some rusty iron keys, a small Priapus and a tripod. When Picchetti was shown the two inscriptions he explained that these had to do not with the town of Pompeii, but with a Pompeian country-house which had once stood there. The historian Bianchini, on the other hand, realised that for sound geographical reasons the inscription must refer to the town itself, and he set forth his views in his *Storia Universale*, published in 1699. But there the matter rested: Picchetti stuck to his opinion, and did not make any more investigations.

Stimulated by these various items of information, another man, Giuseppe Macrini, an explorer of Vesuvius, examined the hill called Civita, where the work on the water-system had revealed ancient remains. In his book *De Vesuvio*, which appeared in the same year, 1699, in Naples, he explicitly maintained that Pompeii was in the region called Civita: "I myself have seen whole houses, ruins of great walls, and some halls made of tiles, partly excavated." But this scholar too had no opportunity of devoting himself to the discoveries. The parts which had been excavated fell in and were covered with greenery again, and after such happy beginnings things were much the same as before. Most of the learned men of the time mistrusted the claims of a few far-seeing writers, and could not bring themselves to acknowledge that Pompeii had really been discovered.

In the meantime a great change in politics had taken place. About the middle of the seventeenth century the France of Louis XIV had replaced Spain as the dominant power in Europe. Continual wars had been followed by a peace in 1697, but three years later, with the death of the last Spanish Hapsburg, the apple of discord was again cast into the European arena. The Spanish inheritance, to which the German emperor Leopold I and Louis XIV had almost equal rights, was at stake. In the ensuing war of succession the Austrians, under the talented Prince Eugene of Savoy, were for the most part victorious, and Count Daun succeeded in taking Naples from the Spaniards. By the Peace of Utrecht in 1713 and of

Rastatt in 1714 the Spanish kingdom was divided, Spain and its American possessions passing to Louis's grandson Philip, while the Emperor Charles VI received Belgium and the Spanish possessions in Italy. After this Austria became the leading power not only in Central Europe but also in Italy, including Naples. Only Sicily was not subdued, and passed to Savoy.

Now it was Austria's turn, under its new ruler, to administer Naples and southern Italy by means of viceroys. The first, Count Martinitz, assumed office on 7th July, 1707; at the same time the city was occupied by German troops. At that time the cavalry colonel, Emanuel Moritz von Lotheringia, Prince d'Elboeuf, a distant cousin of his supreme commander, Prince Eugene, "rejoined the imperial army"[1] in Naples. The strangers were not received with great enthusiasm by the inhabitants. This was made plain at the ceremonial installation of the viceroy. There was a brilliant cavalry procession up to the Castelnuovo, which was occupied by the Austrians, where according to ancient custom the castle commandant had to be installed whenever a new master ruled. Count Martinitz knocked on the gate:[2]

"Who is there?" called the commandant.

"Charles the Third", answered the viceroy, for his imperial master, Charles VI, called himself Charles III of Naples. The drawbridge was lowered as a sign of welcome, and the general commanding the castle received, with the keys of the castle, power over the city. The festival of the installation of Austrian rule was to last three days, and be celebrated by brilliant illuminations, fireworks, banquets and drinking. But Vesuvius stirred again; since the end of July it had shown increased signs of activity, and just at the time of the celebrations the side of the mountain opened and a stream of molten lava appeared. At first it poured towards Resina, but fortunately changed its course. But lapilli and ashes caused a fair amount of damage in the neighbourhood. On 2nd August, just as the splendid viceregal ceremonies were in full swing, there fell upon Naples such a downpour of ashes that at three o'clock

[1] Prince d'Elboeuf on passing through Rome, to the empress of Charles VI, in Vienna, 1707: Vienna State Archives.

[2] Dr Heinrich Benedikt, *The Kingdom of Naples under the Emperor Charles VI*, p. 54 f. Vienna, 1927.

423725

in the afternoon it was quite dark. The white dust covered the city to a depth of many inches when the viceroy commanded a procession to the formed, in which he himself took part, and in which the head of St Januarius was held up towards the mountain in supplication. The following day the eruption ceased. But Count Martinitz could not prevent the people whispering to one another that heaven itself rejected the new masters and that this was expressed by these disastrous natural events. The eruption was the most violent since 1631, and once again the great pine-shaped cloud of smoke appeared over the volcano.

The Austrians soon made themselves at home in Naples, among them Prince d'Elboeuf, who lived in a rented *palazzo* in one of the most elegant quarters of the city. Still unmarried, he lived in great state, providing a succession of banquets and splendid theatrical performances. In 1710 he was made supreme officer of the guard, a post corresponding approximately to the modern major-general, and became engaged to the Neapolitan princess Salsa. He entered on this engagement even though the supreme war council in Vienna looked with little favour on the union of an imperial officer with a Neapolitan, since they knew that there was very strong resistance to the Austrian rule in the highest circles of the city. D'Elboeuf had therefore to overcome some opposition before he could fulfil his heart's desire. He passed the summer in the palace of the Prince of Santo Buono, which was in Portici, northwest of the village of Resina, which it will be remembered was built over Herculaneum, though its inhabitants had no idea what treasures lay buried sixty feet below their dwellings.

One day a peasant, Giovanni Battista Nocerino of Resina, called Enzecchetta, was digging the spring for his house somewhat deeper, since it gave too little water. To do this he had to pierce very hard ground, and in the course of his labour he suddenly hit upon costly stone of all kinds — on white marble and alabaster, and the so-called *giallo antico*, a yellow marble very highly prized in Roman times; while now and then the shape of the fragments showed clearly that they had formed part of ancient pillars and buildings. The peasant did not think much of the matter, but threw away the inferior pieces and took the best home with him, selling them after a

Photo: Alinari

15. Bust of the Roman barker, moneychanger and auctioneer, Lucius Caecilius Iucundus. Naples Museum.

(See page 33)

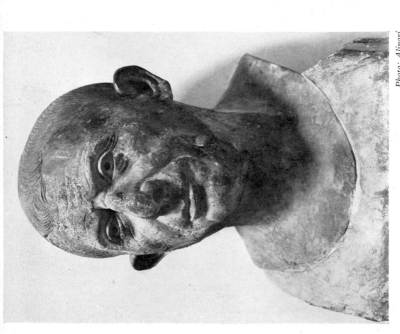

Photo: Alinari

16. A Herm of the Actor C. Norbanus Sorex, found in the Temple of Isis, towards the costs of which he had contributed. Notice the ancient Roman type, which persists in Italy to this day.

(See page 180)

Photo: Alinari

17. Statue of the priestess Eumachia, who endowed the large building on the east side of the forum. The purpose of the building has not yet been ascertained.

(See page 34)

Photo: Alinari

18. Statue of a young Roman woman. This is one of the three statues excavated by the Austrian general, Prince d'Elboeuf, whose discovery led to the exposing of Herculaneum. It was presented to Prince Eugene of Savoy, and is now in the Dresden State collection of Sculptures.

(See page 103)

time to a so-called *marmoraro*, a man who sought out such stones in order to make statues of saints for churches, or fountains and the like for the gardens of the well-to-do.

Now about this time Prince d'Elboeuf, with a view to his marriage, had bought a piece of land from the fathers of the nearby monastery of San Pietro d'Alcantara. On this land, which lay near the sea, he planned to build a little house, a *casino*, which was to have particularly beautiful decorations. For this purpose he fetched a man from France who knew how to make a kind of porcelain putty from pulverised stones and fragments of marble, which formed a material which was not only brilliant but even harder than marble. He and the prince, being on the look-out for the necessary material, got into touch with the *marmoraro* who had bought the stones from the peasant Enzecchetta. The prince saw at once that these fragments were of ancient origin and questioned the man as to where he had got them. The latter took him to the peasant in Resina and bade him show what he still had. The prince there and then bought all that there was, and had the things taken to his villa for closer inspection. D'Elboeuf realised that the peasant's field and well, lying adjacent to the garden of the monastery of the Discalced Augustines, must lie above the site of some classical building. His architect, the Neapolitan Giuseppe Stendardo, whom he had hastily summoned, was of the same opinion. Enthusiastically the pair studied the fragments of pillars and architraves, the ancient red and yellow marble and the polished alabaster which had been removed by the peasant from his well.

D'Elboeuf at once resolved to buy the piece of land and the well, and to carry out excavations there on his own initiative. At that time he had not the remotest conception that this was the site of one of the towns which had been buried in ancient times, the first fragments of which had already come to light. As soon as he owned the field he feverishly set to work to engage workers under his own and his architect's charge, who drove subterranean channels, like rabbit-holes, spreading out in every direction from the well. After some days they came upon a vault, in which they found, besides many fragments of valuable stone, a statue of Hercules in the Greek style, made of Parian marble. This was broken in several pieces, indeed, but otherwise well preserved, and could easily be put together again. Beside it lay pillars of splendid multicoloured transparent alabaster. There was also a statue of a woman, at first falsely taken for Cleopatra, lacking an arm and a foot, which were soon afterwards discovered. Finally, there was an enormous marble slab, about five feet high and fifteen feet long. This was laboriously moved until it could be wound up the well on a windlass, and when it was cleaned it was found to have great letters, almost a foot tall, let into it in metal. It was an inscription in Roman capitals, bearing the name of Appius Pulcher, son of Caius, who lived about 38 B.C., in the year when Caius Norbanus Flaccus was Roman consul. Pulcher was in correspondence with Cicero, and succeeded him as governor of Sicily. This inscription provided a fixed point, and the architect, Stendardus, whose knowledge of Roman history was only slight, immediately betook himself to Naples with these finds in order to consult with the scholars of that city, especially the archaeologists and historians, as to the significance of the discoveries. The famous professor, Dr Giuseppe Valletta, was particularly consulted.[1]

Some scholars, with their confused knowledge of classical mythology, offered the fantastic explanation that the second son of Hercules, called Retino, had built the harbour of Herculaneum on the site of the modern Torre del Greco. The village of Resina, they said, was first called Retina after this same Retino. In classical times this Retino had built a round temple with twenty-four pillars of transparent coloured alabaster, and statues between all the pillars. Inside it (they went on) there was a hall, also with twenty-four pillars of *giallo antico*, yellow marble, and the floor was of the same material. They found support for this explanation in various information derived from classical literature.

Prince d'Elboeuf was therefore led to believe that he had

---

[1] For this find the most important references are *Symbolae litterariae Opusculum Varia*, vol. I, Florence, 1748, Admiranda Antiquitatum Herculanesium Notizia I di alcuni insigni Monumenti antichi, scavati alla Real Villa di Portici l'anno MDCCXI data da D. Giuseppe Stendardo, Architetto Napolitano, al Sig. Bindo Simone Peruzzi, Patrizio Fiorentino; Giornale dei Letterati d'Italia. Tomo quinto p. 399. Venice, 1711; J. H. Keere, Über die Ruinen Herkulaneums and Pompejis, Gotha, 1791; Giuseppe Fiorelli, Giornale degli Scavi di Pompei, Naples, 1860–64; and Beckers Augusteum, Dresden, I, 108–10.

discovered a splendid temple of Hercules, and stirred by these ideas of the scholars, he zealously continued his excavations. Although their views were false, they were right in one respect, in the explanation, namely, that the building had obviously been overwhelmed at the time of the great catastrophe in the reign of the Emperor Titus. At any rate they had the merit of encouraging the prince to continue his labours; and very soon these were crowned with quite extraordinary success.

Some days after the consultation in Naples, during the laborious driving of shafts through the solid stone, three beautiful female statues were discovered, which were comparatively little damaged. They clearly represented a mother with her two daughters, for one statue was draped in a thin under-mantle, with a broad mantle drawn over the head from the back, which heavily veiled the whole figure. This was the customary mode for matrons. The finely formed face had in it ideal traits, and these together with the garments indicated that the original was to be sought in the art of Praxiteles. The Roman sculptor who had executed the work had clearly availed himself of the Greek model. The two statues of the girls, also veiled in heavy draperies, had the heads uncovered, as was customary with maidens. The figure of the matron was broken at the neck and the flank, but was otherwise in an excellent state of preservation.

Prince d'Elboeuf was delighted with his discovery, and, convinced that he had discovered five of the twelve statues which according to the scholars must have stood between the twenty-four outer pillars, he confidently hoped to find the rest. So he continued his labours with the greatest zeal, but fearing that news of the finds might awaken the greed of others, he was careful to keep the matter as secret as possible.

For a long time the prince had wished to win the favour of Eugene of Savoy, who, though probably related to him, had either not properly acknowledged the kinship or considered it too distant for any special recognition or favours. Prince d'Elboeuf lived a luxurious life, spending a great deal of money, and had repeatedly to ask for financial support from the court at Vienna and especially from the Empress. For this reason he very much wanted Eugene of Savoy to speak well of him, if as president of the imperial war council he should be questioned about the man who was applying for this money. So d'Elboeuf hit upon the plan of presenting these priceless and splendid sculptures to the general, who was famed no less for his love of art and the sciences than for his success in war. The objection to this course lay in the fact that the sculptures were damaged; the head of one of the statues of the girls and the hands and toes of the other needed restoration, while parts of the draperies and the fingers of the matron would have to be repaired. D'Elboeuf wanted to present not mere torsos but complete figures. So he resolved to remove the three statues secretly, in returning army convoys, to Rome, where there were numerous sculptors skilled in the work of restoration. To attempt any such work in Naples itself would have undoubtedly given away the secret and perhaps imperilled any further private excavations. Indeed, even at that time the export of ancient works of art was dependent on papal permission; but Prince d'Elboeuf feared a refusal and preferred to smuggle the statues out of the eternal city. In the end he found ways and means to transport them to Ancona and from there by sea to Trieste, thence to Vienna and the Belvedere, the palace of Prince Eugene of Savoy.

The art-loving prince was delighted, and thanked his major-general in Naples by letter for the splendid gift.[1] All the artists and art-lovers in Vienna rejoiced with him, for Prince Eugene had a special room built for the three statues and opened to the public. D'Elboeuf went on with his excavations, and by quite unmethodical digging found various pieces of sculpture, pillars, marble, and so on. He had them taken to his country-house in Portici, where he took up residence with his bride in 1713. But very soon exaggerated rumours of his finds spread through Naples, and in time it became known that the three loveliest statues had found their way over the frontier and abroad.

The matter reached the ears of Cardinal Quirini, the papal librarian and chief of the office for classical art, who learned that the statues had even passed through Rome. Complaints

---

[1] The relevant letter of Prince Eugene is, according to Arneth (*Prinz Eugen*, III/542) dated 1st February, 1713, and to be found in the War Department Archives in Vienna. In spite of careful search, however, I failed to find either the letter or any reference to it in those archives.

were apparently made to the Austrian viceroy in Naples, who urged d'Elboeuf to be more reserved and prudent; and many even maintain that the prince was expressly forbidden to continue the excavations; but the matter probably did not go as far as that. It is more likely that d'Elboeuf, whose financial affairs were continually embarrassed, found the cost of the excavations gradually becoming too much for him, all the more so since the first great success was not followed by others, and the shafts were clearly being driven through places where walls and stairs but not marble statues and similar precious things were being brought to light. Thus in the following years excavation work was much less vigorous, and in the twenties of the eighteenth century there was no real understanding of what had been discovered. The *Giornale dei Letterati*, which appeared in Venice,[1] immediately reported the first successes in the year of their discovery, 1711, but was thereafter completely silent about the whole matter.

In the succeeding years Prince d'Elboeuf was summoned many times to Vienna, where he spent a considerable time before returning to Naples, his wife being unwilling to accompany him abroad. But the excavations were not continued, and the whole enterprise threatened to collapse, especially when the prince, promoted to field-marshal, went soon afterwards to France, and had to sell his villa by the sea. The house came into the hands of the merchant family of Falletti in Naples, who kept it for some years and then on a favourable opportunity sold it.

In the meantime a great change in European politics was preparing. The Emperor Charles VI desired to secure the undivided succession of the empire to his daughter Maria Theresa, who was engaged to Duke Franz Stephan of Lotheringia. That was completely against the interests of the French, who took up arms at the first opportunity, in 1733, on the occasion of a dispute about the succession to the throne of Poland. Two powerful confederacies were at once formed, Spain and Sardinia fighting on the side of the French. Following on this war, which also drew in Italy, the Duke of Lotheringia had to give up his native domain, and in compensation received the grand-duchy of Tuscany — although Elisabeth Farnese of Spain, queen of Philip V, had counted

[1] *Giornale dei Letterati d'Italia*, vol. V, p. 399. Venice, 1711.

on receiving this. She wanted it for her eldest son, Don Carlos, while her second son was to receive the Kingdom of the Two Sicilies and her third son the Netherlands. It was said of that Don Carlos of Bourbon that he was the son of a French prince who was of less worth than a woman and of an Italian princess who was of far more worth than a man. Particularly intelligent by nature, he knew many languages and the most important sciences, with the exception of history. He was finely developed both in body and spirit, only his great hooked nose made him almost ugly. In the course of the war, in 1734, the Spanish troops conquered Naples and the surrounding territory, and the eighteen-year-old infante, Charles of Bourbon, who was a skilled huntsman, was sent there. He was handed two letters, in which his father Philip V, as King of Spain and as conqueror, made over to him all his rights in the Kingdom of Naples. By the end of the year Naples was once again in Spanish hands.

The young prince, whose rule was not yet acknowledged by the defeated Austrians, was at first fully occupied with love affairs and with hunting and fishing. He could the more readily devote himself to these pursuits since he had at his side an outstanding man, the Tuscan Bernardo Tanucci, who gradually became the dominant personality in the State.

The royal youth was anxious to find a place equally suitable for hunting and fishing. The house of the Falletti in Portici, formerly belonging to Prince d'Elboeuf, was offered to him, as providing opportunity for both his pastimes. The property was bought, and when King Charles visited it he found many classical remains, which had been left behind after Prince d'Elboeuf had dug them up in Resina. The King inspected everything with the greatest interest, and resolved, once his reign was consolidated and his stay in Naples assured, to visit the site of the discoveries and perhaps bring more precious objects to light.

And it was in this way that events did develop. The Emperor abandoned any thought of reconquering the territory, and in the preliminary peace of Vienna, on 3rd October, 1735, Naples and Sicily were definitely promised to the eldest son of the King of Spain. The only condition which was attached was that these lands should never be united with the Spanish monarchy. So in his nineteenth year Charles of

Bourbon became absolute monarch of the Two Sicilies, which he could hold at least for the lifetime of his father, until he was called to his Spanish inheritance. When that happened Charles was bound by the peace terms to relinquish the Kingdom to his nearest relations.

See pages 51 and 52.

5

FROM THE ACCIDENTAL DISCOVERY OF HERCULANEUM TO THE DISCOVERY OF POMPEII

1735–1770

THOUGH political affairs affect the destiny of men on earth and influence their life towards confusion or order, eternal nature does not change. It buds and blossoms, ebbs and flows, rages and storms, spreads the blessing of sunshine and fruitful rain, heedless of the battles and struggles of men.

On the gulf of Naples nature had caused Vesuvius to speak in its own way far into the 'thirties of the eighteenth century. In the years 1717 to 1737 the mountainside opened on the seaward slopes and sent slow streams of lava towards Resina and Torre del Greco, to the accompaniment of slight earth tremors. This activity was so continuous that it is possible to speak of an eruption which lasted, with only short pauses, for twenty years, reaching its climax in May 1737. At this time a great cleft opened on the south-west flank of the mountain, out of which a vast stream of molten lava poured towards Torre del Greco, causing great devastation. At the same time a large part of the peak was blown off, and thereby lost so much height that it was lower than the eastern rim of the former crater, now called Somma. So the shape of Vesuvius was changed — which was to happen frequently up till modern times. Then the mountain became quiescent, and its activity almost completely ceased for a long time to come.

During this period of lava eruptions, when the site of d'Elboeuf's discoveries was particularly threatened, no one gave any further thought to continuing the excavations. Fear paralysed all action, even that of Charles of Bourbon, who did not venture to leave his room in the palace at Naples throughout the month of May 1737.[1]

So for the time being the finds made by General d'Elboeuf were the total extent of the discovery. Four damaged statues from that time stood in the villa in Portici, while four torsos were set up for some time in the market-place at Resina, till these too found their way to the King's summer residence. The three loveliest statues, however, known at that time, incorrectly, as the Vestal Virgins, had delighted the art-loving world of Vienna until the death of Prince Eugene of Savoy in 1736. But this delight was not destined to last. The prince had died without issue, and three nephews, sons of his eldest brother, the Count of Soissons, had pre-deceased him. Only a daughter of this brother, Anna Victoria, who was married to a prince of Saxony-Hildburghausen, was still alive. Since Eugene had died intestate, this niece, after strife over the succession, received the inheritance as being the next of kin. Almost one and three-quarter million guilders, wonderful jewels, splendid silver, and an incomparable library fell to her, along with the possessions of Piedmont and Savoy. And all this wealth went to one who was in no way worthy of it. "With a greed which was truly disgusting", writes Alfred Arneth, the distinguished historian and chief of the imperial Austrian archives, "she set about realising as speedily as possible all that her uncle had left. Not a thing was spared, everything was ruthlessly turned into money."[2] The loveliest furnishings of palaces and castles were stripped and the pictures were taken from the walls to be sold to the highest bidder. With much trouble the Emperor succeeded in obtaining Belvedere and saving the library from dispersal, though only by guaranteeing a high life-rent to the heiress.

Among the things put up for sale were the statues presented to Prince Eugene by d'Elboeuf. But though these were admired for their beauty, the significance of their discovery was still not realised. Even while the still unconfirmed rumour of their sale ran through Vienna, "the whole Academy

[1] Michelangelo Schipa, *Il regno di Napoli al tempo di Carlo di Borbone*, p. 76. Naples, 1904.
[2] Alfred von Arneth, *Prinz Eugen von Savoyen*, p. 501. Vienna, 1858.

and artistic world were up in arms".[1] As soon as the matter was confirmed, the well-known sculptor Lorenzo Mattielli, who was living in Vienna, made a plaster-cast of the statues, "to compensate for their loss".

This man was in touch with the art-loving Electoral Prince Frederick Augustus II of Saxony, Augustus III of Poland, and there were negotiations about his going to Dresden. Then the thought struck Lorenzo of drawing the King's attention to the three statues which were for sale in Vienna. The King, who on the occasion of the hanging of the Sistine Madonna in the ceremonial hall of the castle in Dresden is reported to have said, "Make way for the great Raphael!" and with his own hands pushed back his throne, did not enjoy for nothing his reputation for being a lover of all beauty. He did not need to be asked twice, but immediately acquired the three statues, put them into his collection of classical art, and rejoiced in their noble lines, in the fall of the draperies, and the warm yellow marble. But in Vienna everyone looked on with sorrowful eyes as they were carried off to Dresden. So the first really flawless and valuable finds from the district round Vesuvius were now in the far north and as good as lost for ever to Naples. And thus matters rested, as Charles, King of the Two Sicilies, was more interested in carrying home a *living* statue to Naples from Dresden, namely, Augustus's fair daughter, Maria Amalia Christine, who married him in 1738 and entered her new home in July of that year.

The young Queen had been brought up to appreciate the arts. She had seen the three statues many times in the pavilion of the great museum garden in Dresden, where they were displayed. When she came to Naples and saw the other things which d'Elboeuf had brought to light in Portici, she prevailed upon her husband to search for more. Since this fell in with the King's own wishes, and since, moreover, Vesuvius had been almost wholly inactive for a year and a half, since the great eruption in May 1737, he determined to undertake further excavations. On 22nd October, 1738, he gave the order for investigations to be carried out at the place where Prince d'Elboeuf had found his statues. This was undoubtedly a difficult undertaking, since these had lain at a depth of

---

[1] Johann Joachim Winckelmann, *Gedanken ueber die Nachahmung der griechischen Malerei und Bildhauerkunst*. Dresden-Leipzig, 1756.

fifty to sixty feet beneath the petrified mud, and d'Elboeuf had succeeded only with great trouble and expense in driving his narrow, low galleries in a lucky direction.

The King consulted the Chevalier Rocco Gioacchino de Alcubierre, an engineer, originally a surveyor, whom he had brought from Spain to be the commander of the Neapolitan engineers. This man maintained that it was perfectly possible to make such excavations, although great difficulties would have to be expected. There was really nothing else to do but to work blindly, by shafts and holes, as had already been done, though this could now be done, of course, with somewhat greater means and more workers. It had to be remembered, moreover, that the houses of Resina stood on top of the site. In order not to imperil these houses it was thought necessary to fill up the cavities, after examination, with earth and stones. For wherever anything caved in and a dwelling was damaged, there would be innumerable complaints and claims for compensation.

So a beginning was made with work through the well shaft used by Prince d'Elboeuf, whose water surface was about sixty-five feet below the level of Resina. Pickaxes and gunpowder were used. It was not long before two fragments of great bronze horses of more than life-size were discovered. The information was at once taken to the Marchese Don Marcello Venuti, a humanist from Tuscany, who had been entrusted by the King with the care of his library in Naples and of the art treasures he had inherited from his mother, Elisabeth Farnese, after the extinction of the male line of her family. The Marchese went immediately to the site, where in the meantime two enormous marble statues of toga-clad Romans had been discovered, one of them with the features of the Emperor Augustus. There followed brick pillars, painted and covered with stucco, and lastly a third statue, completely preserved and made of the finest marble. Venuti accompanied the royal pair and rejoiced with them at what had come to light. The Marchese lowered himself into the shaft in the presence of his master, and found the workers in the act of uncovering a long stairway. From the shape of the whole place he concluded that they had come on a stage or an amphitheatre. After the discovery of the head and rump of a bronze horse, on 11th December, 1738, they came upon the fragments of an inscription from which it could be read that Lucius Annius Mammianus Rufus had at his own expense built the "Theatrum Herculanensem". This yielded two pieces of information, one, that they had come upon a theatre, and two, more important, that it was the theatre of Herculaneum. The name of the builder and architect was also made known. D'Elboeuf, in other words, in his first finds had all unwittingly hit upon the front of the stage of a theatre, on which there had once collapsed, under the impact of the mudstream from Vesuvius, that wall which served as wings and background, with its marble facing and its numerous statues. This was the explanation of the rich finds at this point. So the statues presented by the Austrian cavalry general to Prince Eugene led direct to the discovery of Herculaneum. Johann Joachim Winckelmann, one of the first men to make a scientific study of classical art and the father of German archaeology, justly said, when describing the three statues in Dresden: "It deserves to be made known to the world that these three divine pieces blazed the way to the discovery of the underground treasures of the town of Herculaneum."

Thus we have the remarkable situation that Herculaneum was discovered, though lying almost sixty feet beneath solid stone, while the site of Pompeii, buried much more lightly under lapilli and ash, was still in question. This had come about because on top of Herculaneum there was a village dependent on a spring of water.

Now Alcubierre, the King's Spanish engineer, set to work. First he employed about twenty men to enlarge and consolidate the corridors and caverns, both those of ancient times and those made by d'Elboeuf. Good fortune attended their labours, for they straightway discovered fragments of a racing chariot and of bronze horses which had clearly been part of a quadriga. From the site of the discovery it seemed as though this quadriga had not belonged to the theatre, but had crowned some other nearby building, and had been carried to its present position by the mud-stream. Other bronzes and pieces of statuary were also found, and rejoiced the King's heart.

Parts of eighteen rows of seats in the theatre had now been uncovered; there followed the discovery of several splendid bronze statues. One of these was very large, and was thought

to represent the Emperor Titus Vespasian. The statue was
filled with lead, and was so heavy that twelve men, working
in the narrow space, were unable to move it. Since there were
now so many fragments of various objects, a rather undis-
tinguished sculptor called Joseph Canart was commissioned
to restore them. He first cleaned the best-preserved statues,
thus removing the patina. But there were innumerable fragments, and Canart, shrinking from the work of piecing them
together, simply melted them down. He even melted down the
torso of the charioteer, which he pronounced to be beyond
restoration, and had it made into medallions of the King and
Queen, figures of saints, and candelabra for the royal chapel,
until the royal pair themselves put an end to his proceedings.
But in this and similar ways much was lost.

The excavations, or rather the cave-diggings, were continued, and on 21st May, 1739, were marked by a specially
fine success. Digging was being carried on not far from the
place where the quadriga had been discovered and a wonderful
equestrian statue of bronze, greater than life-size, was laid
bare; an inscription described it as that of Marcus Nonius
Balbus, one of the most distinguished citizens of ancient
Herculaneum, who had once been governor in Crete and
Africa. Alcubierre was not quite sure where this statue had
been found or in what kind of building. But this did not
matter, his master was delighted with it; and it was at
once set up in the courtyard of the nearby royal villa in
Portici.

Since the King was anxious to keep the story of his successes as secret as possible, only his nominees were allowed
to sketch the discoveries. Nor was anyone permitted to write
about them, so that only a few favoured contemporaries were
able to appreciate the treasures. Among these was Cardinal
Quirini, the art-loving chief of the Vatican collections and
library, who at once declared that this was the finest classical
statue so far discovered, much finer and even better made
than that of the Emperor Antonine in the Capitol (the statue
now recognised to be that of Marcus Aurelius). When the
galleries penetrated, in July and August 1739, into houses
lying near the theatre, charming frescoes were discovered
depicting scenes from the lives of the gods and from Greek
legends.

The Marchese Venuti wrote in raptures about these pictures to a learned friend: "In the excavations near Naples the loveliest thing in the world has been discovered: a painted wall with figures in life-size, splendidly and realistically depicted, much more beautiful than the work of Raphael!"[1]

Venuti was speaking of the picture of Theseus with the slain minotaur at his feet and women and children round him kissing his hands and knees in gratitude. Up to this time about forty such frescoes had been found. They were prised off the walls, and removed from the rooms to the royal villa in Portici, which now possessed an annexe, a real museum, for the reception of the finds. On the advice of a certain Morriconi, the paintings were then covered with a kind of veneer, in order to protect them from fading and peeling, and framed and covered with glass, and turned into a kind of gallery of classical art. It was found, however, that the veneer tended to absorb the colours, then to dry and flake off, thus destroying some of the finest of the paintings. The King, who had watched his collection grow with the greatest delight, was very much vexed. He dismissed Morriconi, but he could not make good the damage.[2] In order to have at least a copy of the discoveries in future, should such damage continue, the King resolved to have copies made of every painting which came to light.

The Queen, too, was enraptured with all the splendid discoveries. A very fine piece of jewellery was discovered, with an emerald with a blood-red fleck in its centre. This was taken to the Queen, who had a picture of Vesuvius engraved on it, with an inscription prepared by the famous Neapolitan professor of Greek literature and archaeology, Abbate Giacopo Martorelli, a conceited, busy, scribacious, but diligent man. The inscription told how the stone came from one of the places which had been overwhelmed by the fires of Vesuvius. The court was as elementary and inexperienced in its archaeological methods as it was jealous of its sole right to carry on the excavations. They were so strict that anyone who dug a

[1] Marchese Venuti to Antonio Francesco Gori, Rome, 31st November, 1739 (Gori, *Symbolae litterariae opuscula varia,* 1748).

[2] In modern times Morriconi has been partly exculpated: many of the pictures varnished by him have been cleaned and show their colours brilliantly preserved.

hole came under immediate suspicion of undertaking un-
authorised work, which was threatened with severe punish-
ments. Without the royal assent no one, not even one of the
workers, was permitted even to paint a copy of anything that
was discovered or to make sketches of it.

The King, however, soon realised that Alcubierre, who was
in charge of the work, though technically very capable, was
quite unable to cope with the scientific aspects: he was an
engineer and not an archaeologist, a technician but not a man
of letters. The most serious errors were made. No importance
was attached to inscriptions, for example: on one occasion
enormous metal letters from an inscription were taken down
and thrown in any order into a basket before the text had
even been read. The King realised that more help must be
secured, and that the engineer must have a scientific assistant
to evaluate, handle, and describe the discoveries. He consulted with his chief minister, Count Fogliani, and by ill-luck
this minister was looking for a good post for a cousin. This
was Monsignor Ottavio Antonio Bayardi of Parma, who had,
it is true, a high reputation for learning, but was in reality a
perverse and muddle-headed fellow, a conceited and pre-
sumptuous scribbler. The little wrinkled, sick old scholar
claimed to have written a history of the Church in forty
volumes. This threw light on his methods of work; but at
first the King was quite unsuspicious. He accepted the man
recommended to him, who inspected the museum at Portici,
but said that his asthma prevented his being personally
present at the excavations. He made the most serious errors
in his descriptions of what was discovered. Typically Hellenic
bronze heads he declared to be Roman. The King, however,
was anxious to satisfy the curiosity of the public, and urged
him to make an exhibition of the discoveries. But what did
Bayardi do? He buried himself in books, wrote and wrote,
and said that he needed many years to prepare his intro-
ductions. Nor could the tedious old man be removed, for his
powerful cousin was still minister.

After the first lucky finds in Herculaneum the difficulties
of excavating in the solid lava began to be felt. The direction
in which the galleries were pushed forward was unlucky and
the yields were meagre. But with the rich material which had
been brought to light within a few years the King was able

to establish a splendid museum, far in advance of anything possessed by any other European ruler. Loggias were built on to the royal palace in Naples to house the works of art, and plans were being considered for a new building to house not only the Farnese treasures but also the finds at Herculaneum.

About the year 1745 the excavations seemed to have reached a dead end: the yields had become very slender. There was also the fear of a new invasion of imperial troops to wrest Naples once again into Hapsburg possession — a fear which was not in fact realised. In any case, Alcubierre stopped the work and considered how and at what point he could undertake fresh excavations which would be attended, if possible, by less difficulties. Now there were living in Naples two men with a very high reputation for learning. One was the canon Alexius Mazzocchi, a scholar who had studied Greek antiquities, and the other was the already mentioned Martorelli, who had been stirred to a quite passionate interest in the finds at Herculaneum. Filled with envy, he had to look on while a non-Neapolitan like Bayardi squandered hundreds of ducats on quite useless work, whereas he himself, the scholar of Naples, had almost to spy in order to get a glimpse of the discoveries and to endanger his freedom in order to make notes on them.

It is true that Martorelli was also very perverse and tedious in his work, but he had always lived on the spot, and now that Herculaneum had been discovered he was feverishly anxious to find Pompeii as well. Fresh rumours arose that workers who were building on the hill of Civita had come upon the vestiges of walls. There were also rumours of smaller finds — a bronze tripod, a Priapus, and the like — and in February 1748 Martorelli, reaffirming the old views of Pellegrino and others, declared his conviction that Pompeii lay buried there. His colleague Mazzocchi, though he was his rival and bitter enemy, held the same views. Alcubierre was obdurate, holding that Civita was the site of Stabiae, but he too had no doubt that *something* lay buried there. So one March day in 1748 he went to the site next the Sarno canal where the finds had been made, and after investigation decided to propose to the King that the excavations at Herculaneum should be suspended and a serious attempt made to

19. Prie-dieu before a Christian cross in the room of a house in
Herculaneum. Discovered in the winter of 1939, this is a proof of
the existence of a small Christian community before A.D. 79,
which prayed in secret before the sign of the cross.

(*See pages* 41, 208)

Photo: Alinari

20. Fresco of a Pompeian man and wife, with a book-roll, writing-tablet, and pen. In the House of the Baker Terentius Proculus. Reg. IX, Ins. 3, No. 10.

(*See page 36*)

Photo: Alinari

21. The only representation of Vesuvius so far discovered in Pompeii. Note the shape of the mountain, completely different from the present. The figure of Bacchus indicates that Vesuvius was then covered with vineyards to a great height. The snake is a symbol of luck. The picture is in the lararium or chapel of the household gods in the Casa del Centenario at Pompeii.

(*See page* 62)

Photo: Alinari

22. Plaster cast of the cavity round the skeleton of the watch-dog of the fuller Vesonius Primus, which was chained up, and choked in the ashes.

(*See page 70*)

work in the area of Civita. The King agreed, and the order was actually given on 23rd March, 1748.

On 1st April, 1748, the experiment was begun with twelve workers, and, as later appeared, at a very lucky spot.[1] But still nobody realised, in spite of the remains of houses which were at once discovered, that they were in the middle of a town; it was still thought that the walls belonged to isolated houses, they were covered up again after a search had been made for objects for the museum, and the digging was started again somewhere else.

Meanwhile the number of workers had been increased. Alcubierre had issued instructions to the burgomaster of Torre d'Annunziata that the workers on the excavations should live in that village. By 6th April there were twenty-four people at work, including twelve convicts who had been sentenced to hard labour. That very day the first splendid fresco was discovered. Joseph Canart was at once summoned, and he cut it away from the wall and had it taken to his studio in Portici. It consisted of coloured garlands of fruit, flowers and vine-leaves, which had clearly decorated a dining-room. An old Roman helmet, oil-lamps, coins and the like were also discovered.

On 19th April, 1748, the first of the dead was discovered, the skeleton of a man lying on the ground, from whose hands had slipped a number of gold and silver coins of the time of Nero and Vespasian. There was no doubt that they had come upon the remains of a Pompeian who had tried to flee from the eruption of Vesuvius with his slender stock of money.

Now the excavations went on with redoubled ardour. Curiosity and greed for plunder were the moving principles of the work and they went together with a complete lack of method. So it came about that digging was carried on now here, now there, spasmodically and unsteadily, with complete reliance on luck and chance. Then work was stopped on this favourable starting-point, and in November 1748 the excavators suddenly turned to the district of the amphitheatre, where the oval depression which appeared in the land suggested that a large building was hidden there. But they had

[1] About two hundred yards from the Temple of Fortuna Augusta in Pompeii, to the left of the Nolan Way and next to the junction of the Stabian and Nolan Ways.

uncovered only one or two parts of the rows of seats when they realised that they had come upon an amphitheatre. Alcubierre, still under the illusion that he had discovered Stabiae, called the building the "Stabian theatre".

But, as before, the search was mainly directed towards articles of silver and gold and bronze statues, and naturally none of these was found among the spectators' seats where they were excavating. So here too excavations were abandoned, and blind digging was begun to the west of the town in the neighbourhood of the Gate of Herculaneum. Here they were lucky enough to uncover a villa, which without any justification was asserted to have belonged to Cicero. It contained delightful frescoes — eight flying bacchantes in streaming robes and a group of centaurs and fauns playing on a tightrope and trying to keep their balance. After these frescoes had been cut out and the few bronze and metal objects salvaged, the house was covered in again. To this day the precise site of this discovery has never been made quite clear. The bacchantes performing their artistic dancing mimes, so much praised in ancient times, excited the King's greatest delight, and he at once had engravings made of them, though these, of course, could not reproduce the tender and lovely colours. These copies, which were at first kept secret, caused the greatest sensation when they were made public.

So the year 1749 began with great promise, but further work uncovered only the remains of some walls, and the expected hoards of gold and silver did not appear. Alcubierre began to doubt the significance of the finds and even declared one day that the excavations at Civita were "now fruitless" and that it would be better to search at other places, such as Pozzuoli, Sorrento, and so on. But a Swiss architect, Karl Weber, a very sensible and hard-working man who had been assigned to Alcubierre, went on working there. By the end of September 1750, when even he had found nothing remarkable, the work at Civita was for the time being abandoned and plans were considered for resuming the suspended work at Herculaneum. Weber had worked diligently, but his methods had not differed in any way from those of his chief. He had acquired experience, however, and was anxious to establish a more scientific and deliberate method of excavation. Alcubierre was in a sense quite pleased at Weber's lack of success, for the Spaniard was jealously anxious to be accounted by the King the only one who could discover anything of value. But one day the news arrived that walls and pillars had been dug up not far from the site of the original finds from Herculaneum — that is, adjacent to the kitchen garden of the Augustinian monks and west of Resina — and these clearly formed part of a large building. This find, too, came to light as a result of the digging of a well through the lava stream of 1631 and the mud stream of the year 79. In the course of this work a semi-circular veranda had been struck, which was decorated with an inlaid paving of coloured marble. This kind of thing was only possible in a very wealthy house.

Karl Weber, who had meanwhile transferred his activity to Herculaneum, and who had received in 1750, with a salary of twelve ducats monthly, "subordinate charge and the right of entry to the underground places and crypts", had just completed the first sensible measure: a map and ground-plan of the galleries and buildings, together with a sketch for the complete uncovering of the theatre. He soon succeeded in investigating the stage more thoroughly. It was not easy for him to work in face of the jealousy of his chief, who even had the props supporting the galleries removed, whereupon the falls which had been feared promptly took place.

Weber much regretted the abandoning of the excavations at Civita and was still anxious to continue them. But when he received the news of the fresh discovery at Resina he eagerly pushed on the work there. And indeed the discoveries were almost miraculous. Suddenly they came upon a great peristyle with no less than sixty-four pillars, and a splendid oblong bathing-pool. Karl Weber's eyes almost started from his head as there was gradually revealed, between the pillars, a perfect gallery of works of art of ancient Roman and Greek masters, in metal and bronze: thirteen great bronze statues, nine of which are among the finest products of the classical world, a group with a drunken and a sleeping faun, dancing-girls, fighters, and forty-seven busts of various kinds. At once it was clear that countless treasures could be discovered in this area. Here in one place were to be found things which the excavators could not have dared to hope for. It was an extensive villa with stately living-rooms, loggias

119

and verandas, peristyles and atria, and all in the richest and loveliest style of decoration. And it had all lain untouched for almost 1700 years and still displayed everything that this jewel of an ancient Roman house contained in the year 79, when the flowing masses of mud stormed over it, filling it and engulfing it.

The first news of the splendid discovery aroused great delight in the court at Portici. The King almost forgot his daily hunt and his beloved sea-fishing. The royal couple hastened to the site and watched the splendid statues being brought up. Whenever Charles III had a few minutes' leisure, he hastened to his museum to talk with the Roman painter Camillo Paderni, who was occupied in setting out the statues. And the Queen, whose boudoir was next to the classical gallery in Portici, spent almost all her day there, receiving her most important and confidential visitors there.

Meanwhile the work in the villa near Resina went on. Excellent imitations of the most various styles and masters of Greek plastic art were discovered, but there were also original works which had obviously been imported from Greece. People racked their brains to decide to whom this wonderful villa could have belonged, when on 19th October, 1752, another surprisingly valuable discovery was made. On that day a small room had been penetrated. Round the walls stood charred wooden cupboards, the height of a man, and in the middle stood a structure open on both sides. In it there were piled on top of one another strange, round, black objects, which looked like piles of briquettes. The workers took some out, and broke or cut them in pieces to ascertain what they were. They came away in leaves, fell to dust, and no one was any the wiser. At last Paderni was summoned when someone thought he had seen some writing on one of the rolls. And soon everything was plain: these round carbonised things were papyrus rolls, the books of Roman times. And since there was a great number of them, what had been discovered was an ancient library. Now the scholars of the whole world hoped that their dreams would be fulfilled, and that the lost writings of Tacitus and Ovid, Livy and Pliny the Elder, would be found. This was all very well; but how could the rolls be unfolded? On a mere touch most of them disappeared in dust, so that all that could be read was what was visible on the outside. It seemed to be impossible to unfold those fragile leaves of the papyrus plant, laid together as they were and quite carbonised. One or two of the rolls, however, had suffered less, and with infinite care it was possible to read separate lines. They were in Greek, and contained the name of Philodemos the Epicurean, who lived at the time of Cicero and Horace. Paderni straightway buried himself in this classical library, and gradually more than a thousand of those rolls were rescued, and their number kept increasing. Now a tremendous technical problem, as well as the linguistic one, was set to the learned world — to which Paderni, the director of the museum, ignorant as he was of Latin and Greek, did not, indeed, belong. It was a problem before which everyone was at first quite helpless.

Years passed before one leaf was unrolled. In 1754 Paderni was still convinced that this could never be done and that single lines were the most that could ever be read. Most attempts ended with more or less damage to the rolls. Then the custodian of the Vatican Library, a Jesuit called Antonio Piaggi, announced that he had invented an apparatus for unfolding the rolls. The King summoned him to Naples, and for decades the Jesuit worked on the precious rolls.

The splendid finds near Herculaneum caused the district of Civita to be almost completely forgotten. For four years almost nothing happened there. It was only towards the close of the year 1754 that there was a change, when some tombs and ancient buildings came to light near the south side of the town, in the course of a piece of road construction. Alcubierre, urged on by Weber, visited the site and again set a few people to work. Though there were only four or five of them, the excavations did begin again, and have been continued, except in time of war, to our own day.

The King, who took ever-increasing delight in his growing museum, wanted at last to have some kind of catalogue. But the worthy Bayardi, who was entrusted with the task of describing the yields of the excavations, went on writing the countless volumes of his *Prodromi*, his introduction and foreword, losing himself in learned Greek, Hebrew, Arabic and other quotations concerning the travels and deeds of Hercules and the mythical origin of the town whose discovery he was meant to describe. And at the same time he was intensely jealous of his exclusive right to present the results of the excavations. In 1748, when Venuti and Gori published their information and, in contrast to Bayardi, went to the heart of the matter, namely, the buildings and objects which had been discovered, Bayardi, with the help of his powerful patron the minister Fogliani, actually had their writings forbidden. So he was able to proceed at his leisure with the compilation of more "preparatory and introductory" volumes, which by 1752 numbered five, of 2,677 pages, without a single reference, apart from in the foreword, to the actual discoveries. The stamp of Bayardi's writing, its Byzantine and fawning flattery, may be appreciated by his praise of the Herculaneum excavations as a mightier work than the deeds of Alexander the Great, for while Alexander's lordship stretched over the world, but only on the surface of the earth, that of Charles of Bourbon had penetrated to the earth's very "bowels"! The Marchese Caracciolo gave the following criticism of Bayardi's work: "So far Mr Bayardi has taken pleasure in burying the ancient world of Herculaneum beneath a much denser veil than that spread over it by the lava."

At last, however, things went too far even for the King, and he demanded forthright from his Prime Minister's favourite, before any further volumes were printed, a catalogue of the contents of the museum. Bayardi could hold out no longer, and in 1755 there at last appeared the first catalogue, very clumsily edited, but beautifully printed and decorated, with an account of 738 frescoes, 350 statues and 1,647 various smaller objects. But even here the scholar did not fail to repeat, in the almost threatening tones of his dedication to the King, that he still needed some years, perhaps many years, to complete his introduction to the description of the finds of Herculaneum. The countless pictures which had been discovered, but judged not good enough for the museum, and destroyed or covered up again, were nowhere described. They were lost for ever.

In the same year, 1755, the Queen brought about the fall of the all-powerful Fogliani, whom she hated, and he had to withdraw to Sicily. This meant also the end of Bayardi, who departed for Rome. It was high time, for people were beginning to blame the King, in spite of his deep interest and zeal, for the many incredible ineptitudes and damage done in the excavations and in the evaluation of the finds, though naturally he could not keep his finger on everything. In Florence people had even gone so far as to assert that the whole stir about Herculaneum was just Neapolitan humbug and a mighty hoax.

In order that things should not reach such a pass again, and that there should be a serious scientific assessment of the discoveries, the King resolved, on the advice of Fogliani's successor, the talented Tuscan Bernardo Tanucci, a former university professor, to found the Academy of Herculaneum. This was done on 13th December, 1755, and it was intended to include all the learned men of Naples interested in classical antiquities and experts in classical literature. Who were the first members of this Academy? First there was the happily departed Bayardi, but he died shortly after his nomination. But along with some fine collectors, lawyers and numismatists with a humanist background there were only very few archaeologists, for archaeology was in its infancy; Mazzocchi was outstanding among them. Martorelli, who was also canvassing to become a member of the Academy, published in 1756 a work in two volumes and 652 pages in which he attempted to prove, mainly by means of an inkwell which had been dug up ten years before, that Greek and Roman books were not in rolls, but rectangular like our own. And this, though years before a whole library of carbonised rolls had been found in the villa near Herculaneum and Martorelli himself had seen and examined them! In addition he developed in great detail his views of what this inkwell showed regarding the Greek origin of Naples.

The founding of the Academy was well meant, but its composition caused it to be stillborn. There were hot talks, jealous feuds and intrigues, and wanderings in all kinds of learned irrelevancies, while the heart of the whole enterprise was neglected. The greatest service rendered by the Academy was that on the instigation of Mazzocchi and some other members digging went on somewhat more energetically in the district of Civita. And in June 1755 there was brought to light the house of Julia Felix, containing countless statues, fine frescoes of Egyptian gods, delightful representations of the Muses, and the famous tripod, supported by bronze satyrs. But the Academy did not exert the slightest influence on the method of excavation. Many more paintings were destroyed, no value at all was set on the architecture, and the remains of the houses were covered in again as soon as their contents had been systematically plundered. Even the publications which the Academy, as Bayardi's successor, was supposed to bring out did not appear, for every member wanted something different, until finally one of them, old Francesco Valetta, took the matter in hand, had the most important paintings sketched, and published them in 1757, at the royal press, in a single folio volume with the title *The Antiquities of Herculaneum*. The publication cost the King 12,000 ducats. So a beginning was made with giving the world the facts about the great discoveries.

A particularly vexed problem was the deciphering of the papyrus rolls, and little progress was made in this, since the fantastic machine of the monk Piaggi was of little help in unrolling the carbonised writings. The machine was like "a frame of the kind used by wig-makers to prepare their wigs"; it had to be handled very cautiously, and after four years' work only three rolls were completely unfolded, while many others had been wholly destroyed. With infinite care and tenderness the leaves were slowly unrolled and laid on under-lying paper. Line after line appeared, and if the luck held in this painfully tedious operation, one leaf, one page, was saved in the course of a month. "Sometimes the King came to the museum and watched the monk for hours, as he peeled the black leaves, thin as a wafer, from the charred cylinder, and the parallel columns, corresponding to a normal page in a book, became visible on the strips stuck one on top of the other."[1] After four years of continuous work all that had been secured was a part (39 columns) of a philosophical treatise by Philodemos on music. So the Academy was not able to publish anything definitive, but it was a great gain that each of the rolls was carefully salvaged, the number in the course of time reaching 1,800.

The painful slowness of all the work connected with the excavations stirred the public, who had no conception of the difficulties, to mockery and scorn. In Naples it was maliciously

[1] Justi, *Winckelmann and his Contemporaries*, II, 171. Leipzig, 1898.

said that Vesuvius, whose activity had been resumed in 1755 with lava bursting from its side, was spitting so much because men were taking so long to explain what it had done to the earth in the course of two energetic days.

At this time, in the year 1756, Johann Joachim Winckelmann came from Dresden to Naples. This man was the thirty-nine-year-old son of a poor cobbler who had wanted his child to follow the same craft, while the lad himself was determined to study and become a "bookman". And he reached his goal chiefly by learning to value time and to use every minute of the day in action and study, raising himself out of miserable poverty and becoming a librarian. He had early shown an interest in historical remains. Even as a schoolboy he had taken his companions with him to the mounds lying outside the city, which contained the graves of Huns, in order to search for urns and other relics.

In 1755 he arrived in Rome with a royal pension. From that time onwards he was in his element. There, and in Florence and Naples, in the following thirteen years he acquired his admirably comprehensive knowledge of classical sculpture and his conviction of the "noble simplicity and tranquil greatness" of ancient Greek art. With no academic career behind him, he had little use for the professors of his time, and he found Naples and its learned men, as well as the method of excavation and evaluation of the finds, so repugnant that he roundly condemned the whole situation, and indeed often went beyond the mark in his strictures.

The daughter of the Saxon king being Queen in Naples, more had been heard in Dresden than elsewhere about the discoveries of Herculaneum, and people there were agog for further information. When Winckelmann received his pension to enable him to go to Italy, not the least important motive in its bestowal was the desire to learn more details from him. He was to write letters about the discoveries in Herculaneum, which were to be sent to the electoral prince, who was specially interested in excavations. Winckelmann also carried letters of introduction to the sister of the prince, the Queen of Naples. But at first the archaeologist was so entranced with Rome that in his first work from there, *Thoughts about the Imitation of Greek Painting and Sculpture*, the only mention of Herculaneum was of the three statues which Prince d'Elboeuf had

125

sent to Prince Eugene in Vienna. And since his knowledge of this matter was only from hearsay, many of his statements, for example concerning the year of the discovery, were incorrect.

Towards the end of 1757 he decided to make use of the recommendations to the court at Naples and to examine in person the state of affairs concerning the treasures from Herculaneum and the other finds. But despite his letters of introduction it was not so simple a matter to be received in audience. The Queen was a difficult character. Jealous almost to madness for her position, easily angered and very violent in her temper, she treated the whole court, including those of the highest standing, like slaves. Even high-born ladies could wait upon the Queen only on their knees. The Queen was aware, moreover, how jealous her husband was of everything concerning the excavations, which as time went on took a more and more central place in his affections. This Saxon who asked for an audience was very likely a painter who had simply come in order to spy in the museum, to make sketches of the contents, and thus to forestall the planned publications of the Royal Academy. It was a long time before the foreigner succeeded in being received, and finally in being invited to the royal table. It was an even longer time before he received permission (on 27th February, 1758) to visit the museum, and was presented with the first Academy volume on the painting. Even then Winckelmann had to undertake not to make a single sketch, and to be content just to look at everything in peace and comfort.

The archaeologist now resolved to ask for a lodging in the Augustinian monastery, in order to be as close as possible to the museum in Portici. He gained his end with the help of the papyrus-worker, Father Piaggi, to whom he had a letter of introduction, and who had in fact become the chief scholar in the museum. This monk, who for years had been well provided from the royal treasury, while achieving very little, was naturally considered by Alcubierre, Paderni, the director of the museum, and all who had some part in the excavations, to be a parasite and a good-for-nothing. He repaid this by making merry at the expense of Alcubierre and Paderni and their method of handling their finds. Piaggi influenced Winckelmann, who was given access only to the museum and

126

not to the site of the excavations, in the most partial and malicious way against everyone who was at work there. Granted that great errors were made, these were more or less excusable in view of the novelty of the enterprise and the absence of any technique based on experience. Winckelmann let himself be too strongly influenced by Piaggi. He went often to the museum; and this must have made a much deeper impression on him than he showed in his report on it. The wonderful bronzes and marbles, the portraits of the Emperors, the equestrian statues of the family of the Balbi, the numerous frescoes which had been cut out and were now gathered in a single gallery, the mosaic floors and pillars of precious marble which had been so skilfully set up in Portici, and the rich collection of tripods, candelabra, vases, lamps, and the like — all these confirmed Winckelmann in his view that "the spirit of Greek art was not alien even to the craftsmen". But all this should have warned Winckelmann to have more respect for the excavators. For it was they — Alcubierre, for instance — who had to be thanked for the discovery of quite new sites. And the passionate concern of the King, who provided the means for the whole undertaking, should have been properly honoured. On the other hand, Winckelmann was justifiably annoyed that he was not permitted to draw anything or take notes; immensely interested as he was, he tried to spy out and inspect everything. At that time the rumour spread through Naples that highly lascivious paintings had been found. The ancients were infinitely freer in their reproduction of things that in our modern view are considered indecent. The organs of human reproduction were for them symbols of energy and beauty as well as of the will of nature to produce new life; they were signs of blessing and exuberant health, which they delighted to represent in stone or marble for all to see. Paintings would show lovers in the act of love; a very fine piece of marble statuary was even discovered which showed a satyr and a goat coming together. This was immediately sent to the court in Caserta. With the strict injunction that no one should be allowed access to it, the King entrusted it to the royal sculptor in Portici, Joseph Canart. Although Winckelmann used to bribe the watchmen, who showed him many things which the King wished to keep secret, even he was unable to see such things. He left Naples again and returned to Rome, there to set down his experiences in a letter.

Meanwhile the villa where the papyrus rolls had been found continued to yield costly works of art, the Resting Mercury, for instance, which remains to this day one of the best known pieces of classical sculpture. The King was delighted with this discovery, and it was one of his last joys as the ruler of Naples, for Ferdinand VI of Spain died on 10th August, 1759; before his death the government had to be entrusted to his ministers, since he had fallen a victim to incurable insanity. The heir was Charles III of Naples and Sicily, his step-brother, who was now obliged to relinquish his kingdom and ascend the Spanish throne. He committed the Kingdom of the Two Sicilies to his third son, who was only eighteen years old, with Tanucci as regent till the majority of Ferdinand IV, as the young king was now called. The eldest son could not be considered, as he too was hopelessly insane, and the second son was the Spanish Crown Prince. The third son, now King of Naples, was very backward compared with other lads of his age, and had shown in his boyhood inclinations which did not promise well.

With a heavy heart Charles III left the kingdom which he had grown to love well. With his excellent qualities he had done much good. He had built the splendid San Carlo theatre in Naples, and founded a workshop for Gobelin tapestries as well as the famous porcelain works of Capo di Monte. And it was he who had ordered the resumption of the excavations undertaken by Prince d'Elboeuf, which had led to the discovery of Herculaneum with its splendid treasures and of the sites on the hill of Civita, though no one was as yet quite sure what really lay hidden beneath that hill. It was the King who had to be thanked for these undertakings, with their yearly expenditure of 8,000 to 9,000 ducats, which had brought to light those wonderful classical works which now adorned a museum more splendid than that of any other prince. Nor did the King desire to keep anything for himself; just as he required of everyone else that they should look on every discovery on these classical sites as the precious possession of the nation and the state, so he never regarded the museum as his own property. Once he himself found among the rubble of Pompeii a lump of pumice-stone in which several coins of the time of Nero were embedded, as well as a gold ring with a chalcedony stone, which he afterwards wore on his finger and loved to show to his princely guests. On his departure for Spain he drew this ring off his finger and left it in the museum, for he considered that he had no personal right to it.

Vesuvius in the meanwhile was still active, and at the end of September 1759 severe tremors presaged a more serious eruption. Torre del Greco as well as Portici were specially threatened, and in Naples public prayer for nine days was at once ordered, together with the exhibition of the head of St Januarius. The people prayed that Vesuvius, from which lava had flowed as far as the sea in the last days of September, might cease its activity. Towards the end of the year, just at Christmas-time, there was a violent explosion. Three miles from the sea a long cleft appeared in the mountain-slope, and molten lava streamed from it in the direction of Torre d'Annunziata. The eruption lasted till 7th January, 1760, and much needless destruction was caused, for instead of helping themselves many people entrusted their goods and chattels in prayer to the care of some saint. Thus the Neapolitan lawyer Masserante lost his new dairy-farm with its equipment, which had cost him 20,000 ducats. As the lava slowly advanced, people advised him to have his goods removed on a wagon, but he replied: "But my villa has a lovely chapel dedicated to St Januarius." "All the more reason", they told him, "for rescuing the chalices and pictures from it." But he replied: "I have dedicated this place to the saint, and he must protect it." Then he went and threw the key into the molten lava. So everything was burned.[1]

After the departure of King Charles III the fate of the excavations depended on the new ruler, who was in effect the minister Tanucci, and he commanded that they should be carried on. At that time about forty convicts were employed on the excavations. In consequence, much that was found, especially gold coins, was not delivered up, but suddenly appeared on the market somewhere. Tanucci was therefore compelled to issue a warning that any worker who stole the smallest article would be first whipped till the blood came

---

[1] *Narrazione istorica di quel è avvenuto nel erruzione del dì* 23 *dicembre*, 1759.

and then condemned to hard labour for life in the galleys of Malta. That put an end, at least for the time being, to the widespread and lucrative thieving.

The Herculanean Academy, whose most important members had already died, gradually faded out. Tanucci, burdened with government affairs, had no more time to attend the meetings, and these were discontinued. But perhaps this was as well, for the care of the publications came in this way into the hands of Tanucci's secretary, the active and enthusiastic Pasquale Carcani, a man with an insatiable appetite for reading and for action. He said of himself that work was such a necessity of life to him that he thought it would be easier to die than to sit idle for an hour.[1] On Tanucci's behest he continued the publication of the volumes — on behalf of the Academy which now existed only in name — with their engravings of the pictures and statues and other discoveries.

Meanwhile Winckelmann had finished his report and in 1762 his first *Letter* about the discoveries in Herculaneum appeared. By this time the Academy volume had become known in Europe and had almost created a fashion for classical art. Bronzes, woodcuts, jewellery, even furniture were made *à la Herculaneum*, everyone was interested in the discoveries, and all this caused Winckelmann's *Letter*, inexact and superficial though it was, to be read with avidity, taken up and praised beyond expectation. Admittedly Winckelmann gave the first account in German of how d'Elboeuf had transported his finds from Herculaneum and how laborious had been the excavations of the underground corridors. But his account omitted all mention of the participants in the work, notably of the Spanish engineer Alcubierre, who had, to use the Italian proverb, as little to do with classical antiquities "as the moon with Cancer". Winckelmann too believed that it was Stabiae that had been discovered beneath the mount of Civita, and he just criticised the slowness of the operations. In 1762 he prophetically said that "with such indolence there would still be digging and discovery awaiting posterity to the fourth generation." Winckelmann also related how the parts of the gilt iron horse and of the charioteer belonging to the broken quadriga had been treated; how they were found in

[1] Justi, *op. cit.*, p. 203.

November 1738, how the fragments were taken to Naples and unloaded in a corner of the royal courtyard, where they lay for a long time. Then he told of the medals of the royal pair which had been struck from the metal, and of the King's final command that at least one horse should be restored out of the remaining fragments of what had been once six bronze horses. This was at last done, but was naturally a sad botching of the original splendid fragments. The horse which was put together in this way stands to this day in the museum at Naples.

With delight and ill-concealed pleasure Winckelmann went on to relate how a Venetian painter, Joseph Guerra, after the first volume of the *Antiquities* had appeared, painted pictures resembling those found in Herculaneum and actually offered them for sale as genuine antiques to no less a man than the learned Jesuit who was head of the Roman College. That trustful man acquired no fewer than forty such fakes at a high price. Winckelmann did not suspect that a similar trick would be played on himself in no very distant future. Guerra, who lived in Rome, could imitate the Pompeian style, and slyly implied that the pictures had been secretly taken from Herculaneum. But in the end he made such great mistakes — providing Epaminondas, for example, in the battle of Mantinea with armour which belonged to the Middle Ages — that the whole matter was ridiculed in Rome and throughout the world. In Winckelmann's account, with its mere 96 pages, the pictures and statues were given only about ten pages, while, thanks to his friendship with Piaggi, the account of the papyrus rolls took up a third of the whole book. One interesting piece of information was that one of the deciphered parts contained a treatise by Philodemos on music in which he tries to prove that music is harmful to morals and to the State. This *Letter*, with all its errors and partiality, contained much that was significant and novel to the outside world, its special importance lying in the fact that it was the first reasonable and unpedantic account, even though it was based on insufficient information.

Meanwhile the work, at Tanucci's behest, had been continued. The twelve-year-old King was very backward, and had no interest in the proceedings. The Austrian Imperial ambassador, Graf von Neipperg, reported very strange things about the Neapolitan court, which gave little promise for the future of the young monarch. The Count complained that the King's education and upbringing were below the level of any reasonable criticism. "The King's apartments are like those of a child of two or three years of age, filled with innumerable silly games and dolls, models of coaches and the like. Apart from these childish pastimes the hunt takes up almost all the rest of his day, and is the only thing his nurse and other attendants are diligent to entertain him with. In short, his education is a mis-education, laying in a store of ignorance and depriving him of all useful knowledge, stifling the good qualities and gifts of this tender, gay, obedient and lovable little prince, who would be capable of acquiring the best culture."[1]

In such a situation there was little hope for the future, and the ground was certainly not prepared for awakening the prince's interest in antiquity and his zeal for the excavations.

The rich finds in the house outside Herculaneum, now commonly called the "Villa of the Papyri", gradually petered out; but in the region of Civita there were fresh successes. In 1763 a gate with three entrances (the Gate of Herculaneum) had been discovered, a find which strengthened the belief that a complete town lay behind it. In the direction of the sea excavations laid bare a large inn, the skeleton of a mule with fragments of a wagon, and a great quantity of household objects — water-jugs of bronze, bottles, glass and keys, pots and casseroles. There were five skeletons, four of them almost embracing one another. A great pillared building was at first thought to be a temple, but was soon found to be the mausoleum of the distinguished Pompeian family of the Istacidii, standing near the last resting-place of the priestess Mamia, with its semi-circular seat. The excavations had penetrated the centre of the Street of Tombs beyond the Gate of Herculaneum, a fact established by an inscription on the back of that seat.

Meanwhile the worthy Swiss, Karl Weber, had proposed various reforms in the excavations to the minister Tanucci. He suggested that it would be better not to strike sporadically

[1] Graf Neipperg to the Empress Maria Theresa, Naples, 26th July, 1763. State Archives, Vienna.

Photo: Alinari

23. Equestrian statue of Marcus Nonius Balbus the Elder. Marble sculpture from Herculaneum.

(See page 113)

Photo: Alinari

24. The bronze horse constructed in Bourbon times from the fragments of four horses of a shattered quadriga found in Herculaneum.

(See Pages 112–113, 131)

Photo: Alinari

25. Sale of Cupids (Erotes).
Wall-painting from Herculaneum.

Photo: Alinari

26. One of the dancers from a Pompeian house, falsely thought to belong to
Cicero, which was discovered about 1750 and covered in again after the frescoes
had been cut out and other objects removed.

(*See page* 118)

27. Bronze bust of Dionysos.
Probably Greek. Found in the museum of statues and busts in the Villa of the
Papyri near Herculaneum, which was rifled in the years 1750–65.

(*See pages* 40, 119–120)

here and there, but to conduct the investigations according to some plan, starting from a single point and proceeding step by step and yard by yard. For years Weber had also pressed for a cessation of the work at Resina, which had in recent times had no results, and for concentration on the area of Civita, where such a great number of paintings and buildings had already been found. At the beginning of the year wonderful mosaic figures had been brought to light, which put everything else, even the discoveries in Rome, in the shade. Camillo Paderni's activities were stopped, and the frescoes which he judged too poor for the royal museum were no longer hacked off the walls. Charles III of Spain maintained from afar his interest in the diggings, and it was one of Tanucci's chief concerns to send full accounts and drawings with every courier who departed for Madrid.

On 16th August, 1763, a discovery of the greatest importance was made: on the Civita site a statue of white marble was dug up, of a man in a toga, and nearby a pedestal with the inscription, "In the name of the Emperor and Caesar Vespasian Augustus, the tribune T. Svedius Clemens has restored . . . to the public possession of the Pompeians those places which belonged to them and had been taken into private possession."

This was the first written and indisputable proof that the site of Civita, where the digging was being carried out, was none other than that of buried Pompeii. Now it was clear that a whole town had to be raised from the depths, and the order was given that all buildings discovered from that time should remain uncovered. Unfortunately Karl Weber died suddenly that same year, and it was again a Spaniard who took his place, an officer of engineers called Francesco La Vega. He took over the conduct of the work in April 1764, at a time of famine in Naples owing to the failure of the harvest. The thirty men working at Civita also suffered, and their progress was very much hindered.

Winckelmann had meanwhile dared to revisit Naples and the museum at Portici, in spite of his *Letter*, which had appeared in German and had not yet reached Naples. He wanted material for a second and more comprehensive account. Tanucci alone had some idea of the contents of his first *Letter*. When Winckelmann appeared before the minister in Naples

10   133

he was very coolly received, which seems to have sundered friendly relations between them. In his second *Letter*, addressed to Heinrich Füssli of Zurich and published in 1764, he made explicit reference to Pompeii and to the inscription which had dispelled any doubt about the identity of the site. It had to be added, however, that though a gate, dwelling-houses and tombs had been discovered, there was so far no trace of a capitol.

Winckelmann was the first to point out that the Pompeians had returned in great numbers, after the town had been overwhelmed, in order to save what they could. The *Letter* was much less sharply worded than the first, and contained only a few perfectly justifiable attacks on the Royal Academy, which was now no more than a name without significance. Winckelmann's annoyance at not being made a member of the Academy could, however, be clearly seen in his account. This time he had been to the site of the diggings, and had even crept around in the narrow corridors of the subterranean theatre of Herculaneum, but he had met with opposition and reserve from the authorities and did not feel as happy as before.

Meanwhile a storm was brewing which was to undermine Winckelmann's position and for the time being put an end to his visits to Naples. The news of the amazing excavations had roused enormous interest abroad. In France the man most interested was Anne Claude Duc de Caylus, a collector of works of art, an archaeologist, and a veritable Maecenas, famed for his writings on art and his etchings of frescoes by Raphael, Michelangelo and Titian. He was avid for news about Pompeii and Herculaneum, furious at the secrecy of the court of Naples, and delighted at everything which "escaped the attention of the dragons guarding that rich golden fleece". Although Winckelmann's *Letter* appeared in a very small edition, Caylus succeeded in laying hands on a copy, and he translated it into French and had it published. Since it contained so much that was hostile to the court of Naples, with which the Duke himself had come into conflict, its publication was a deliberate provocation. The French edition became known at once in Naples, and provoked a veritable storm of indignation against Winckelmann. The previous rulers had known very well why this man was to be distrusted from the start. This was his thanks for the permission he had received to inspect things! Paderni and Piaggi, who were mentioned by name in the *Letter*, were ruthlessly exposed. In brief, the ground was prepared for the biting lampoon which was written against this "Goth" who had believed every lie told him with airs of secrecy by "some slanderer or galley-slave working on the site". And this fellow was still boasting that he had discovered things concealed from everybody else. The lampoon undoubtedly went too far, and it ignored Winckelmann's services to the knowledge of classical art. But the indignation was also understandable when it is remembered that it was directed against a complete stranger who had entered the Neapolitan wasps' nest with the express purpose of writing his *Letter*. "This publication", wrote Winckelmann in February 1765, about the lampoon, "has barred my way to the museum of Portici."

It would have been even more interesting for the scholar to have visited the new excavations in Pompeii. For on 11th August, 1764, a human skeleton was found on a threshold, clutching a glass jug with two handles and a piece of iron whose purpose could not be determined. Further search revealed a wall which was part of a theatre, as could be seen from inscriptions. This was the so-called covered theatre or *odeon*, chiefly used for concerts.

As a result of these successes instructions were issued, on 9th February, 1765, for work on Herculaneum to cease and for all forces to be united at the newly discovered Pompeii. These instructions were the more readily given since in recent times fumes of an earth-gas had become perceptible in the corridors and caves where the men had to work at Herculaneum, and these gases had affected the workers' health. The new order and the consequent increased activity soon led to remarkable success.

Since December 1764 digging had been going on in the neighbourhood of the Temple of Isis, and in June 1765 the temple of the goddess was hit upon. The workers pressed forward into the pillared court, and the first things they found were the carbonised remains of figs, pineapples, chestnuts and other nuts, oats and dates. When the sanctuary was uncovered the statue of Isis came to light; crowned with a gilt wreath and adorned with precious bracelets, it stood behind a great altar. The pictures on the walls depicted in Alexandrian style scenes of animal and plant life on the Nile; everything indicated Egypt. In a room behind the sanctuary lay a skeleton and nearby a plate with fish bones. The pictures in the rooms were on the whole well preserved, with scratches here and there where the entombed people had desperately attempted to break through.

On 20th July, 1765, an inscription was discovered which stated that N. Popidius and N. F. Celsinus had rebuilt the Temple of Isis after its destruction in the earthquake. This made the nature of the discovery completely clear. The whole place was beautiful and noteworthy, and the frescoes were splendid. The bones of the last animal sacrifice lying on the altar, and the skeleton of the priest who had tried to cleave a way out with the help of an axe, witnessed so directly and vividly to the sudden advent of the catastrophe that even the young King set aside his hunting and fishing and his childish pastimes and betook himself to the site in order to be present at the excavation of the rest of the temple, especially of the splendidly decorated priest's house. The pictures were so fine that the artists who were commissioned for such work were instructed to copy them at once.

At that time the two chief artists in the royal service were Filippo Morghen and Giovanni Battista (or Alvise) Casanova. The latter, who had been trained in Dresden and Venice, and in 1752 became the pupil and companion of the famous painter Mengs for ten years, was the younger brother of the world-famous Giacomo Casanova, the author of the intimate memoirs. Giovanni Battista was one of the best artists in Rome, and had known Winckelmann during the time he worked in the Vatican Library. Casanova had made a profile study of Winckelmann and had prepared many of the sketches for his publications on classical antiquities.

In the spring of 1765 so many frescoes were discovered in the houses near the recently uncovered theatre that they could not all be removed to Naples, and it was left to Casanova to decide which were the best preserved and finest, to be cut out and made ready for removal. And now he was delighted to be able to copy the splendid pictures in the Temple of Isis.

Meanwhile he and Winckelmann had quarrelled, after he had prepared many etchings for Winckelmann's chief work, the *Monumenti Antichi*. For, like Guerra, Casanova and Menges had prepared three pictures, one representing Jupiter and Ganymede, the others dancing-girls and an ancient legend. He sent them to Winckelmann in Rome with a note that they had been taken from the walls of Pompeii after being accidentally discovered by a foreigner, Diel of Marsilly in Normandy, a former lieutenant of the French Grenadiers. The officer, he added, had not succeeded in removing the pictures as a whole, so he had broken them off piecemeal and taken them secretly to Rome, where they had been reconstructed. Winckelmann was enthusiastic and gave the fable of their discovery, and a description of the pictures themselves, in his *History of Ancient Art*, in the fifth section entitled "The painting of the ancient Greeks". In this account he spoke of the Ganymede picture as "incomparable". "Jupiter's favourite", he said, "is undoubtedly one of the loveliest pieces which has survived from antiquity, and I consider the features to be beyond comparison: so much desire glows in it that its whole life seems to be a kiss."

He then went on to draw the conclusion that the garments of one of these figures proved it to be the oldest of all known classical figures. This appeared, then, in his *History of Ancient Art*, to be read and known everywhere. When the truth was revealed and Winckelmann was exposed, he was furious, and would have nothing more to do with Casanova's work, that "artist turned rogue, or rather, artist born rogue". It was he himself who suffered most, however, for now he had to seek the help of another artist. Soon afterwards the scholar had the satisfaction of hearing that Casanova, who had in the meantime married the daughter of a French innkeeper in Rome whom he had seduced, was charged with embezzlement, and found it convenient to leave Naples and Italy and to return to Dresden. There he was made professor at the Art Academy, since the story of the embezzlement in Rome was not taken seriously in the Saxon capital.

Once more Winckelmann, ardent and indefatigable in his investigations, and still the archaeologist for Dresden, succeeded in entering Naples in spite of the enemies which his *Letters* had made for him. For in 1764 Sir William Hamilton had arrived in Naples, and his interests lay less in politics than in everything connected with art. He was slenderly built and thin, with a prominent aquiline nose and dark, thinning hair. He was an intelligent and distinguished man, and possessed of great means, which had come to him through his wife, who was of noble birth. He made an eager study of the discoveries at Pompeii and Herculaneum, and ransacked Rome and Naples for classical objects, which he bought and set in his house. In spite of the veto, he secretly initiated certain private excavations. He also carried through some very successful deals with his finds, meeting with little interference from the court. He knew how to keep on good terms with the young King, joining in his follies and accompanying him through thick and thin on his hunting expeditions. In the course of time he had collected, among other things, some fine classical vases. Hearing of Winckelmann and his archaeological knowledge, Hamilton invited him to Naples to help in the publication of a book about classical vase-painting. Winckelmann told him of his fears on account of the hostility he had brought upon himself, but Hamilton promised to put the matter in order with Tanucci. And in fact, when Winckelmann entered Naples in 1767, in order to prepare for a journey to Sicily, he was none too badly received at the court. The chief minister, who was the deciding person, did indeed reproach him for his former conduct at a banquet given to foreign emissaries, mentioning the relevant points in the *Letters*, but he put no obstacles in his way. He had heard that the scholar was slowly winning a world-wide reputation and he rightly judged that Winckelmann would in future be more careful and prudent. In this way, too, Tanucci was able to please Hamilton, as well as Great Britain, of which Hamilton had been made plenipotentiary in March 1767.

So Winckelmann succeeded in inspecting the sites of the excavations and the newest finds in Pompeii, where all energies were now concentrated. Not far from the covered theatre, with which a beginning had been made in July 1764, a remarkably decorated helmet had been discovered, with an iron peak and richly ornate greaves, like those depicted on vases. A great heap of weapons was found nearby, almost all of them being highly ornamented. In October 1766 further digging uncovered a large building in front of the theatre, with a great courtyard surrounded by innumerable pillars, and many little rooms opening off it. While Winckelmann was visiting Pompeii many skeletons were also discovered, among them that of a woman with parts of her clothing, a gold-worked cloth, and costly jewellery still clinging to it. In an open room used as a prison-cell shackles were discovered, and the skeletons of four prisoners and the remains of a harnessed horse: never before had the remains of so many dead been discovered in a single building.

Winckelmann had just arrived, and took part in the attempts to solve the riddle of the building's purpose. Some thought it was a gymnasium, others barracks or a market-hall; today it is fairly generally agreed that this former annexe to the theatre had been used as barracks for the gladiators in the years preceding the catastrophe. This is borne out not only by the many ornamented weapons, but also by drawings on the pillars and walls of various gladiatorial combats.

The old method of impatient, casual searching had not yet been given up. Scarcely was the purpose of some building or other half-settled than the unfinished work of excavation was abandoned and digging was begun elsewhere. The dominating motive was still the search for treasures, for jewellery and objects of silver and gold.

At this time, towards the end of October 1767, the really responsible agent, the mighty Vesuvius, which had been quiescent for almost six years, renewed its activity. This was, it is thought, the twenty-seventh time since the great catastrophe that the heart of the mountain had burst open. Stones were again hurled out to a height of a thousand feet, once again the pine-shaped cloud appeared over the mountain, and lava flowed into the valleys from the sides of the mountain as well as from the crater, dividing into several streams and crushing the buildings in its way as though they were houses of cards. Added to all this were a thunderous roaring, storms of lapilli and ash, and earthquakes — in short, all hell seemed to be let loose. Sir William Hamilton watched this eruption from the immediate neighbourhood. He had climbed Vesuvius many times in order to investigate its activity, and on this occasion he was in the valley between the Somma and the peak of the mountain and had to run for his life before the lava as it rushed down the hillside. Winckelmann watched it all from Naples, and was thus able to construct a picture from his own experience of how Pompeii and Herculaneum had been engulfed, for even in Naples the small pumice-stones rained "thick as snowflakes, so that the sun was darkened".

The King had to flee from his palace in Portici to Naples. In Naples prayers were once again offered in the churches, and processions were held with the picture of St Januarius, the patron saint of Naples. He was implored to check the terrible fury of the mountain. His miraculous liquefying blood was expected to help. Whether the change in the saint's blood is to be ascribed to a miracle or a chemical process, the people certainly regarded it as miraculous, and when the blood liquefied hoped that all misfortune and evil would cease. The Swedish traveller Jakob Jonas Björnstähl tells of this occasion that the people stretched out their arms to the picture and addressed it, "sometimes threatening it if the miracle did not quickly take place". Once the mob even wanted to throw the statue of the saint into the sea if Vesuvius did not quickly cease its work of destruction. In fact, the eruption did not last long, for by the end of October the fire-belching mountain was again at rest.

Winckelmann, however, did not fulfil his plan of describing in a new *Letter* the latest finds and excavations, and the new eruption of which he had been an eye-witness. He had to leave the latter task to Hamilton. In 1768 he had to under-take a visit of some duration to his native land in order to see, among other things, to the German edition of his *History of Art*. In May 1769 he planned to return to Italy via Ancona. The well-dressed, distinguished, and well-provided stranger arrived in Trieste, where he put up at a simple inn; in the adjacent room a traveller, without money or luggage, had arrived the day before from Venice. Below in the public room, during his meal, Winckelmann enquired about the prospects of a ship for Italy. His neighbour joined in the conversation, and in this way the archaeologist made the acquaintance of the stranger, who offered himself as Winckelmann's guide in Trieste. This man was an Italian with a very doubtful past, who even at the age of sixteen had stolen from his masters in Florence and Vienna, had spent three years in jail in

Vienna, and for some time had joined forces with a woman of the streets to carry out confidence tricks in Venice and Trieste. Winckelmann knew nothing of all this, but the man was also quite uneducated, and it seems strange that the scholar should have spent several days almost exclusively in his company, gone walks with him, and even taken dinner with him in his room. He told the man of many events in his life, of how, for example, he had been received in audience by the Empress Maria Theresa and had received from her and from the chancellor, Prince Kaunitz, great gold and silver medallions as souvenirs. The stranger, who saw from Winckelmann's dress and adornments, as well as from his stories, that he was well-to-do, perhaps even very wealthy, asked Winckelmann to show him the gifts from the Empress. When Winckelmann agreed to do so, the decision formed in the criminal's mind to murder him and gain possession of his goods. To this end he secured a rope and a heavy kitchen-knife.

Winckelmann's ship was due to leave on 8th June, and he passed the time in writing directions for the new edition of his art history. The evening before his departure he had removed his wig, cravat and jacket and was sitting at his writing-table. He had just written the words "There must" when suddenly the back doors were flung open, the Italian rushed in, and wound the rope round Winckelmann's throat. The scholar jumped up, and there was a brief struggle with the attacker, who had now turned to his knife. Winckelmann had almost succeeded in overpowering the evildoer when he slipped and fell on his back, whereupon his attacker struck him six fatal blows.

The noise brought one of the inn's staff hurrying up. The assailant fled, but when the waiter saw the wounded man he did not help him, but ran off in terror in order to fetch a surgeon. Winckelmann dragged himself down to the first storey, where a chambermaid, seeing him pale and bleeding, likewise rushed off in terror. Other people passed the dying man as he painfully made his way down the stairs, but they all fled at sight of him to their confessor, or for a doctor, or God knows where, till at last one sensible man arrived, who took charge of Winckelmann, put him to bed, and tried to apply some emergency dressings. But the unfortunate man was too badly wounded, and only able to murmur some last instructions before he died. Thus a criminal devoid of morals or understanding had murdered a great scholar, who besides his other services to the study of classical antiquities was also, despite all his errors, the first to spread through Europe information about the excavations at Herculaneum and Pompeii.

6

THE RESURRECTION OF POMPEII DURING THE REIGN OF KING FERDINAND, AND THE NAPOLEONIC INTERLUDE

1770–1815

O N 12th January, 1767, the young King Ferdinand of Bourbon, for whom Tanucci had acted as regent, entered on his sixteenth year, and by the custom of his house had reached his majority. His father was already thinking of his marriage, and had sought the hand of one of Maria Theresa's daughters for him. Since the Empress was anxious to find *établissements* for her numerous children which would suit the political interests of the house of Hapsburg, she was very willing that the sixteen-year-old Archduchess Josephine should become the Queen of Ferdinand of Naples. Ferdinand too was willing, and only asked for her picture, since he had of course never seen her. When he received it, the ambassador related that he "had seen how the picture had given His Majesty the greatest pleasure".[1]

The wedding was planned for October 1767. Vesuvius was active at the time, and one day, as Kaunitz reported, "lava poured from five different places in the heart of the mountain, accompanied by fearful crashing and roaring. When in a few hours it had advanced far on the road to Portici, the King and all his court fled to the city an hour after midnight."[2] Superstitious as everyone was, even in the highest circles, this was taken to be a bad omen, and in fact the sad news

[1] Ernst Graf von Kaunitz-Rittberg to his father, the Reichschancellor Kaunitz, 24th January, 1767. Vienna State Archives.
[2] *Ibid.*, 20th October, 1767.

arrived shortly afterwards that the King's bride, the Archduchess Josephine, had died of smallpox. The imperial physicians, in spite of the fact that Maria Theresa herself had just suffered from this terrible disease, had advised against the new practice of inoculation for the Empress's children.

The Empress, however, did not alter her general purpose after this misfortune. On the day of Josephine's death she sent the sad news to her ambassador in Madrid with instructions to put before King Charles the proposal that Josephine's fifteen-year-old sister Charlotte might be Ferdinand's bride. A similar instruction was sent to Naples. The young King, according to Kaunitz's report, "was of the same mind", so that, as the ambassador said, "all that had to be done was to change the name in the marriage-articles".[1]

King Ferdinand profited by the change, for the Empress herself had once said of her daughter Josephine: "Her features are not attractive and her behaviour is the same"[2]; while of Charlotte the Empress had written, a short time before, that of all her daughters she was the most like her.[3] The Empress did not hide the fact that her child was being sacrificed to politics, for from Kaunitz's reports she knew very well what sort of a man she was giving her daughter to. "His Majesty knows nothing of public affairs," wrote Kaunitz of him. "His indolence is unlimited. He has no idea how to spend his time in his own apartments, since there is never any question of reading good books; he has no understanding of music or drawing, or even of a single game or anything that demands movement. There is nothing at all by which he can be entertained in his own rooms, and his only recourse is the hunt, which he follows every day, no matter the weather. But since this occupation cannot fill all his time, he passes the remainder, till he goes to bed, in childish games and nonsense in the company of his attendants."[4]

When Kaunitz was received in audience the King would often not listen to him at all for a long time, but would tease

[1] Ernst Graf von Kaunitz-Rittberg to his father, the Reichschancellor Kaunitz, 28th October, 1767. Vienna State Archives.

[2] The Empress Maria Theresa to the Countess Terchenfeld, 1763. See Eugen Guglia, *Maria Theresia*, II, 202. Munich, Berlin, 1917.

[3] *Letters of the Empress Maria Theresa to her Children and Friends*, ed. A. v. Arneth, IV, 488, 1881.

[4] Graf Kaunitz to his father, 20th January, 1768.

and tickle him till the Count was forced to escape, and the childish King imagined that this was a "good method" of treating an ambassador.[1]

In March 1768 the young King was sent a miniature of his new bride, and Kaunitz reported that the King "loved her Royal Highness the Archduchess Charlotte more than the Archduchess Josephine of blessed memory, as he thinks her portrait is very lovely; added to this is the continual talk of Her Majesty the future Queen's liveliness and brightness, which pleases him very well, as for all his sixteen years he is just a child and supposes that Her Majesty will like to join in his favourite pastimes."[2]

So in April of the same year the marriage of the Archduchess Charlotte to the young King took place by proxy in Vienna. From the characters of the young couple the Empress had every reason to hope that her daughter, with a mind and nature far superior to her husband's, would be able to exert on the government of the southern kingdom an influence which would be very profitable to the house of Hapsburg.

When she arrived in Naples the young Queen assumed the name of Carolina. Imbued though she was with a strong sense of duty, she did not know what to say of her husband. After the first weeks of her marriage she wrote to a friend that only her faith in God had prevented her from committing suicide. Now she was making an effort to come to terms with her fate, and to seek diversion by studying her new kingdom, its beauties and its circumstances, and to find peace for her heart by restless activity. She tried to take her husband as he was, as an irresponsible child, and for the rest she cultivated an interest in the life and history of her adopted land. Even in her old home she had heard much about the splendid discoveries and excavations of ancient times. When she arrived in Naples the great open theatre of Pompeii had just been uncovered, and shortly afterwards the smaller closed theatre slowly came to light. The young Queen was at once conducted to the site, where she sat on the circular stone seats and inspected the monuments in the Street of Tombs outside the Gate of Herculaneum. She received each new item of information with enthusiasm, and would have gone much oftener to

[1] Graf Kaunitz to his father, 27th July, 1768.
[2] *Ibid.*, 15th March, 1768.

the sites if she had not had to give so much time to her husband; for example, he demanded her company on his hunting expeditions. Since these were his main occupation she was often compelled to sit for hours in the fields, waiting patiently, without herself partaking in the hunt. Her first letters to her friends at home sounded so pitiable that in April 1769 the Empress Maria Theresa resolved to send to Naples her twenty-year-old son Joseph, the young Queen's brother — who had been for the past four years the Holy Roman Emperor and co-ruler with his mother — to see if everything was in order. The Emperor soon afterwards reached Rome from Florence, and met with such inquisitive attention that a little poem was circulated about it:

> To see Rome, to go to Rome, the Emperor was keen,
> But Rome now has more of him than he of Rome has seen.

Joseph remained a fortnight in the eternal city, then went on to Naples, which he reached after a coach journey lasting twenty-seven hours. He proceeded at once to the royal palace, and Carolina rushed to meet him and, half-dressed as she was, threw herself into his arms. The King reproached her for this. "But she is my sister", interjected the Emperor.

The royal guest stayed with the ambassador, Kaunitz, hoping to be less disturbed there than in the palace. He then proceeded to acquaint himself more thoroughly with conditions in Naples, and in particular with the person of its ruler. By a complete contempt for ceremony — he threw himself, for example, on the carpeted floor of his brother-in-law's room and invited Ferdinand to do the same — and by his witty, playful tones Joseph sought to gain the affections of the King. It was not long before they were on the most familiar terms, calling one another Don Fernardo and Don Pepe. In spite of the greatest restraint, Joseph was often rendered speechless by the childishness of the eighteen-year-old King. Thus he stood by smiling when the young King, who loved to crack his whip, showed him this pretty game again and again, indoors and outdoors. Ferdinand also loved to put ice in the pockets of the courtiers and jam in their hats, and the like. Any serious occupation was far from his thoughts, and he even complained to his guest of the Queen's fondness for reading, which he hated not only for himself but also for everyone else. Once when Joseph was speaking with his sister about her husband she said good-naturedly: "Oh, well, he's a good sort of fool."[1]

The Emperor would have liked to pay more attention to many interesting things, but he too had to accompany the King on his perpetual hunting expeditions, where he watched ironically how the wild boar and the fallow-deer, which had been penned in readiness, were driven into a path closed off by a net, while Don Fernando shot into their midst in the most sportsmanlike manner. Joseph had also to watch the King fishing in a little pond near the sea, which was filled beforehand with a stock of fish. The hunt had at least one advantage, that it took the Emperor to Portici and the neighbourhood of the excavations, which he rejoiced to inspect. He had mentioned to Tanucci how much he should like to see the thirty-four human skeletons which had been found on 16th April, 1768, between the great theatre and the Temple of Isis. The minister at once ordered La Vega to put in more workers and cover up a house which had been discovered, where there was likely to be a skeleton, and so to arrange things that it could be dug out as though for the first time, before the Emperor's eyes.[2]

Early on 7th April the Emperor Joseph went up Vesuvius, lingered on his return on the site of Herculaneum, inspected the well where d'Elboeuf had brought to light the first traces of the town, and towards evening entered Torre d'Annunziata, where the royal couple had just returned from the hunt and were awaiting him. There they dined, so that it was eight o'clock before they visited Pompeia, as it was called at that time. While the young King of Naples hurried through the sightseeing "very superficially", as Joseph remarked, the Emperor himself was exceptionally interested. He was led at once to the arranged place, and the first spadeful revealed a bronze vase, little silver objects, coins, fibulae and terra-cotta figures. At first the visitor was surprised, but he soon doubted the genuineness of the finds, suggesting that they had been placed there beforehand and only lightly covered up, so that

[1] Emperor Joseph II to the Empress Maria Theresa, Florence, 21st April, 1769. Vienna State Archives.

[2] This was the house which is today classified as Regio VIII, Insula 2, No. 39, and is still called the "House of the Emperor Joseph II".

fortune might be seized by the forelock. The chief of the excavations, the engineer La Vega, made an embarrassed attempt to "explain" to the Emperor, who remained mistrustful, though still intensely interested. Sir William Hamilton, who was of the company, along with Kaunitz, gave the necessary explanations with such fire that even the King was interested and pleased. The Austrian guest did not miss the opportunity of encouraging Ferdinand's interest, and representing to him how profitable and how reputable the whole enterprise could be for himself and his country. The young King then said that he wished to come more often and bade La Vega tell him whenever there were signs of some new discovery. In such a case he was even ready to give up a whole day, even if it meant missing his beloved hunting.

Meanwhile there was laid bare, in the presence of the two rulers, a house of several storeys, such as had rarely been found in Pompeii. It had not only a richly decorated atrium, a bedroom with frescoes and a picture of Juno, the tutelary deity of the mistress of the house, but also a bathroom and a great underground bakery lit by means of a round opening. A way was made into the bakehouse, in the north-east corner of which stood the oven, with a great bowl in the centre for moistening the bread. On a heap of lapilli there was the skeleton of a man, half-seated, half-lying, who had sought shelter from the falling stones and, like all who had tried to save their lives in this way, had been suffocated. Nearby lay several coins. For a long time the Emperor stood reflectively before these tokens of an intense human drama, which were eerily illuminated by the light of the torches. The Queen in her lively way was quite carried away by the discovery; she wanted to see everything as quickly as possible and she took away as much as she could in her carriage.

Then the company turned to the covered theatre, where a small part of the stage had been laid bare. Joseph asked La Vega how many workers were employed on the operations. "Thirty", said La Vega, this being more than the normal.

But the Emperor nevertheless thought it so small a number that he at once asked Don Fernando:

"How can you allow such work to be carried on on *così languendo* (so languidly)?"

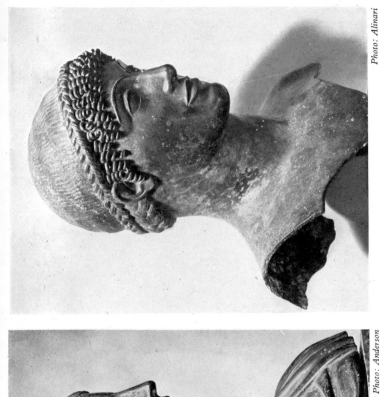

Photo: Alinari

29. Bronze Bust of an athlete. Perhaps a Greek original. From the Villa of the Papyri near Herculaneum.

(See pages 40, 119–120)

Photo: Anderson

28. Bronze bust of a beautiful woman (so-called Sappho) from the Villa of the Papyri near Herculaneum.

Photo: Alinari

30. Very naturalistic bronze bust, found in the Villa of the Papyri near Herculaneum, falsely called Seneca.

(*See pages* 40, 119–120)

The King replied: "Oh, it must be done *poco a poco* (by degrees)."

"No," replied Joseph. "It is work which should employ three thousand men. There is nothing like it in Europe or Asia or Africa or America, and it is besides a matter of honour for the kingdom. Who is in charge of the excavations?"

"The Marquis Tanucci," replied the King. And the Emperor thought to himself, as did La Vega, "Oh yes, the man who does everything." But the Queen, who did not care for Tanucci, agreed with all that her brother said, and joined with him in urging the King to keep a close watch on Tanucci, in order that the work might be pushed on more quickly.

From the theatre the company moved on to the Temple of Isis, which, with its graceful façade and the four pillars, its inscription over the entrance and its frescoes with their Egyptian motifs, delighted the Emperor. He reiterated his representations to his brother-in-law that more value should be attached to the excavations and that they should be furthered in every possible way. He was especially interested in the marks left by the wooden doors of the temple, which could be seen quite plainly on the stone. Further on they inspected the houses to left and right of the Gate of Herculaneum, and looked out towards the Street of Tombs. But it was now late, and to the Emperor's regret they could not explore further.

Joseph had heard earlier from another source that individual buildings had been covered up again after their contents had been removed. When La Vega now showed him a plan with the excavated parts of Pompeii marked on it, that he might have a general view of the whole operation, the Emperor cautiously asked: "Then what of the houses I have not seen, though they have been recently brought to light? Have they really been covered up again?"

"Yes," La Vega was forced to reply, shamefacedly.

"Why did you allow that?" said Joseph, turning to the King.

"It happened in the time of my father."

"That is so," put in La Vega. "It was done in the twenty years while nobody realised that they were working in the middle of a town. But now that, for the last six years, we

11   149

have known from an inscription that we are in Pompeii, we leave the buildings which we uncover; before that people were only interested in getting things for the museum."

At a quarter past eleven their majesties finally left Pompeii. They entered their carriages, and the Emperor made use of the long drive to urge on his brother-in-law once more the necessity for supporting and developing such a wonderful enterprise in every way. He then went on to expound to Don Fernando the great task of ruling a people, how it was his destiny to make them happy, and he laid it on his conscience to take his calling as a ruler very seriously.

"Since he was in good humour," Joseph later reported to his mother, Maria Theresa, "I put some weighty considerations before him. I spoke to him of his duties to the State, of his fame and good name, and of freedom. Finally I tried to discover his taste for affairs of State, whether he hoped or whether it was likely that the humiliating position in which he was placed, his slavery and tutelage to Spain, could ever be shaken off. There is no doubt that all these feelings are dimly present in him, but at the same time he shows such an obvious repugnance for anything new, such a tremendous indolence of spirit, and such a marked lack of all reflection, that I am almost ready to swear that this man has never in his life given a single thought to himself, his physical or moral life, to his position, his interests or his country. He does not know a thing about the past, nor does he know the present; he has never thought that there is a future — in brief, he just vegetates from one day to the next."

The Emperor Joseph's impression of his royal brother-in-law was certainly not of the best. On the other hand, his sister's state of mind and her resignation to this strange marriage were much better than he had expected. With her good sense and her cleverness she seemed to be adapting herself to the circumstances. And he thought that even if her vivacity and other qualities were to bring her into difficulties in the future, it was still to be hoped that she could exercise a healthy influence both on her husband and on the government. The Empress's purpose in arranging the marriage, the maintenance of the Hapsburg influence in Naples, would therefore in the course of time be achieved. In matters of culture, including the fate of the excavations, the very best results could be expected from the Queen, who was enthusiastically in their favour. Joseph made these impressions known in Vienna in a very long report of sixty-three pages to his mother the Empress.[1]

His visit did in fact bring about a remarkable invigoration of the work in the buried towns. Since the interest of the royal couple and especially of the Queen persisted after his departure, there was an increase of activity at the excavations. Everyone wanted to find something, and pick-axe and spade were impatiently used at ever new places. At that time work was being carried on outside the Gate of Herculaneum, where the frescoes of the bacchantes and the rope-dancing satyrs had been discovered and cut out, in the so-called villa of Cicero which had been covered in again. Suddenly the workers chanced on a large new villa, which had possessed before the catastrophe something which had been lacking in most houses inside the town, namely, a generous allowance of light and air. It was the country-house of that man whose unhappy attempt to save his family in the cryptoporticus had only led to his death and that of all his household. In the course of these excavations, as the great peristyle, supported by four-sided pillars, the wonderful baths, and the bedrooms and ante-rooms came to light, for the first time in Pompeii three remarkable windows were discovered, set in a semicircular wall. At another point round apertures like peep-holes were discovered, which let the light in through thick glass. This was the first proof that the Romans had used glass in their windows. It is true that they were exceptionally rare, very expensive, and to be found only in splendid and luxurious buildings. But all their luxury had been of no avail to their owners.

In March and May of the year 1771 the workers came upon eighteen skeletons of adults and two of children, who had been choked by the clammy ashes in the cryptoporticus almost 1700 years before. The ashes had completely enveloped the bodies of the unfortunate people, perfectly modelling the outlines of their recumbent figures. The excavating party was at a loss what to do with these moulds, made long ago in the quickly solidifying ashes. The form of the young daughter of

[1] The Emperor Joseph II to the Empress Maria Theresa, Florence, 21st April, 1769. Vienna State Archives.

the house, who must have been very attractive, could be exceptionally well seen. She had drawn her fine linen dress over her head to protect herself, and the ashes had preserved this outline as well. The girl had also exposed the upper part of her body, the delightful youthful bosom, the round full arms, as well as her shapely legs and feet, and all these had been preserved in their tender forms by the ashes.

The excavating party stood, deeply moved, before these signs of the transitoriness of all earthly life, even the fairest; but all they could do was to save the imprint of the girl's breast and arms in the hardened ash (that is, a kind of negative). Soon they came upon the skeleton of the householder himself, with his key, together with that of his slave, in the garden near the gate, where fate had overtaken them. The key and the moulds were at once taken to the museum, where they may still be seen today; the moulds hint at such attractive figures that they inspired Gautier, the French writer, to write his novel *Arria Marcella*.

While the diggings were being carried on with such success, Tanucci's secretary diligently and enthusiastically continued his work of publishing the findings of the Herculanean Academy. In addition to the catalogue, which was contained in a splendid volume, there were by 1772 three volumes describing, with illustrations, the paintings which had been discovered and two volumes on the bronzes. These included the statues which had been found in the villa of the papyri — for example, that wonderful representation of the drunken satyr, a Roman copy of a Hellenic original, and that of Alexander the Great fighting on horseback, which had been reproduced for the book by Giovanni Casanova. The young sleeping faun, from the same villa, and the resting Hermes, as well as a dancing satyr and many others, had been reproduced by the painter Vanni. Morghen too had made some illustrations of bronze statues for this work. Its publication, however, was attended by great difficulties. For despite the efforts of the Emperor Joseph and his sister the Queen, the King had in fact no great interest in classical antiquities, and this became particularly clear when money was required. Ferdinand of Naples had ordered as early as 1770 that the publications on Herculaneum and Pompeii, each volume of which, richly adorned with engravings and splendidly bound in leather, cost 16,000 ducats to produce, should no longer be part of the royal expenditure, but should be handled by a publisher like any other book. Each volume then cost, in the Austrian currency of the time, twenty guilders, a very large amount, which affected the sales to private individuals.

Reviews of these publications were not exactly favourable. The artists who had reproduced the pictures and bronzes were blamed for having given what were admitted to be splendid engravings, but what in comparison with the originals were "very defective", even falsifications. The notes on the reproductions were also considered positively stupid. "Who would expect to find, in the note on a nymph whose sex is uncertain," wrote, for example, the scholar Heinrich Cramer in his account of the Herculanean discoveries, "a discussion of the question whether there are such creatures as hermaphrodites, yet that is what these commentators have actually done."[1]

Meanwhile the excavations continued, with varying fortunes. Tanucci put an end to the aimless treasure-hunting which had persisted till then, and in 1775 he ordered systematic digging to be carried on from the Gate of Herculaneum towards the centre of the town. He also remarked that in the last two or three years the work had been less diligently pressed forward. La Vega, who as Alcubierre grew advanced in years was almost in sole command of the excavations, retorted by complaining that now everything in Pompeii had to be left exposed, and this made a great difference, since they were compelled to remove the excavated material to some distance. In the time taken to clear forty-eight rooms in the past, only eight could now be dealt with. The reproaches levelled against La Vega were not completely justified; he devoted his whole life to the cause and had also been the first to prepare plans which enabled a fairly accurate survey of the excavated sites in both towns to be obtained.

Queen Carolina took La Vega's part the more readily as she did not like Tanucci and worked to bring about his fall. Since the birth of a Crown Prince in 1775 her position had been greatly strengthened in the Kingdom, and with her husband's nature as it was, she began to exert an increasing influence on the government. And in 1777 she brought about

[1] *Bemerkung Rambach*, p. 5. Halle, 1773.

the fall of the minister who had been almost all-powerful, and in the time of the regency had been the sole arbiter of the destinies of Naples. But this event did not have a good effect on the progress of the excavations, for Tanucci had taken a personal interest in them, which had been fostered by his secretary, the author of the Academy volumes. The minister's successor knew very well that the King himself had no taste for antiquities or the fine arts. This was confirmed by the Swedish scholar Björnstähl, who was staying in Naples at the time, and endeavoured to stir up the King to send either soldiers or galley-slaves to Pompeii. Thus despite the desire of the Queen and of the former King Charles, in Madrid, for active prosecution of the excavations, after the downfall of Tanucci they fell off considerably. "I have been told", wrote Björnstähl, "that the King of Spain was very dissatisfied if he did not get something new for his museum every week. Now months, even years, pass without anything of value being brought into the museum, the work goes on so lamely."[1] But for the future better things were to be expected, through the Queen's influence. At this time she came under the influence of Prince Caramanico, who was thoroughly conversant with Italian history and art. She gathered about her a group of highly cultured people and was encouraged by Caramanico in her concern for the recovery of the buried towns.[2]

In 1780 the veteran of the excavations, Alcubierre, died. His signal achievement lay in transferring the work to the area of Civita, and this outlives all his errors of inexperience and lack of archaeological training.

Vesuvius had meantime shown signs of moderate activity, first in August 1776 and again, as a kind of "centenary celebration"[3] of the great catastrophe, on 8th August, 1779. A violent explosion hurled a new storm of stones and ashes out of the crater. The wind carried lapilli once more over the excavated parts of Pompeii, so that the fear arose that the whole area, including Portici, with the royal villa and the museum, might one day be buried again and destroyed. The newly founded Academy of Science and Fine Art in Naples

---

[1] J. Bernouilli, *Additions to the Latest News from Italy*, p. 293. Leipzig, 1778.
[2] Alexander Polovtsoff, *The Call of the Siren*, p. 136. London, 1939.
[3] Alfano and Friedlaender, *op. cit.*, p. 41.

therefore urged on the King, after its first meeting, the necessity of bringing into the capital not only the Farnesian Library but also the whole museum or "Herculanean Chamber of Antiquities in Portici", as it was then incorrectly termed. This in fact was done, and amid the jubiliation of the populace the great bronze statues, the pillars and treasures of all kinds were transported in a long convoy on wheeled carriers specially made for the purpose to a building lying at the foot of the hill of Santa Teresa. This building had been built as royal stables in 1586, then about 1600 it was transformed into a university by the architect Fontana, the engineer of the water-system which ran through Mount Civita. It later housed the Jesuits until their expulsion from Naples, so that the former stud building, known as the *palazzo degli studi*, was free to receive the treasures from Portici. To this day the building, though changed and restored, still houses the now world-famous collection of Pompeii and Herculaneum. By this union of books and pictures from the Farnese legacy with the classical treasures it was hoped that "the long extinct taste for the beautiful would at last be revived" there.[1]

The news of the success of the excavations had meanwhile spread far and wide. Everyone interested in what was valuable in science and art, and able to make the difficult and expensive journey to Naples, came to see with his own eyes the treasures of antiquity. Among these was Goethe, who visited Pompeii from Naples in the course of his Italian journey, on 11th March, 1787. It was a gay little company of artists which undertook this excursion: the painter Johann Heinrich Wilhelm Tischbein, a cousin of that Friedrich August who was recommended by the Prince of Waldeck to the court of Naples and later had the privilege of painting Queen Carolina. Then there was Jacob Philipp Hackert, a landscape-painter and an accomplished Mannerist, whose reputation was perhaps greater than it deserved to be, who was staying in Naples at the time, and forging those connexions which heralded his most brilliant years as court painter. The great poet and the two artists entrusted themselves to the guidance of the Marquess and Marchioness Venuti, who were of the same family as that Marcello Venuti

[1] Count Lamberg to Prince Kaunitz, Naples, 31st August, 1781. Vienna State Archives.

who had, while in Charles III's service, had a hand in the first excavations at Herculaneum and described the first discoveries in 1749.[1]

On the journey from Naples to the buried towns, Goethe was delighted by the glorious views. He had known them till then only in drawings and pictures, but now he saw them as they appeared in actuality, brilliant in the sunlight. But when they reached the sites he was at first somewhat disillusioned, for his expectations had been too great. "Everyone is amazed at Pompeii's smallness," he wrote in his *Italian Journal* on Sunday, 11th March, 1787. "Narrow streets . . . tiny windowless houses. . . . Even public buildings, the bank at the gate, the temple, as well as a villa nearby — they are more like models and doll's houses than real buildings. The rooms, corridors and galleries, however, are very gaily painted, the wall-surfaces are all alike, with a splendid picture in the centre, now usually broken away. . . . In its present desolate condition — first overwhelmed by stones and ashes, and then plundered by excavators — the town still reveals a delight in art and paintings such as even the keenest people today have no idea, or feeling, or need of. If the distance of this place from Vesuvius is considered, then it is clear that the volcanic material which covers it cannot have been hurled here or carried by the wind. It is more likely that these stones and ashes drifted for a long time like clouds, till they finally settled on the unfortunate place. To have a picture of how this happened one should think of a snowed-up mountain village. . . ."

After Goethe and his company had visited some "small, cramped houses, but all of them containing the most beautiful paintings", they proceeded to the "remarkable town gate" (the Gate of Herculaneum), in the Street of Tombs, where work was going on apace. Here Goethe and his friends sat down on the semi-circular seat at the gravestone of the priestess Mamia. They enjoyed a wonderful view towards the sea, the islands swimming in blue and the shores of the gulf of Naples lost in haze. While Goethe was resting on the seat, the sun sank into the waves in a veil of gold and purple. "A glorious spot, well worth remembering", wrote the poet.

[1] Marchese don Marcello de Venuti, *Descrizione delle prime scoperte dell'antica città d'Ercolano*. Venice, 1749.

After so much poetry, however, hunger and thirst soon asserted themselves, and the little company turned into a nearby inn. "We washed from our spirits the strange and half-unpleasant impression of this mummified town," says Goethe, "as we sat in an arbour near the sea, in a poor inn, and ate a frugal meal, and rejoiced in the blue of heaven and the brilliance and light of the sea, hoping to return by the time the vine-leaves appeared. . . ."

The good bottles of Lacrimae Christi, the splendid wine from the slopes of Vesuvius, had excited the visitors, and when they strolled on the shore for a while before going home everyone was merry and happy, quite unlike people who had just visited a town destroyed by a terrible catastrophe. They joined in a gay skirmish with the sand, and Tischbein caught the scene in a little sketch.

When Goethe returned to Naples, he was haunted by the tragic reason for these discoveries of ancient times. In his imagination he peopled the places he had seen with their former inhabitants, he thought of the life and activity, the art and the culture, whose remains were now coming to light, and he gave his final judgment on the visit in the following words: "There has been much evil in the world, but very little that has given so much delight to posterity. I cannot easily think of anything more interesting." Yet he was quite aware that his stay there had been too short and fleeting for a proper impression to be obtained. He emphasised this in a letter, saying that it was clear that the enchantment of the town came home to you only after a longer stay and thorough study. Goethe had travelled incognito, and therefore did not meet La Vega, the leader of the excavations, who kept a record of proceedings. These notes, begun as far back as 1748, on the most important discoveries and events, such as the visits of the royal couple or of distinguished strangers, say nothing of the poet's visit.

If Goethe had gone several months later, he would have been shown the scene of one of the countless human dramas which took place at the time of the catastrophe, which might have inspired him to a poem. For in August of the same year, 1787, there was found, in the cellar of a house beside the town wall, a human skeleton and that of a dog. On closer examination it was discovered that the human bones were not lying all in one place, but were scattered in different parts of the room, and had been gnawed. But the skeleton of the dog lay completely preserved in one corner. It was clear that the walls had collapsed and imprisoned the two. The human being had died first, and the dog had lived on for a time and had fed on the human flesh until it too died of suffocation or of thirst. On the gnawed arm-bone of the dead person, who was plainly a woman, there were a metal bracelet and some coins.

Meanwhile the so-called Herculanean Academy, without being actually dissolved, had disappeared from the scene, silent and unsung. It was even removed from the Court and State Almanac, where it figured long after it had ceased its activities. But in 1787, under the influence of the Marchese Domenico Caracciolo, who was the minister and for a time the viceroy of Sicily, it was summoned to life again, with the concurrence of the King. The English ambassador, Sir William Hamilton, had also had a great deal to do with this. His wife had died in the meantime, and in addition to his diplomatic duties he still pursued his study of Etruscan, Greek and Roman antiquities, undertaking observations of Vesuvius, and preparing a description of the Phlegraean fields in the district round Naples.

He was fifty-three years old when he became acquainted with Emma Lyon, the mistress of his nephew, the Hon. Charles Greville. Two years later an arrangement was made whereby Greville ceded his mistress to Hamilton, who in return paid his nephew's debts. Emma resented this scheme, but acquiesced. Her beauty and charm obtained for her such a hold on Hamilton that in 1791, in spite of her reputation, he married her. He had just sold his Neapolitan classical collection, which contained many objects from Herculaneum and Pompeii, for a very large sum of money (£8,400) to the British Museum, and it was popularly reported that he had done this because he had spent so much on the fair Emma. There was a great deal of gossip about the unsuitable marriage of the British ambassador. But he did not care: "a pin for the world", was his reply, and in one of his letters to his young wife he wrote: "My study of antiquities has kept me in constant thought of the perpetual fluctuation of everything. The whole art is, really, to live all the *days* of our life;

and not, with anxious care, disturb the sweetest hours that life affords."[1] The happy lover found heaven on earth in his hobbies and in his charming twenty-six-year-old wife.

At first Neapolitan society would not receive her at all, but when the Queen, attracted in spite of everything by the charming and lovable young wife of the ambassador, invited her to the court and even singled her out for favour, there was nothing for the proud nobility to do but to accept her in their circle. She had had no schooling, and her education, begun by Greville, was continued by Hamilton. He used to take her on his numerous visits to the buried towns, where she would sit on the steps of the great open theatre, the excavation of which had been completed on 2nd December, 1789, by the efforts of the Academy. Everything else had been brought to a standstill, and all the workers were concentrated there. That was a notable advance, for which the new Academy was to be thanked; and it also saw to the publication of the unrolled and deciphered papyri. This was done in two large and expensive volumes, the first appearing in 1793, containing the fragments of the papyri in facsimile. Photography had of course not been invented, so that this publication, which made available some extracts of writings by unimportant Epicurean philosophers, was produced only at great cost and with much labour.

Meanwhile important events had taken place in the world. From 14th July, 1789, the day of the storming of the Bastille, the dungeon-fortress of the French monarchy, the Revolution, with its infectious ideas, had stormed across Europe. Every royal court trembled, among them that of Ferdinand and Carolina, who were even less inclined to revolutions and novelties than other princes. And when the life of the royal pair in Paris was seriously threatened (and Marie Antoinette was the sister of Carolina), hatred of the new tendencies reached its height in Ferdinand's court. The ambassador of the newly created republic, whom no one wished to acknowledge, was the first to feel this; on the other hand, the court feared the threat of the French fleet to Naples. But when the news came that Louis XVI had been guillotined in January 1793, then, in the words of the Austrian ambassador, Count Esterhazy, it was "impossible to describe the mounting

[1] Polovtsoff, *op. cit.*, p. 145 f.

loathing and hatred of the French nation, which had perpe-
trated . . . this fresh outrage."[1] The fury reached its height
when in October of the same year Marie Antoinette also fell
a victim to the terrible axe.

The time that followed was full of suspense and fears.
Some hope was placed in England and in the Emperor in
Vienna, and there was a desire to join in the war against the
French revolutionaries. In December 1793 the French fleet
appeared before Naples, threatening death and destruction;
and there was nothing to oppose to it. But as soon as the
warships had sailed away again, the desire to fight the revolution was revived, and Naples joined in the grand alliance
of its foes. There was fear and unrest in the city, and in
March 1794 a conspiracy against the King and Queen was
discovered. Its aim was "summarily to assassinate the royal
family, proclaim liberty and equality, in a word, to bring
about a revolution on the French model."[2]

In the course of these years it was naturally impossible for
anyone to trouble much about the excavations. Even Hamilton, whose position in recent times had enormously gained in
importance, since everyone saw in England the last bulwark
and hope of salvation, was too much engaged in politics to
devote himself to his favourite avocation. So Herculaneum
and Pompeii lay more or less desolated and abandoned, and
the work was carried on by a few convicts. Vesuvius, however,
took no notice of war or revolution, and on 15th June, 1794,
the south-west slope opened in no fewer than six new places
and erupted such a quantity of steam, stone and ashes that
the whole horizon was darkened. The following day, when
the thundering of the earthquakes and the streams of lava
continued, the cardinal archbishop of Naples ordered the
statue of St Januarius to be carried in a ceremonial procession to the region of Vesuvius, and the divine help be
implored. Meanwhile the lava had reached Torre del Greco,
covering the whole town, and had flowed on to the sea. For
the third time since 1631 the little town had fallen a victim
to a fiery stream of molten magma.

[1] Count Esterhazy to Prince Kaunitz, Naples, 9th February, 1793.
Vienna State Archives.
[2] Count Esterhazy to the Foreign Minister, Franz Freiherr von
Thugut, Naples, 29th March, 1794.

After this eruption, which lasted till 21st June, Vesuvius was quite a new shape. Its peak had completely collapsed, and was now an immense circular crater. Fear and anxiety reigned again in Portici. Anonymous letters, warning the King and Queen of attempts being planned on their lives, increased the uneasiness which pervaded the court.

Meanwhile, in the great coalition war carried on in Italy in 1796, General Bonaparte had gained the supreme command and led the army to victory. In the peninsula, in Lombardy, Genoa and the Papal lands, one republic after another was formed on the French model. The next step was the establishment of a Roman republic in the Papal capital. It was clear to everyone that in a short time Naples would go the same way. It was true that Napoleon, who was unwilling to carry on the war at such a distance, had concluded a special peace with Ferdinand in 1796. But during the Egyptian campaign General Berthier entered Rome in 1798 and drove out the Pope. King Ferdinand attempted to anticipate the threat which was hanging over him, and marched with an army against Rome, aiming at restoring the Papal authority. He was encouraged in this not only by the English ambassador, Hamilton, but also by Admiral Nelson, who had come to Naples covered with the glory of the Battle of the Nile. But the campaign against Rome completely failed, the Neapolitan army was annihilated at the end of 1798, and the King was not only forced back into his capital, but he and the Queen were obliged, with Nelson's help, to flee to Sicily.

The news of the approach of the French had encouraged the revolutionary movement in Naples. Only the most necessary and most precious things could be taken with them in their flight, and these included some specially valuable coins and small objects from the museum of classical antiquities. Everything else had to be left behind, in the knowledge that the French invaders might well remove the bronze statues from the Villa of the Papyri and the wonderful paintings brought to light over so many years with such labour. But what was to be done? At this time the royal couple were glad even to save their lives, with the help of Nelson and Emma Hamilton.

The French occupation followed immediately after this flight. General Championnet appeared in Naples with a weak

161

force, proclaimed the house of Bourbon deposed, and established the so-called republic of "Parthenope". This was accomplished not without some skirmishes in the city itself. By chance a cannon-ball destroyed the head of the splendid statue of the son of Marcus Nonnius Balbo of Herculaneum, which the sculptor Brunelli was commissioned to replace. "Still, it was better than if the head of one of us had been knocked off", said the Neapolitans.

On the very day that the French army entered Naples, which was incidentally the sixth anniversary of the execution of Louis XVI, Vesuvius showed signs of a minor eruption. A Paris account observed that this was more a kind of welcoming bonfire than a proper volcanic eruption. Of course the excavations had completely ceased as a result of the war, and on 5th January, 1799, the workers were dismissed. But Championnet, who was a cultured man and had heard much of Pompeii and Herculaneum, was interested. Scarcely were the necessary arrangements made in Naples to form the new republic on the French pattern than he made his way out to the buried towns and gave instructions for the work to be resumed. In the course of the operations five houses[1] were uncovered which are still associated with the name of General Championnet. In one of them was discovered a female skeleton with bracelets, rings and necklaces of gold, and in the others it could be clearly seen how the last occupants had so disguised the original Doric columns of the peristyles with stucco that they looked like Corinthian columns. These houses, situated on the outskirts of the town, south of the basilica and towards the sea, possessed hanging gardens with a wonderful prospect over the gulf.

French rule in Naples, however, lasted only a short time. Napoleon had been too long out of the way. A new alliance between Russia, Austria and Great Britain had arisen; upper Italy was lost to the French, and with their going the new republics with their fine names disappeared one by one. When the Roman republic likewise collapsed and the Pope returned to the Vatican, the republic of Parthenope had also had its day. In June 1799 Naples was evacuated; the King could have returned at once, but he stayed on in Sicily for the time being, intending to await events.

[1] Regio VIII, Ins. 2, Nos. 1–5.

When the French left, excavations in Pompeii and Herculaneum came practically to a standstill. It was emphasised that order must first be created and the rubbish cleared away — in brief, the "damage done by the revolution" had first to be restored. In addition to this, money was completely lacking; nothing could have been done, since the means to do it did not exist. In December 1799 Francesco La Vega made urgent representations to the Finance Minister, saying that the expert artists whose task it was to carry out the work of restoration on the ancient sites were dying of starvation. In the past year they had not received a penny, since no work had been given them — and this in spite of the fact that during the now defunct republic they had proved themselves unswervingly loyal to His Majesty.

But without a royal mandate the authorities remained niggardly, and the King still lingered in Sicily. That great champion of the excavations, Sir William Hamilton, had also been summoned home from Sicily. This was a heavy blow not only for the work on the buried towns, but also for the royal couple, who had formed such intimate relationships with the ambassador and his wife, and through them also with their saviour, Nelson. These friendly feelings received special expression at a royal garden party held in September 1799. In the brightly illuminated park of the Castle of Palermo a temple of fame was built; in it there was the statue of the King, and before it three statues in wax, Lord Nelson in the centre, with Sir William Hamilton and his wife on either side. As the members of the court went into the park the young Crown Prince stepped forward and laid a laurel wreath on the head of the statue of Nelson. In this way the King honoured his rescuer. It was specially hard for Hamilton, when he was treated in this splendid fashion, to leave his post in Naples, where he had not merely spent thirty-seven years, but had also been able to enjoy to his heart's content the main cultural interest of his life, and to give full play to his collector's instinct.

But in the world of politics another great change had suddenly taken place. When the French republic, threatened with defeat in every theatre of the war, saw a great new coalition arrayed against it, it recalled General Bonaparte, and in one stroke the whole picture was transformed. When he got back Napoleon overthrew the government of the Directory in Paris, and made himself First Consul with absolute powers. Then he took the field, and after the victory of Marengo over the Austrians there followed the peace of Luneville in 1801, and a little later peace with Great Britain. Naples, which had belonged to the second coalition, likewise gave way, yielding to all Napoleon's demands. At that time King Ferdinand handed over to the French government as a gift to Napoleon a number of treasures found in Herculaneum. In this way a great many works of art, including a fresco in nine parts depicting Apollo and the Muses,[1] found their way to Paris, to the house of the First Consul, who later presented them to his brother Joseph. They are to this day in the French capital, but no longer in Bonaparte possession.

In June 1802 the King and Queen of Naples returned to their capital, but all the changes, together with the still threatening state of affairs, kept people so preoccupied and restless, that in spite of the Queen's interest in the buried towns and their secrets, nothing substantial was done in the next few years. And in fact, after Napoleon had been raised to the position of Emperor of the French in 1804, the cycle of wars began once more, to last, with short intervals, for ten years, until the great man's overthrow.

In the third coalition war of 1805 Naples was again ranged on the side of Napoleon's enemies. Carolina, who bitterly hated the Corsican upstart, was quite clear about the consequences, should he triumph. "We are in a very painful position", she wrote in July 1805, "Bonaparte has sworn to bring about our downfall. Under the guise of mildness he is the perfect chameleon, the greatest criminal among men."[2] The Queen's foresight was accurate. Her friend Nelson had a great victory, it is true, at Trafalgar, but he fell in the battle, while on land Napoleon smashed the enemy alliance at Austerlitz, at the battle of the three emperors, on 2nd December. This time Naples' fate was sealed. Despite the resistance of Great Britain the Emperor sent General Massena to Naples with troops, Ferdinand had to flee once more to

[1] Found on 20th July, 1755.
[2] Queen Carolina to Ruffo, Naples, 16th July, 1805. Vienna State Archives.

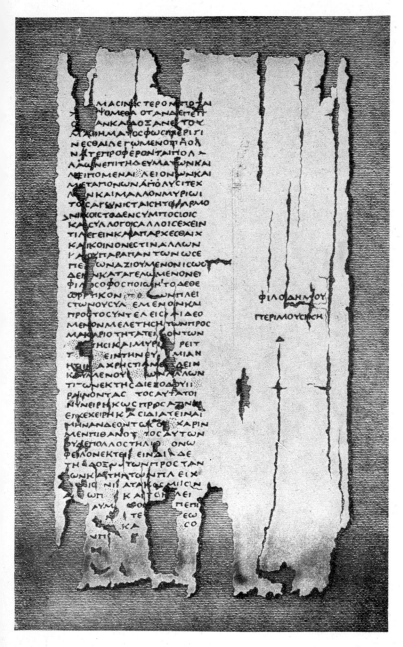

31. Unrolled title and first column of a carbonised papyrus roll found in the Villa of the Papyri. From a work by Philodemos entitled *Concerning Music*.

(*See pages* 121, 124)

Photo: Alinari

32. Wild boar attacked by hounds.
A well-preserved bronze group from Pompeii.

Sicily, and the brother of the Corsican, Joseph Bonaparte, was made King of Naples.

On 14th February, 1806, he arrived in Naples, just two days after Queen Carolina had followed her husband to Palermo. Joseph was the most cultured and intelligent of Napoleon's brothers. He had scarcely been king a fortnight when on 2nd March he drove out to Pompeii, inspected the excavations with the greatest interest, listened to the explanations and firmly resolved to do all he could to further the enterprise in the interest of science and culture. He commissioned one of his ministers, Cristoforo Saliceti, the Chief of Police, who was thoroughly hated on account of his arbitrariness and hardness, to have the care of the operations. This man's well-known ruthlessness promised at least that the work would be directed with some energy. Fifty men were at once set to work next to the basilica of Pompeii, and Saliceti was to be found in person at the excavations. At first excavations were carried on unmethodically here and there. Soon, however, King Joseph himself appeared, and inspected the work on the Temple of Fortuna and in the House of Sallust, on the Street of Consuls leading from the Gate of Herculaneum to the forum. In a short time over one hundred and fifty workers were employed.

In 1807 the King, recognising the disadvantages of disorderly and unmethodical digging, ordered the director of the royal museum, Cavaliere Don Michele Arditi, to prepare an exact plan for the improved conduct of the excavations. He, the King, would see to it that the necessary number of people was made available.[1] Arditi at once set to work and soon laid his proposals before the King. His chief advice was that the whole area beneath which Pompeii and its surroundings lay should be bought up from private owners. Work should not be carried on here and there, but a squad of workers should be put into the country-house of Diomedes before the Gate of Herculaneum, and another in the House of Sallust on the Street of Consuls, and the two parties should dig towards one another in the direction of the Gate of Herculaneum. He also asked for a daily budget of twenty ducats. King Joseph agreed in principle to all those proposals; but though he made an order regarding the buying of the land, this was at first,

[1] See Henri Thédenat, *Pompéi*, I, 34–5. Paris, 1928.

owing to lack of money, not carried out. Even the daily expenditure was not possible, and in the time of Joseph the work was confined to the area of the House of Sallust and that of Apollo on the Street of Mercury on the northern outskirts of the town. There, indeed, the work was rewarded with the discovery of some very fine frescoes, one of which depicted Athene's invention of the flute. The House of Apollo got its name from the many pictures of Apollo which were found there; in the courtyard there was a miniature stream, and a tiny toy-like waterfall. Joseph Bonaparte spent a lot of time in this house, admiring the frescoes and the other things which had been brought to light.

But the new King's position in Naples was very uncomfortable. The populace were passively opposed to him, and even on occasions took up arms; and the conquest of Sicily recommended to Joseph by his imperial brother in Paris was completely out of the question. On the contrary, with assistance from England Bourbon troops were pushing into Neapolitan territory. In such circumstances the peaceful work of excavation was naturally bound to suffer, however much the King would have liked to promote it. And meanwhile Napoleon, having defeated Prussia and concluded the peace of Tilsit and then conquered the capital of Spain, ordered his brother Joseph to assume the Spanish crown. On 22nd May, 1808, Joseph left Naples, not in the least pleased, but doubting from the start the issue of his task of turning Spaniards into good Frenchmen. If this had not been possible in Naples, how much less would it be in that larger and even more fanatical land.

In July 1808 new rulers entered Naples: the French Marshal Joachim Murat, till then Grand Duke of Berg, and another Carolina, his wife, the twenty-six-year-old youngest sister of Napoleon. The Emperor had been dissatisfied with his brother's rule in Naples and expected more from his general. "Murat is a beast", he said of him, "but he has drive and audacity. He has waged war all his life. He is a beast, but he is a hero!"

There was war in Naples too, and the Kingdom had to be conquered all over again. But Pompeii and Herculaneum nevertheless gained from the exchange of dynasties, for Murat was interested. He took up the plans made by Arditi under Joseph, which had not yet been executed, and brought them nearer realisation. At first a hundred workers were employed, and the number rose in the course of his reign to five hundred. Murat was so filled with enthusiasm after his first visits that he would have liked to rebuild the amphitheatre completely, and firmly intended to do so. The full extent of the town of Pompeii was now established, when the walls were excavated. The King had the rubble cleared away, and, carefully following the line of the street, had it cleared in the area lying between that great villa beyond the Gate of Herculaneum and the House of Sallust, just as Arditi had proposed. The work, however, was carried on only from the side, room after room and house after house being cleared, with the digging sometimes being deliberately from below upwards; and this led to the collapse of many buildings whose interiors had been cleared, and the destruction both of the buildings themselves and of their contents.

Queen Carolina Murat was even more enthusiastic about the excavations than her Bourbon namesake. The Archbishop of Naples, Giuseppe Capece, who was a good student of classical antiquity, knew how to introduce her to the secrets of the two buried towns in such a way as to arouse her passionate interest. Again and again she went to the working sites. Those who conducted the excavations encouraged her fancy by every means in their power, including that same trick which had been used on the Emperor Joseph II. When the Queen and the Crown Prince announced a visit for 27th October, 1808, an ancient Roman shop was "prepared" for uncovering before the eyes of the distinguished visitors. When some ancient bronzes and many terracotta jars were found in two rooms of the house, the place was noted and the things lightly covered over again, to await the moment of "discovery" before the Queen.

Carolina Murat mentioned these visits in innumerable letters. She had been given three amulets from the Temple of Isis, bearing inscriptions which told of victory. "I send you, my dear Hortense", she wrote to her sister-in-law, the Queen of Holland, "two genuine talismans which were found in the Temple of Serapis. Please give the third one to the Empress, from me. Two of the inscriptions, as you will see, signify 'Victory', and you will agree that that is very suitable for the Empress. I had excavations made, I was present myself, and have seen ashes which are two thousand years old, and many rare jars, which I have sent to the Empress." [1]

Queen Carolina took into her own home everything that was found and could be moved, and almost made a special museum of her apartments. And she did not rest until her husband and his minister went to Pompeii, on 3rd October, 1810, and she was able to give them a personal explanation of the importance of furthering the work. The Queen was delighted when a triclinium, or dining-room, was dug out while they were there (probably this too was arranged beforehand), with the walls gaily painted from top to bottom with fish, birds and game of every kind, and when she could see, from the three stone couches, how the ancient Romans had sat round the little table for their meals. Only the wooden surface of the table had disappeared, though its three marble feet were still there. This was very different from Herculaneum. The light and porous covering of lapilli and ash was not able to preserve any wooden objects from decay and disintegration, whereas the mud which covered Herculaneum turned into stone beneath whose protection wood was fossilised and carbonised, and preserved in its original shape.

In the presence of her husband, the Minister of the Interior, the Cavaliere Arditi and La Vega, who was still in charge of operations, the Queen expressed her deep interest in having the whole town brought to light as speedily as possible. Urgent consultations followed on what had to be done in order to realise her wish. The Finance Minister was pressed to do everything in his power to make this task possible — for in the end it was really a matter of money.

Everyone present on the occasion of that visit had the liveliest impression of the Queen's intense interest in the classical sites. Everything connected with them, even the volcano itself, interested her. "I am now in Portici", she wrote to her sister-in-law Hortense some days after this visit, "and as you know quite near Vesuvius, whose eruptions vary in appearance from day to day. . . . Like you I see very few

---

[1] Queen Carolina Murat to Queen Hortense, Portici, 14th November, 1808. *Lettres et documents pour servir à l'histoire de Joachim Murat, 1767–1815*, vol. VI, p. 407. Published by Prince Murat, Paris, 1908–11.

people, I read and work a great deal. I have had excavations made, and that, my dear Hortense, is my pastime."[1]

And in fact the Queen turned up at the excavations every week, she urged the people on, she raised their wages, she gave them money herself and was overjoyed at even the smallest find which she was able to take away with her. After the visit along with her husband and the others, the *Monitore Napoletano* gave a full account of it on 7th October, 1809; in consequence, a serious examination was made of the possibility of buying the sites from their private owners. In 1811 two-thirds of the land was acquired for the State. The royal pair were so interested that their influence was almost too eager and feverish for thorough work. The Queen behaved almost like the chief of operations. She planned to spend two thousand ducats monthly, and in addition to the hundreds of workmen, who were carrying on the work under a lessee, she even succeeded in having army pioneers put to work. Carolina Murat asked for two progress reports a week. The main work was now in the Street of Tombs, and many skeletons were found of Pompeians who had tried to flee in the direction of the sea. Another difference between Herculaneum and Pompeii could be seen here: hundreds of skeletons had already been found in Pompeii, though only a very small part of the town had been explored, while in Herculaneum only twelve skeletons in all had been found.

The Queen was also anxious that the amphitheatre and the basilica should be completely uncovered. It was a source of great delight to her to take her guests to Pompeii and show them the latest discoveries. Thus on 6th April, 1811, Carolina came with the sister-in-law of the Russian emperor and inspected the excavations in the House of Apollo. It soon became generally known what a high value the Queen set on everything connected with the buried towns. An abbé, Domenico Romanelli, the head of the library of the royal children, dedicated to the Queen in the same year the account of a journey from Pompeii to Herculaneum via Paestum. François Piranesi, an accomplished artist and archaeologist, sone of the famous engraver and architect Jean Baptiste Piranesi, who had engraved the monuments of Rome,

[1] Queen Caroline Murat to Queen Hortense, Portici, 12 October, 1809, *op. cit.*, vol. VIII, p. 58 ff.

published in two volumes, in 1809, his enormous *Theatre of Herculaneum*. The Queen loved to present this to her guests, as well as the publications of the French architect F. Mazois, who at the expense of the court of Naples and under the Queen's patronage had published a splendid work on Pompeii.[1]

One day, on 11th January, 1812, two skeletons were found in the Street of Tombs not far from the town gate, just at the point where the lapilli gave way to water-ash. One lay face downwards, and by its side lay no fewer than 69 gold coins and 115 of silver, which had fallen out of a purse completely ruined by the years. The gold coins were quite new, of 22 carats, from the reigns of Tiberius, Nero, Otho, Vitellius, Vespasian and Domitian; they looked as though they had come straight from the mint. The second skeleton lay on its back with its arms stretched wide open, but had nothing beside it. Not far away there was a third skeleton. The impression of all the dead had been left behind in the ashes. But at that time there was no way of preserving such moulds, and they were simply destroyed.

The chief of the excavators, Arditi, at once took the treasure to Zurlo, the Minister of the Interior, who drove with the fortunate discoverer in his carriage to the Murats. They received them with great delight, inspecting the rare coins again and again, and were only sorry that they had not been present in person when the discovery was made. This feeling was strengthened when the Queen learned that on 12th May, 1812, again in the Street of Tombs, and not far from the so-called villa of Diomedes, the skeleton of a young woman had been found, wearing the most splendid rings and charming ear-rings decorated with pearls. She had pressed her child to her breast; not far away two young girls were lying.

The chief of the excavators now ordered that the next discovery should not be advertised, but everything should be immediately covered in again and brought to light only in the presence of Queen Carolina. Soon afterwards the pioneers who were working alongside the men uncovered a skeleton,

---

[1] Charles François Mazois, *Les ruines de Pompéi, dessinées et mesurées par F. M., architecte pendant les années 1809–11*. Paris, 1812–1838. *Continué par M. Gau, architecte.*

which was covered in again, and on 21st November, 1812, it was uncovered before the Queen and her children. Beside the dead Pompeian lay something, which gleamed like gold. On closer examination this proved to be a heap of no less than 360 silver coins and 42 of bronze, which were scarcely recognisable on account of the rust (patina). In the midst of the collection there were eight fine imperial gold medallions, which looked fresh from the mint. They had been in a dark brown bag of coarse linen, some fragments of which were still preserved. One piece of this was safely transferred to the museum, but the rest crumbled to dust as soon as it was touched. These bodies were ten feet above the layer of ash and covered only by a thin layer of mixed lapilli and ash.[1]

Carolina Murat was now led to a second "prepared" skeleton, and further digging revealed four dead, among them a child, of which nothing had been known, so that the Queen at last experienced a genuine find made in her presence. These victims too had pearl ear-rings, and garnets set in gold rings in the shape of snakes, while coins were scattered everywhere. The Queen was as pleased as a child, and on 30th November in the same year she went back with a small donkey, which was laden with all the finds, attached to the royal coach, and brought back to Portici. The happy Queen presented the workers and pioneers that day with two hundred chinking ducats.

While Carolina Murat was thus eagerly occupied with the excavations which produced in the last months of 1812 many monuments in the Street of Tombs, such as that of Scaurus with its representation of gladiatorial and animal combats, this ambitious and clever woman did not forget politics. She was now regent, as her husband was taking part in the campaign of the *Grande Armée* against Russia, which was launched in June 1812 and by November was in complete collapse. Their position was bound to suffer under this misfortune of her brother the Emperor. From this time are to be dated the struggles of the Murats to retain the throne they had come to enjoy so much, struggles which even made them betray the man who had given them their throne and everything else. Murat and his wife loved royal power, and they loved

[1] I. de Clarac, *Fouille faite à Pompéi en présence de S. M. la Reine des deux Siciles le 18 mars 1813.*

the splendid city of Naples, not least on account of the joy they had in the excavations. In February 1813 a very fine monument was discovered in the Street of Tombs, which had been erected by a Greek freedwoman called Naevoleia Tyche for herself and her lover, the merchant Munatius Faustus. This Munatius was highly esteemed, for he had been given the honour of the *bisellium*, that is, of a seat of double width in the theatre, an honour which was noted on the monument.

Immediately this monument was found, its entrance was walled in again without further search, so that it could be laid open in the presence of the Queen. On 18th March she appeared, accompanied by the sculptor Canova, and the monument was brought to light. Two glass urns were found, containing cremated bones in a mixture, which had not completely dried up, of water, wine and oil. The glass urns were protected on the outside by a covering of lead, and it was this covering which had preserved them for 1700 years. The Queen had them sent to Portici with no fewer than 900 coins which had been discovered recently, and presented the pioneers with another two hundred ducats. It can be readily appreciated that this was a great incentive to the soldiers to make new discoveries. Queen Carolina was impatient for success and things were sent to her so promptly after their discovery that little time was spent on their careful examination.

While her elder brother and protector, Napoleon, was fighting in Germany throughout the year 1813 for the preservation of his power, even Austria, joined to him though it was by marriage ties, began to fall away. The Murats were very anxious about their own future, but they did not put a stop to the excavations. In September 1813 there were 532 men at work, chiefly on the basilica and the amphitheatre, as well as in the preparation of places which were to be dug up in the presence of the Queen. It also took a great deal of time to repair the streets and roads along which their majesties would be led to the finds. Towards the end of the year their visits were more frequent, the Queen often coming several days in succession.

Meanwhile the position in the military arenas of Europe had grown more acute. The occasional French victories had been dearly bought, and Napoleon had to draw on troops and reinforcements from wherever he could. Naples had to provide 20,000 men for the army of the Emperor's step-son, the viceroy Eugene in upper Italy. Napoleon wrote repeatedly in the most vigorous terms to his sister and Murat about these reinforcements. One of these admonitions arrived just as the pair were visiting the excavations at Pompeii. Scarcely had the King read the missive than in the sight of everyone he angrily tore it across, trampled it underfoot and cried: "Not a single company will I send!" Then he summoned his ministers in Naples and said furiously: "Gentlemen, it is unheard of! The Emperor treats me from above as though I were a corporal!"[1]

In the autumn, events followed one another in swift succession. From the 16th to the 18th of October Napoleon suffered defeat at the Battle of the Nations at Leipzig, and had to retreat across the Rhine towards the interior of France. Now it was high time for Murat and his wife to consider their plans in the event of the Emperor's final defeat. They would have preferred to go on with the excavations at Pompeii, for in November, 1813, they had just reached the forum, and were beginning to lay it bare. For a whole year Murat had been toying with the thought of going over to Napoleon's enemies, and securing his kingdom in good time against the coming collapse. To achieve this, he was ready to go to war against his brother-in-law and benefactor. In January 1814 Murat broke with Napoleon, and thus with France, his native land. The allies first planned to use him to throw the rest of the French out of Italy, and then to turn against the traitor. This marshal who had become a king had the vague idea of uniting Italy and playing the part of a national hero. But it was all a dream, which was dissipated by hard facts. His correspondence with Napoleon, banished to Elba, was censored, and showed the allies that Murat was playing a double game; and this gave them the necessary grounds for dropping him completely in spite of his treaties with Austria.

Then on 1st March, 1815, Napoleon, who had secretly left Elba, landed on French soil. This marked the beginning of the flood of triumphs and victories which swept him to Paris, to draw new armies from the land and once more to throw

[1] Freiherr von Helfert, *Queen Carolina of Naples and Sicily in the Struggle against French Hegemony*, 1790–1814, p. 522. Vienna, 1878.

down the gauntlet to the allies, who were in counsel and in conflict at the Congress in Vienna. When this news reached him Murat forgot all that had happened. All he saw was the star of his imperial lord, whose genius for leadership he had admired in countless battles and campaigns, once more in the ascendant. In a moment he forgot all his treaties, took the field with his Neapolitan troops and fought the enemies of Napoleon wherever he met them.

In Naples the Queen anxiously awaited news of her brother's and her husband's audacious enterprise. The best means she knew for calming herself and her strained nerves was a visit to Pompeii. The arena of the amphitheatre had just been completely uncovered, and on 11th April the Queen came out from the castle at Portici, where she had moved after Murat had left for the army, in order to inspect this success. She specially admired a fairly well-preserved cloth bag containing a bronze lantern, which had been found beside a skeleton in the right-hand aisle of the amphitheatre. After this visit instructions were given that new houses had to be most carefully prepared for excavation, "in order that the Queen might be entertained". All the workers who had been busy in the amphitheatre were now concentrated at one point, where five houses were treated in this way. On 17th April she showed the excavations to her brother, the former King of Westphalia, and on the 18th to the Spanish royal couple. But that was her last visit.

Meanwhile Murat's campaign had gone badly. Austria had again made an alliance with Ferdinand of Bourbon, and shortly afterwards, on 2nd and 3rd May, Murat was defeated in the Battle of Tolentino. On 10th May the British fleet arrived before Naples and delivered an ultimatum demanding the handing over of all warships and arsenals. The danger of popular revolt in the city was mounting, but Carolina Murat kept it in check by appearing fearlessly before everyone at a review of the *garde nationale*. On 18th May, at nine o'clock in the evening, her husband returned in despair. "All is lost", he said to her, "except my life. I was not so fortunate as to find death. All that is left me to do is to flee to France, in order to offer my sword to Napoleon, wherever possible." And in the night Murat left the city, clad in plain clothes and with only a few trusty companions. Two days later Carolina gave herself up as a prisoner on board a British ship. She was taken to Trieste, relinquished her honours, and under the name of Countess of Lipona sank into the obscurity of private life.[1]

Now the way for the return of the Bourbon king, who had fled to Sicily, was once more open, for the foreign power was decisively broken. So far as the buried towns were concerned, however, the French rule, thanks to the interest of the royal house, had been of advantage. If the work had gone forward with the same speed as in the last few years, all Pompeii would have been brought to light in a comparatively short time.

A great drama had been played to an end, and now throughout Europe the attempt was made to turn back the wheel of history.

[1] The ex-Queen Carolina Murat died in Florence in 1839.

7

POMPEII AND HERCULANEUM
IN MODERN TIMES

1815–1940

THE Congress of Vienna settled the return of the Bourbon Ferdinand to the throne of Naples on the one condition, which was very agreeable to this king, that he should get rid of all novel French ideas of freedom, and never grant a constitution. The King, whose wife Carolina had died in exile in Vienna at the beginning of the Congress, made preparations to return to his capital of Naples. He could not help smiling when Arditi, acting for La Vega, who was sick, presented reports on Pompeii in which the newly fled queen, the sister of Napoleon, was referred to simply as "Madama Murat". Her return was certainly not to be feared, for her husband, after the defeat of his brother-in-law at Waterloo in September 1815, had made a desperate attempt to reconquer Naples from Corsica with a weak force. The enterprise failed completely; Murat was captured on landing and summarily shot.

Arditi, nevertheless, had every reason to regret that "Madama" no longer had the say in Naples. For now that the Bourbon Carolina was also dead, there was no one, in default of any interest on the King's part, seriously concerned about the whole enterprise and with the necessary powers to further it. La Vega died in 1815, and under these unfavourable circumstances the architect Antonio Bonucci took over the conduct of the excavations. He did try to carry on the work, but the amount of labour at his disposal grew steadily smaller. Pompeii now sank to be just an interesting place of entertainment, a kind of open-air museum to which one could take

176

guests for their amusement. The expenditure was cut by half, and several lots of land, bought by Murat's orders, beneath which lay parts of Pompeii, were even put up for sale again. Only forty to one hundred men were fitfully employed. In December 1818 there were only thirteen, for the lessees could no longer meet their expenses, and would have preferred to let the whole thing die a natural death.

For things unconnected with the excavations which interested the court, however, there was always money and labour. One day the King announced that it was too tedious to have to walk in Pompeii, he wanted to be able to drive his princely guests through the town, and measures had to be taken at once to make this possible. So for a week everything else was brought to a standstill to make it possible for the King to drive along the Street of Tombs and the Street of Consuls to the forum. The ancient shape of these roads had to be changed, and the great stepping-stones removed which lay here and there in the street to help people to cross dry-shod. The ancient high-wheeled chariots surmounted these without difficulty, but the low-sprung royal coach of modern times would have come to grief on them. So on 11th April, 1818, King Ferdinand of Naples was the first after so many centuries to drive through the ancient town. Pompeii was looked on as not much more than a plaything for the King's personal amusement.

From this time the town was increasingly used as a place of entertainment for the members of the royal house and for visiting princes. When many different kinds of surgical instruments, a sign of the flourishing art of Roman doctors, were dug up in one house, the find was covered up again and freshly "discovered" on 31st October, 1818, in the presence of the Prince of Salerno and the Prince of Württemberg. The same kind of thing happened on 13th May, 1819, when the Emperor Francis I of Austria and his fourth wife, Queen Carolina Augusta, visited Pompeii in the course of their Italian journey. But they experienced more than the beauties of Naples and interesting discoveries in the buried towns, for they were also able to see how bitterly the populace felt about the retrogressive measures of the government. And in fact in 1820 the rebellious masses did compel the nomination of their councillor, General Pepe, as supreme commander of the

Neapolitan army, and the King had to grant a constitution on oath. This was a threat to the "principle of legitimacy" and to the principles laid down, since Napoleon's defeat, by the dominating figure in Europe, the Austrian Chancellor Prince Metternich. A congress of the Great Powers was therefore arranged in Laibach, to which Ferdinand of Naples was also summoned. He had scarcely crossed the frontiers of his rebellious land when he proclaimed that the constitution had been forced upon him and gave his approval to Austrian troops "creating order" in Naples. So the country was occupied by the imperial General Frimont till December of the year 1826.

Throughout this time digging had almost ceased, and the work was only resumed after the successful occupation of Naples. The Quartermaster-General of the Austrian army in Naples, Franz Freiherr von Koller, took an active part in the resumption of the excavations. He was the same officer who in 1814 had accompanied Napoleon to Elba and had lent the fallen hero his general's coat to prevent his being recognised. A highly cultured man who had a great love of the arts, Koller spent much time on the site of the excavations, accompanying the Kings of Sweden and Holland on a visit to Pompeii and assembling a splendid collection of classical vases, which in 1828 were bought for the museum in Berlin.

In October 1822 Vesuvius again showed signs of great activity. On the 22nd a stream of lava flowed down from the crater, and soon there followed an eruption which was so violent that the famous pine-shaped column of smoke rose up to a height of two miles, while black ashes mixed with lapilli were scattered over the land, some falling once more on Pompeii. Those who were at work on the site had to flee to Torre d'Annunziata; then the crater fell in, the summit of Vesuvius was lowered by 600 feet and the width of the opening extended to about two and a half miles. The rain of ashes fell on Naples as well. But the eruption lasted only a short time, and the damage was slight. None the less, this episode had seriously disturbed the work, and the fresh ashes had to be cleared away. This was all the more difficult, as there had been no lessees since 1823, and the excavations on the forum, especially in the house of Eumachia, went forward very slowly. Nor was there any money to spare, and this was so serious that on one occasion explicit royal approval had to be obtained for the cost of transporting one chest of articles to the museum.

A general survey of the results of the excavations up to the year 1823 shows that it was in the Bourbon time, despite everything, that the heart of Pompeii had been discovered: the forum with its surrounding buildings, the theatre quarter with the gladiatorial barracks, the town wall to the west, the western parts of the town as far as the Gate of Herculaneum, and the greater part of the Street of Tombs; besides these, there was the amphitheatre lying apart in the south-east corner, and scattered here and there on the northern edge of the town and on the Stabian Way private houses had been excavated. In 1824 work was going on in the Temple of Fortuna and in the forum baths, where more circular windows, like portholes, of thick glass, were found, as well as 778 Roman oil-lamps — a proof that the baths were also used by the Romans after nightfall.

As was natural with Austrian troops in occupation, it was chiefly Austrian visitors who now came to the excavations. Thus Marie Louise, the daughter of the Emperor Francis and Napoleon's widow, now Duchess of Parma, came to Pompeii; but as was to be expected from one of her character, she was not very much impressed.

On 4th January, 1825, Ferdinand of Bourbon died, after a reign which had lasted no less than sixty-six years — though the power had mostly been in the hands of others. He was succeeded by his son Francis I, a sick man when he ascended the throne and without any great influence on the course of events in the kingdom. Nevertheless, he had more understanding for the excavations than his father, remembering his mother's interest in them. In his reign the main work was on the houses north of the forum baths, especially on a large building which had belonged to a Pompeian merchant. It had a large bakehouse, and (bakers in ancient Roman times being also millers) three large mills, in which conic stones had been ingeniously set up; these were turned by slaves or small donkeys, and ground the corn which ran through between them. In the mill-house a lucky sign was painted on the wall — *Hic habitat felicitas* ("Here happiness dwells").

Another building was discovered nearby about the same time, which was given the misleading name of "The House of the Tragic Poet". The name was given after the discovery of a large mosaic showing seven people rehearsing a play. Another picture apparently depicted a scene in which the tragic poet was reading from his work. In reality this was a representation of a messenger of Apollo, the god of oracles, proclaiming from a papyrus roll that someone must give up his life for King Admetus if the king was to escape death from the wrath of the goddess Artemis. And the wife of the king, Alcestis, died for her husband. This is the story which Euripides used for his play *Alcestis*. The little house was made the dwelling of the hero, Glaucus, in Lord Lytton's novel *The Last Days of Pompeii*, and has in consequence become world famous.

The new King enjoyed visiting Pompeii, and in September and October 1826 he passed several evenings there with the Queen, walking by moonlight among the ancient buildings, and watching the uncovering of a mosaic fountain. In his reign the practice of excavating in the presence of distinguished visitors was further extended. Not only for princes but also for other prominent visitors, special "prepared" excavations were arranged.

At the end of December 1826 the evacuation of the kingdom by Austrian troops was completed, and that winter countless "distinguished strangers" streamed into the lovely southern city. Besides many princely guests, such as Leopold, later King of Belgium, there were also many wealthy English visitors, who were particularly impressed and enthusiastic. At the end of September 1827 another spectacle was prepared for the royal house of Naples, five human skeletons with gold bracelets and coins being "discovered" in their presence on the threshold of a house near the forum. In the Temple of Isis a bust of the famous actor C. Norbanus Sorex was discovered; he had contributed towards the building of the temple. In such ways the interest of the King and Queen was stirred, and when the proposal was shortly afterwards made to them that the excavations at Herculaneum should be resumed, King Francis made the most important decision of his short reign with regard to the excavations. In 1827 an ancient vault had been accidentally discovered on a country estate near Resina, and this aroused fresh hopes of successful diggings. When this was made known the King gave orders

Photo: Anderson

33. View of the Temple of Apollo near the forum of Pompeii,
in its present condition.

(*See pages* 11, 49)

34. Bronze statue of a dancing faun. It is not known how the statue was set up; it was found lying in the atrium. It is one of the finest pieces found in the buried towns. Naples Museum.

(*See page* 13)

that work should be begun on the part of Herculaneum which slopes down towards the sea. In the eighteenth century investigations had been carried on there, but the buildings had been covered in again. The decision now reached was that the former method of carrying on the investigations in Herculaneum, by means of shafts and galleries, should be replaced by a thorough exposure of the houses and the land, so far as such work did not conflict with the life of the village of Resina. This was the beginning of the more extended operation of uncovering Herculaneum, which had been at a standstill for almost sixty-three years and which was now to continue, though with many interruptions, till 1855.

The visits of princes developed into a ceremonial affair; the mere announcement of their coming was enough for the officials carrying on the excavations. It soon became customary for houses to be named after the distinguished visitors in whose presence they were uncovered. Most of them, however, showed little understanding of the splendid discoveries. One exception was the great art lover, Ludwig I of Bavaria, who was travelling in Italy in 1829, accompanied by the Counts of Arco and Seinsheim. He loved the land, its inhabitants, and its treasures as no other German did, and his understanding was brilliant. Afire with eagerness he visited Pompeii, where he stood out among the many other royal guests, whose curious but irrelevant and naive questions were just material for new witticisms. Ludwig of Bavaria showed, in the words of the chief of the excavations, "at every step such exceptional knowledge and enthusiasm for the precious monuments of antiquity as beggars description." Some years had passed since his last visit, and he wanted to see what had been recently brought to light, in particular the baths. In his presence a great many things, such as coins, oil-lamps and jars of all kinds, were discovered in an ancient shop in one of the streets. The King's enthusiasm was so kindled that he wanted to take an axe and a pick and join in the work. "He should be our king", said the architect Carlo Bonucci, "then we should get on very much better."

In his many visits to Italy King Ludwig returned again and again to Pompeii, though it must be admitted that these visits had much to do with the fair Marchioness Florenzi. In his enthusiasm he later had a Pompeian house built in

Aschaffenburg, on the model of the country-house beyond the Gate of Herculaneum; this was to preserve for all time a living example of an ancient Roman house. Francis of Naples had helped his guest in every possible way to increase his delight in the discoveries. But he himself was a sick man, and he died on 8th November, 1830, after a reign of five years. He was succeeded by his son Ferdinand II. The new king, who at first behaved in a more liberal fashion than his father, was less interested in Pompeii and Herculaneum, in spite of the fact that just before he ascended the throne a very promising building was discovered, the house of a wealthy Roman, called after its charming fountain figure the Villa of the Drunken Faun. It was the architect Bonucci who found the splendid building, not far from the temple on the Street of Fortuna. The lovable but unfortunate August von Goethe, son of the poet, was present at the discovery. But he was fated not to see the whole of this splendid building with its painted atrium and charming peristyle, for he died of small-pox in Rome soon afterwards, in October 1830. The drama of the mistress of the house was revealed at the same time. Her skeleton was found, surrounded by treasures which had been hastily gathered together. A sackful of coins, bracelets of heavy gold, ear-rings and rings set with precious stones, lay all around her, and the position of her limbs indicated the terrible death-agony which she had endured.

It was a whole year, however, before, on 24th October, 1831, the wonderful Alexander mosaic was reached, in the loveliest room of the house, showing the great emperor fighting with Darius in the Battle of Issus. Unfortunately one corner of the mosaic had suffered rather badly, but different signs and preparations for improvement showed that the damage had not occurred in the year 79, but earlier, probably in the earth-quake of 63. Even today we can say what August Mau said in 1900 in his well-known book on Pompeii, that this picture as well as the other mosaics in this house, pictures of the fauna of the Nile, of a horse, a crocodile and an ibis, "are far and away the loveliest mosaics preserved from antiquity".[1] The splendid picture of the battle, a mosaic reproduction of a famous picture painted about the third century B.C., and attributed to the Greek master Philoxenos of Eretria, was

[1] August Mau, *Pompeii in Leben und Kunst*, p. 273. Leipzig, 1900.

very large — measuring about fifteen feet by eight feet — and was composed of about one and a half million coloured stones each about two to three millimetres in size.[1] After some months' labour the great mosaic was cut out from the floor, and on 21st August, 1832, was ready to be removed, having first been inspected by the royal pair. At the same time they were shown the mosaic of Mediterranean fishes and sea-creatures. Scientific study of these mosaics was at once arranged. The scholars were long in disagreement about which battle the Alexander mosaic was meant to represent, and it was many decades before there was general agreement that it was Issus. In the garden of the House of the Faun there was found at the same time, in a nest which had been overwhelmed by lapilli, the bones of a dove which had been sitting on its eggs; the tiny skeleton of a chick just about to break from its egg was still recognisable.

The news of the mosaics excited great interest throughout the artistic world. Goethe's opinion was that the discovery was a landmark in the history of our knowledge of classical art, and on 10th March, 1832, he wrote as follows to Professor Zahn, who had sent him a coloured sketch of it: "Neither this time nor times to come will suffice to comment properly on this wonder of art, and after all our explanations and examinations we are forced back on sheer admiration."

Despite this success, which awakened the desire to push on more speedily with the excavations, the need for heavy expenditure weighed so sorely on the progress of the work — the King and Queen having no real interest in the matter — that there was little progress to record. Once again there came a period of dubious and spasmodic treasure-hunting. First, work was carried on at the extreme south-west corner next to the Porta Marina, then in the north on the Street of Tombs, then again near the House of the Faun — in short, quite unmethodically and with very few workers. Only when an important visitor was imminent, as for example on 7th November, 1838, for the young Queen Victoria of England, was something hastily done. Those in charge of the excavations, including the architect Bonucci, strove without success to rouse more interest in their labours. The number of those

[1] Ernst Pfuhl, *Meisterwerke griechischer Zeichnung und Malerei*, p. 59. Munich, 1924.

employed had shrunk pitiably, so that the far-travelled and mocking Prince Pückler-Muskau ironically said, after paying a visit to Pompeii at that time, that he had counted thirty workers, namely fifteen mules and fifteen children.

Years passed and the digging went painfully on. The uneasy years of revolution in 1848 and 1849 were no help, especially as the unrest began in the Kingdom of the Two Sicilies. The reigning monarch had returned to the reactionary ways of his grandfather, and stood immovably for the principles of Metternich, which had now entered their last decline. The Sicilians rose against the suppression of liberal tendencies, and on 28th January, 1848, the King was compelled to grant what he and Metternich so heartily loathed — a constitution for Naples. When rebellions broke out in France, Vienna, Berlin and Upper Italy, and fears of war spread over Europe, it was soon apparent that the measures which had been adopted had all been forced upon the rulers. Ferdinand II of Naples began to fight the rebels; in May 1848 he dissolved the Parliament of Naples, threatened the resisting Sicilians with force of arms, and laid Messina in ruins. In this way he succeeded in suppressing revolt in Sicily.

Meanwhile Pope Pius IX had had to flee from the revolution, and towards the end of 1849 he made his way to Naples, where the King had consolidated his power by persecution of the defeated liberals. It was clear that in such disturbed times the work in Pompeii and Herculaneum was bound to come almost to a complete standstill. Only in October 1849, when the news arrived that the Pope intended to visit the two towns, were a few small excavations in Pompeii hastily prepared, to be exhibited to the Holy Father. And Pope Pius IX appeared on 22nd October, inspected everything with great interest, and, standing on the raised pedestal of the Temple of Jupiter, gave his blessing to the country folk who had streamed in from the neighbourhood into the forum.

When peace returned in 1850 a somewhat better time began for Pompeii, with more than twenty workers; but this was not really of great significance. No real change could be expected so long as there was so little interest among those in power. At this time digging was going on at the Stabian baths, and the Stabian Gate to the south was discovered; but for the rest the old habit was resumed of regarding the town as a place of entertainment for foreign guests and of undertaking some work on the site only when such a visit was imminent. Thus on 12th August, 1851, the brother of the Austrian emperor Francis Joseph, Maximilian, who was later shot in Mexico, was a guest there. He had climbed Vesuvius and inspected the Bourbon museum in Naples. His feelings were mixed: "What has been removed from Pompeii to the glass cases of the Bourbon museum", Maximilian writes in his memoirs,[1] "shows the mere outline of the life once lived there; the spirit has been taken from these things, and they have been prosaically dissected — perhaps from a scientific point of view with perfect justice. . . . Pompeii is charming with its ruins, but also terrible, like painted corpses the little rooms still glitter in their garish colours; the yesterday still clings to the walls which was followed by a night of almost two thousand years till today arrived. The whole effect, however, is more of a desolate, burned-out place than of a careful excavation; and it is certainly not a grand place; moreover, we were all more or less disillusioned. . . . Besides, only one quarter of the town is known. . . . Only two things affected me, the massive stone-built arena and the city of the dead, the Street of Tombs. Though the arena is much smaller than that of Verona and Pola, it has something grand about it: it is a sad ruin, such as I love, grey and stony, with fresh greenery luxuriating in its midst, and surrounded by a truly glorious view, lit in the southern evening by the colours of paradise into a picture of purest longing. The Street of Tombs, as darkness began to fall, made a solemn and spiritual impression without being terrible or uncanny." The arch-duke also discovered that practically nothing was being done in Pompeii; in the last years of the Bourbon rule the work was reduced to insignificance. Even Vesuvius seemed anxious to share in the universal idleness. From 1840 to 1850 it had been slightly active, only at the beginning of February 1850 did it show signs of increased activity. In 1855 the excavations in Herculaneum, which had gone on very slowly and without great results, were again completely abandoned. Since 1828 parts of two house squares, so-called islands, had been laboriously laid bare. The best of these was the completely exposed and well-preserved peristyle of the Casa d'Argo.

[1] *Aus Meinem Leben*, p. 111 ff. Leipzig, 1867.

Once again it was evident how incomparably more expensive and laborious the work of uncovering houses in Herculaneum was than in Pompeii.

One of the triumphs of the Bourbon excavations was the House of the Fuller, brought to light in Herculaneum in 1855, with its two enormous cauldrons with their fuel arranged beneath them and still well preserved. In a vault of the house there was found in a leaden vessel a great quantity of dried-up vermilion paint, such as one sees used on the walls of Pompeii.

The dissatisfaction of the people of Naples led to a plot on 8th December, 1856, against the life of King Ferdinand II, whereby he was severely wounded. He died of the effects three years later, at Caserta, on 22nd May, 1859. He was succeeded by a king whose reign was destined to be short. The events of the year 1859, the war of Napoleon III and the Sardinians against Austria, and the movement for the unification of Italy which was inaugurated by these events and thenceforward advanced irresistibly, drew the Kingdom of the Two Sicilies into their maelstrom. As a consequence of the political events the diggings in Pompeii naturally came to a complete halt.

Meanwhile the bold leader of the free party, Giuseppe Garibaldi, took ship at Genoa with a thousand volunteers, landed on 11th May, 1860, in Sicily, defeated the Bourbon troops, and in a short time had conquered the whole island. The following August he crossed from Sicily to Calabria, in order to bring Naples back into the common united fatherland — with the tacit agreement of the government in Turin. The people, as well as many of the royal troops, enthusiastically joined Garibaldi in his advance. Francis II, along with the remnants of his troops and with his brave wife, Maria, the sister of the Empress Elisabeth of Austria, was forced to withdraw to the naval base of Gaeta, and on 7th September Garibaldi entered Naples. The fortress of Gaeta held out for a time, thanks to the inspiring courage of the Queen, but on 13th February, 1861, the defenders were forced to lay down their arms. The reign of the Bourbons in the Two Sicilies was at an end, and now nothing stood in the way of uniting these lands with the rest of Italy.

During the equipping and arming of Garibaldi's Thousand

a famous French novelist, Alexandre Dumas, had been of great help to the Italian patriot. Dumas was then fifty-eight years of age and had had a rich and adventurous life, both in the literary world and in his other successes and failures. He had placed himself at the disposal of Garibaldi during the campaign as mediator, messenger, and general handyman. When the campaign ended happily and Garibaldi's authority in Naples was for a short time unlimited, he rewarded the writer's loyalty by entrusting him with the conduct of the museum and the excavations. The dictator also gave Dumas the palazzo Chiaramonte to live in. The novelist eagerly set to work at his new task, although he had very little knowledge of archaeological matters. He brooded over the plans of the town, visited the unexplored sites, and planned to invite French scholars in great numbers and to entrust them with the work of excavation. The foreign writer, however, met with great opposition in Naples for those very reasons. Men who were more suitable for the work than he sought to supplant him in his post, and the Neapolitans objected to his living a splendid life at the expense of the city. Matters came to a head in a hostile demonstration before the palazzo Chiaramonte, which made an unforgettable impression upon Dumas. He remained for many years more in Naples, but the delight he had in his position was gone.

His patron, Garibaldi, whose ideas about the unification of Italy did not coincide with those of King Victor Emmanuel II and Cavour, had meanwhile withdrawn to his little native island of Caprera and left the field free for the House of Savoy. The royal liberator of Italy regarded it as his patriotic duty to resume the work which had been so neglected by the Bourbons, and carried it on with increased energy and zeal. He not only gave immediate approval to the payment of a considerable sum of money for the excavations, but he did much more, the best, in fact, that could be done. For he appointed someone to be in charge of the work who was eminently suitable for it. This happy stroke led to the unexpected development and flourishing of the undertaking, and to outstanding improvements both in the technique and the systematisation of the work.

The man who was entrusted by the King with this important task was the thirty-seven-year-old archaeologist and numismatist Giuseppe Fiorelli. He had long been interested in the classical finds in Neapolitan territory, and even before 1848 had from time to time taken a share in the excavations at Pompeii and in describing the coins and other discoveries. In the storms of the revolution of 1848–49 he came under suspicion of liberal tendencies and was accused of political conspiracy by his opponents and imprisoned. He lost his position and on his release from prison found himself penniless. One day the brother of the Bourbon king, the Count of Syracuse, whose sympathies, so far as his position allowed, were liberal and who was a lover of the arts and of the work of excavation, summoned him to his presence. This prince had been told that some ancient bodies, with heads well-preserved, had been found in Cumae. But this was a deliberate fraud which Fiorelli exposed, proving that the faces of the dead bodies had been recently formed from wax. The Count, very pleased to be rescued by Fiorelli from this deceit, talked with him, heard the story of his sufferings, and asked him if he knew where one might undertake other excavations, outside Pompeii, with some hope of success. Fiorelli took him to a site where he had long suspected classical remains might be found; an investigation was put in hand, and many valuable things, tombs and so on, were in fact discovered. The prince took him into his employment as secretary, and there Fiorelli remained until his patron's death. In this position the scholar was protected from political persecution, since the reigning monarch naturally had to preserve his brother's interests. But after the prince's death Fiorelli was again thrown on the world without a penny and was unable to find a new post, since he was not *persona grata* with Francis II. When Garibaldi made an end of the Bourbon power and Dumas had also resigned from his position as leader of the excavations, which in any case no one had taken quite seriously, King Victor Emmanuel put Fiorelli in charge. He was made Professor of Archaeology in the University of Naples, and director of works at Pompeii and Herculaneum. He was now able to turn his mastery of the excavations to good account. During his imprisonment he had begun a history of the discoveries in Pompeii,[1] which is still the main

[1] Giuseppe Fiorelli, *Pompeianarum Antiquitatum Historia*. Naples, 1860.

source for the exact illustration and description of the diggings.

On 20th December, 1860, Fiorelli took up his duties, and by 7th January, 1861, no fewer than 512 workers were employed. In September of the same year a new lessee's contract was made. From 1861 onwards Fiorelli published a *Journal of the Excavations of Pompeii*,[1] which was much more sensible and fully edited than the previous journal and was no longer confined to descriptions of royal visits and lists of the discoveries. The most important improvements introduced by Fiorelli, however, concerned the method of digging. Till then the practice had been to lay bare a house here and there, then the next house a little further on, while the intervening area was untouched. The mounds of earth and lapilli were moved to one side and there heaped up, and any visit to the uncovered sites involved laborious clambering over these heaps. The newly uncovered walls, pillars and paintings which were thus suddenly exposed to the weather were also in great danger.

Fiorelli's first action was to clear away the masses of rubble and lapilli, to protect the uncovered buildings by means of roofs from the sun and the rain, and to restore the connections between the individual houses and temples. Only when these things were done did he proceed to further excavations, but he went about this too in his own way. From the parts of the streets which had already been laid bare he decided on their probable course underground, and marked this on his map. Then he did not first excavate the street, as had been the custom, and then proceed, from below, to work on the houses to right and left — a method which led to the danger of the houses collapsing — but he worked from above, from the roofs of the houses. A tiny railway removed the rubble immediately. It was Fiorelli too who divided the town into regions and blocks, so-called islands, giving the houses numbers. In this way a simpler and more systematic understanding of the work was made possible. He was also the first to leave the paintings where they were, at the same time protecting them from exposure to the light, the air and the weather. When the most necessary steps had been taken to these ends, further excavations were begun. But now the work was no longer

[1] *Giornale degli scavi di Pompei*. Naples, 1861, 1862, 1865.

directed to districts which promised specially rich finds, but, the western part being almost wholly uncovered, the work was carried methodically towards the east.

An interesting discovery of this time was the lupanar, or brothel, in a little street in the centre of Pompeii, whose purpose was unmistakable from the cells with their stone supports for beds, and from the indecent pictures which adorned the walls. Unashamedly outspoken writings on the walls praised the erotic qualities of certain men and of women, often described by their first names alone. In this house there was also found a basket with carbonised beans and onions. Immediately this dubious place was discovered it was arranged that only a minimum of visitors should have access to it.

About the same time a completely intact bakery was brought to light on a street leading to the Temple of Jupiter.[1] Fiorelli himself was present at the excavation. He personally took no fewer than eighty-one rolls out of a sealed and almost air-tight oven, into which not a particle of ash or lapilli had penetrated. Their form was perfectly preserved, though they were quite black and hard as stone. Without a doubt they were put into the oven on that unhappy day in the year 79; they had the characteristic round shape of Roman loaves, which usually weighed about a pound. The loaves were divided into eight sections. To this day the bread in Naples has almost precisely the same shape.

In this way new insight into the life and customs of the ancient Romans was obtained. Every sign was now carefully studied for what it could yield of exact information. Fiorelli was careful to see that every step was taken with intelligent foresight. The abilities of the man appointed by King Victor Emmanuel II, the wise and fortunate ruler of the new Italy, were soon recognised in Pompeii in each and every one of his undertakings.

One day in 1864 digging was going on near the Stabian baths when the workers suddenly found, in a narrow little side-street leading from the baths to the forum, a cellar in which there seemed to be a skeleton. Fiorelli, who feared that the workers might carelessly destroy something important or beautiful, had given instructions that on the first signs of

[1] Strada degli Augustali, Regio VII, Island I, No. 36.

anything unusual the digging should be stopped and he should be informed, and the work resumed only in his presence. This was what happened on this occasion. Fiorelli hastened to the place, inspected the hole in the ground and had it sufficiently enlarged to obtain a better view. When the head of the skeleton came into view he thought of filling the cavity in which it lay with plaster of Paris. This was done, and only when it had hardened was the cellar opened from above. In this way moulds of four human figures were obtained; the position of their limbs, and even the expression on their faces were reflected with remarkable faithfulness. Here was pictured their horror as the ashes poured round them and buried them. Four plaster casts were obtained of the actual skeletons, two of them apparently a mother and daughter of gentle birth, for their limbs were delicate and fine. Beside the older woman there were three pairs of gold ear-rings, more than a hundred silver coins, and two iron keys. On the bones of her hand she still wore two silver rings; one arm was broken, the other was raised to her head as though to ward off a blow. Behind her lay her daughter, fourteen years of age, her head resting on her arms. Not far away was the body of a third woman of simpler origin, indicated by the iron ring she was wearing on one finger. Still farther behind lay a huge man, also with an iron ring on his finger and with sandals on his feet which were still clearly recognisable.

Through Fiorelli's happy idea, which has been used many times since then, a moving picture of the terrible misfortune was obtained. This was made possible by the fact that the ashes which buried the bodies solidified while the bodies were still intact. They preserved the outlines of the body, which then of course broke up and decayed, leaving only the skeleton inside the solid mould which had arisen in this most natural way. The photograph shows the casts of the young girl and the older woman, which may be seen today in the small museum in Pompeii. The little side-street in which these bodies had been found and then "reshaped" came to be called the *vicolo degli scheletri*. They were practically death masks, with this difference, that not merely the head but the whole body of those who were suffocated and sank down in the ashes had been reproduced. This can of course only happen with those who perished in the damp ashes; of those who sank down into the heaps of lapilli or were suffocated in cellars only the white bones remained.

In 1869 King Victor Emmanuel honoured the excavations at Pompeii with a visit, and Fiorelli was his guide. He was so satisfied and interested with all he saw that in addition to the grants made for the furthering of the excavations he made a personal contribution of 30,000 lire. Fiorelli made use of this opportunity to ask that Herculaneum might also be taken again into the sphere of operations. The King gave his consent and issued the necessary instructions for work to be begun on two more house blocks or "islands" in Herculaneum, and especially to the south of the baths. In 1875, however, the work there had once more to cease, for many houses in Resina threatened to collapse, and the owners of the properties were bitterly opposed to the excavations which involved the destruction of their fields, their trees and meadows. Moreover, results had not been up to expectation.

This new pause coincided with the departure of Fiorelli, who was called in that year to Rome as general director of all museums and excavations. This was a heavy blow to the work on the two towns; but it was lightened by the fact that his successors in office, first Michele Ruggiero and later Giulio de Petra, were his loyal and learned pupils, who maintained the meaning and spirit of his work.

On 3rd July, 1875, there was another interesting discovery. Till this time no writings apart from those on walls and houses had been found in Pompeii. Whereas papyrus rolls had been preserved in carbonised form in Herculaneum, they had been completely destroyed in Pompeii by the ashes and lapilli. So all hope had long been abandoned of finding anything of this nature in Pompeii. Then suddenly, in the house of Lucius Caecilius Iucundus, in an iron-bound broken-down chest there were found the well-known wooden tablets, as described by Pliny, the inside coated with fine wax on which writing was impressed with a metal pen. They had been protected by the way in which they had been stored, and had escaped the fate of other wooden articles in Pompeii; though quite carbonised, they were in all other respects well preserved. The seals were still easily recognisable, and some of the wax was still there. Since the impression on the wax had penetrated to the wood, it was possible to decipher 127 of the 132 tablets. They were mostly receipts given by Iucundus — who conducted all manner of business and could be described as the "Jewish man of business" of the great Pompeian families — in A.D. 55–60. They all bore the signatures of witnesses, often of relations of those people who had held official positions in the last years of Pompeii. This was a find which stirred the learned world to great enthusiasm and a renewal of the hope that in Pompeii, as once in Herculaneum, well-preserved papyrus rolls could be found — a hope which has, indeed, so far not been fulfilled. For since that time only individual small finds of waxen tablets have come to light in Pompeii.

In the time that had passed since their discovery great efforts had been made to unroll and decipher the rolls discovered in the Villa of the Papyri. This was a laborious undertaking without much success. Other governments and learned academies endeavoured to give their help. Thus in the time of the Bourbon rule the Prince of Wales, as he then was, later King George IV, had requested permission to have some of the papyri unrolled and copied at his own expense. He sent a certain Hayter to Naples, who in the years from 1802 to 1806 unrolled with more or less success about two hundred rolls, copying ninety-six and taking them to Oxford, where parts of them were published.

The French rule which followed put an end to this English effort in Naples. Later the restored Bourbon government made over more papyri to England as well as to France for further work on them, and these had varying fates. In England, for example, a certain Sickler offered his services in opening the rolls in a new way. In 1819 a commission was set up, before whom he was to demonstrate his abilities; in the course of this demonstration the man completely destroyed seven papyri and would have spoilt them all if the commission had not called a halt to the proceedings. By 1879 only 341 papyri in all had been unrolled, only eighteen of which were in Latin.[1] All the rest were in Greek, and many works of Epicurus were given identically in several rolls. Here too the new circumstances in united Italy had their effect, and in course of time a special department was set up under the guidance of the Naples museum to study the papyri.

[1] *Herculanensium voluminum quae supersunt collectio altera* 1862 *to* 1876. Of the 341 opened papyri 195 had been published up to that time.

This department, now under the National Library in Naples, continues to this day with this infinitely difficult and hitherto rather thankless task. Nevertheless the hope persists that more valuable papyrus rolls will be discovered, particularly in the still unexplored parts of Herculaneum. The future will show whether this hope is justified.

The main purpose of the excavations, of course, was to lay bare the two towns, of which a great part still lay unexplored, and this was the end to which all labours and manpower and money were directed. As we know, however, Vesuvius had since A.D. 79 buried not only those two towns but also other villages, as well as innumerable houses scattered through the countryside. One day, when a certain Signore Pulzella was laying the foundation of a wall in the fields near the village of Boscoreale, which was to mark the boundary of his land towards the road, he found traces of ancient buildings, and a great number of large wine-jars and oil-jars. When Fiorelli heard of this in Rome he at once concluded that it was a Roman country-house, where grapes were pressed. A few workers from Pompeii were immediately sent to the place to begin orderly excavations. And soon they had exposed a room with a mosaic floor, an ancient Roman kitchen and a stable. But that was as far as they could advance on Pulzella's small property, and further work meant entering the vineyard of his neighbour, an old clergyman called Angelo Andrea de Prisco. But he opposed any "devastation" of his property, so that at the end of 1876 the work there had to cease. No one had any notion of what further excavations there would one day bring to light.

In 1879 a ceremony was held in remembrance of the misfortune which had destroyed flourishing towns and villages and brought great suffering on the people 1,800 years before — but which had also so faithfully preserved for posterity the irreplaceable monuments of Roman life and Graeco-Roman culture. In that year Giulio de Petra, the head of the excavations, collaborated with Domenico Comparetti to publish a valuable memorial volume with interesting essays.[1]

In the following years, when work at Herculaneum had completely ceased, all efforts and resources were concentrated

[1] Giulio de Petra and Domenico Comparetti, *Pompeji e la regione sotterrata dal Vesuvio vel 79*, 1879.

on laying bare more of Pompeii. The technique of the excavations was continually improved, the work was more careful and scientific, and the earth which was cleared away was sifted. This method had great advantages, but of course it did not advance very quickly, and it cost a great deal of money. Nevertheless, progress was steady, and new evidence was obtained for our knowledge of the last sad hours of the people of Pompeii. Thus in 1880–81 there were found, south of the town and towards the sea — perhaps at the former mouth of the River Sarno, whose course has since altered — the skeletons of countless fugitives and a great quantity of valuable gold objects. In Pompeii itself house after house and street after street were brought to light, which we have no space to detail here, but of which the many guide-books, among them the most recent, that of Professor Maiuri, give precise descriptions. When a specially beautiful house was found, as, for instance, in 1896, that of the Vettii in the Street of Mercury, the news of it travelled round the world, always rousing great interest and stirring even private individuals to make large donations of money.

In that house of the Vettii there lived two brothers, well-to-do merchants who did business in many things, but chiefly in wine. On the amphoras found in the house the names of the consuls were clearly marked, thus giving us the vintage year and the number of amphoras filled from each harvest. In the kitchen of this house the ashes of the fuel were found and pots on tripods containing the bones of the meat prepared for a meal more than 1,800 years before. The peristyle and the garden were charming, the many little statues and the friezes of Cupid and of dwarfs, made by no ordinary man but by a genuine artist, were delightful. They are a visual lesson in Roman culture: for example, there is a representation of the production of perfume, from the flower to its use by the fair ladies of Rome. In another picture dwarfs are working as goldsmiths and jewellers, along with their elegant clients, who are seen displaying the wares conceitedly on their arms and then taking fright at the high prices. In modern times the house of the Vettii has been almost completely restored, and is today one of the finest sights in Pompeii. A little room with specially daring frescoes and a marble statue of Priapus seems to have been a private room dedicated to love. The money-chests bound with iron and bronze stand in the same place as they did of old; in the garden the same flowers and shrubs (known from various carbonised remains) which adorned it 1,800 years ago are blossoming again, and the water wells out from the ancient lead-pipes for the garden and its fountains.

Thus year after year passed in slow but deliberate work on Pompeii. The old abbot, the owner of the land at Boscoreale, died. On 10th September, 1894, his much more intelligent heir began further excavations, which were conducted in the most exemplary manner. A great country-house was uncovered, containing dwelling-rooms, baths, rooms for the making and storing of wine and olive-oil, as well as a yard for the pressing of the fruit. This house had belonged to Lucius Herennius Florus, who had lived in luxury on the fruits of his wine business. A seal found in the rubble gave us his name.

The excavators had found a house whose fittings and furnishings were completely unimpaired. Everything had been in its place, untouched for more than 1,800 years. Bronze baths resting on lions' heads came to light, as though ready for immediate use. In one great chest there were discovered no fewer than fifty keys, as well as some silver vessels. In the kitchen the dog was still attached to its chain, in the stables were the skeletons of several horses, most of them still tied up, only one of them having succeeded in wrenching free. In the yard for the wine-press the first three dead were discovered, one of them a woman with wonderful ear-rings of gold and topaz, who was perhaps the mistress of the house. From the way in which everything lay, it was possible to construct a vivid picture of the last moments.

The chief find in this villa, however, took place at Easter, on 13th April, 1895.[1] The workers were to have some days' holiday, and only a few were kept back in order to clean the two shafts of the wine-press. A man called Michele climbed down into the narrow space. He quickly returned, saying that there were poisonous fumes. Consequently no one wanted to go down, and the foreman abandoned the cleaning of the shafts. Everyone left the site except Michele. He lingered

---

[1] See Antoine Baron Héron de Villefosse, *L'argenterie et les bijoux d'or du trésor de Boscoreale*, Paris, 1903, and August Mau, "Ausgrabungen von Boscoreale", *Römische Mitteilungen*, XI, 1896.

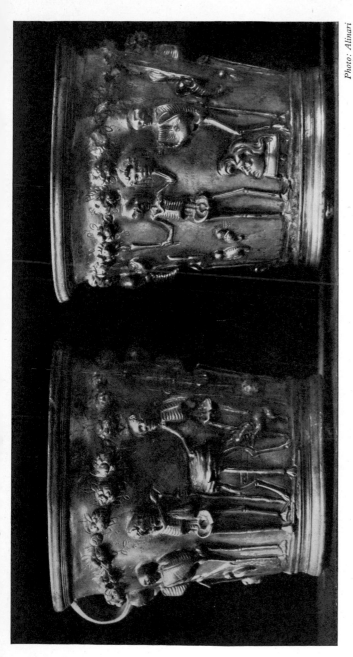

Photo: Alinari

35. Silver flagons, the 'skeleton' jugs, from the Villa of Boscoreale, midway between Pompeii and Vesuvius. The Greek inscription warns us to enjoy life while we have time and are not yet skeletons.

(*See page* 198)

Photo: Exclusive News Agency, Ltd.

36. A tavern open to the street, where cold and hot drinks and food were served. The airtight bronze kettle in the foreground, right, contained some liquid from the year A.D. 79 which had not wholly solidified. Names of girls

behind, went to the owner of the house and said: "Sir, I found the wine-vat quite empty; there was just one dead man in it, and round about him the most wonderful silver vessels, bracelets, ear-rings and rings, a double necklace of heavy gold, and a sackful of countless gold coins."

The owner pledged the man to secrecy and made him stay the night. When it was quite dark they climbed down into the wine-vat, armed with lanterns and baskets, and their eyes nearly started from their heads when they saw the treasures spread out round the skeleton, which was crouched face downwards on its hands and knees. Besides innumerable beautifully wrought silver vessels there was a leather bag with the name on it still recognisable, with no less than a thousand gold coins in an unbroken series from Augustus to Domitian, the latest being of A.D. 76. Among these coins were some from the reigns of the Emperors Galba, Otho and Vitellius, which are among the rarest of all Roman coins, since these three men all reigned within one year, each for only a few months. The coins of Augustus and Tiberius were much worn, but the 575 coins of Nero were very well preserved. Some of them looked so new that they might just have come fresh from the mint. The gold was flawless, while the silver was somewhat blackened and tarnished.

The lucky finders hid the treasures away in all secrecy. They planned to turn their find to account by circumventing the ban on the export of finds such as these. Michele was rewarded, however, receiving a heavy bribe as the price of his silence; but he proceeded at once to the public-house and got drunk. The wine loosened his tongue and he began to boast of the discovery. The news spread through the district like wildfire and reached the ears of the authorities, who at once instituted an investigation. The treasures, however, had already safely passed the frontiers: 117 silver articles and the bag with the coins were in Paris by May 1895, where they were offered to the Louvre. The sellers asked for half a million francs, but the museum wanted to pay only half that amount, in five annual payments. So the negotiations were broken off. The articles were then offered to Count Edmond von Rothschild, who bought them, and keeping back only a little for his own collection gave 109 of the silver vessels and all the coins to the Louvre.

14   197

Among the silver vessels found in Boscoreale there are two of especial interest, so-called skeleton flagons, whose representations of mortality are meant as an exhortation to enjoy life while there is time. On the one flagon the dramatist Sophocles, the Platonic philosopher and tragic poet Moschion, and the Epicurean Zeno are depicted, and on the other the skeletons of Euripides, Menander and the cynic Monimos. These represent poetry, music and philosophy, while the other skeletons on the vase represent mankind in general. Moschion and Menander, who unveiled the mysteries of love, are holding female masks signifying the heroines of their poems. Inscriptions in dotted Greek letters describe the individual figures. The whole composition presents the Epicurean view of life of the Alexandrian and Hellenistic age. "Enjoy, while you are alive", runs one inscription in Greek, "for tomorrow is uncertain. Life is a show, enjoyment is the chief good, lust the best treasure, be merry while you are alive." So the skeletons on the silver flagons, intended to contain rare wines, bring death to the notice of the happy guests at table, and say to them: "Look at these sad bones; drink and enjoy yourself as long as you can, for you will look like them one day, when you are dead."

The sale of the treasures, including these remarkable vessels, had a sequel in the Italian parliament; but the pieces were now abroad and in the possession of a third party, so that nothing could be done about it. In 1900, in the neighbourhood of Boscoreale, another villa was discovered, containing fine pictures of the second style, among them the portrait of a seated woman playing the lute, while in the background, behind her chair, a young girl is listening to her playing. It is perhaps the portrait of the owner of the house and is one of the loveliest frescoes that has ever been uncovered in that district.

The news of the splendid finds in Boscoreale had again roused universal interest in the excavations of the buried towns. Royal visitors and other distinguished strangers streamed into the land. The Empress Elisabeth of Austria came repeatedly in the course of her Mediterranean journeys, always visiting the museum at Naples and at Pompeii. She was so delighted with the bronzes of the two athletes in combat, which had been found in the Villa of the Papyri in

Herculaneum, that she had casts made in 1896, which she put on the terrace of her wonderful villa in Corfu.

There was general regret throughout the cultured world that there were not enough means at the disposal of the excavators to hasten the progress of their work and to uncover Pompeii and Herculaneum at least in a comparatively short time. So the idea of international co-operation began to take root in the first years of the new century. An English archaeologist, Dr Charles Waldstein, took up this idea and made an effort to realise it. He prepared a great plan for the technical as well as the financial execution of the whole task of excavation. His first plan was to uncover Herculaneum alone — but undoubtedly with the ulterior thought that once a beginning was made there the plans could be enlarged to include Pompeii. He wanted to arrange for a little army of archaeologists, technicians, and labourers, who could resurrect Herculaneum in the briefest possible time — supported in their work by contributions from the wealthiest men in the world. But the project was not begun very tactfully. Obviously, certain sensibilities had to be watched, and as a matter of course the Italian monarch and the Italian government had to remain at the head of the whole undertaking.

At the beginning all doors in Rome were opened, there was in fact real enthusiasm for the affair, and the busy Waldstein travelled to the United States in order to interest wealthy patrons there. He planned to go to Pierpont Morgan and ask him to take an active share in the matter. Two days before he landed a New York evening paper published a telegram from Rome, which officially stated that the Englishman had no authority to handle the matter. It was further asserted that the Italian government was against the plan. The sudden change in Rome was to be traced to unfortunate gossip among newspaper men to the effect that Waldstein had offered the presidency of the international society for the excavation of Herculaneum to the President of the United States, Theodore Roosevelt, and that he was inclined to accept. Now the presidency would naturally fall to the King of Italy, and in fact no one had seriously considered any other possibility. The plan, however, was in this way turned into a question of national honour: the excavations were regarded as a matter of Italian prestige, and it was decided that they should be carried on independently at Italian cost, even with the risk of their taking longer than they would with international support. This decision was a good one, for only in this way was it possible for the conduct of the excavations to remain exclusively in the hands of those learned and experienced Italians who had given, and still give, their whole life in the service of the work.

Meanwhile the activity of Vesuvius had varied, though it had been more or less active for a long time. Its shape was continually altering. At the turn of the century and in the first years of the twentieth century there were several violent eruptions from the crater. In 1905 the peak was about 4,000 feet high,[1] the highest recorded. In April 1906 there was another violent eruption. On the eighth day of the month a pillar of cloud and smoke rose to what was said to be a height of 40,000 feet, rising up as though from an exploding kettle with a great roaring. Enormous quantities of gases were hurled forth, followed by grey and white ashes. Great masses of erupted material were thrown into the air, and Vesuvius lost 300 feet in height. Heavy damage was caused in several places, such as Ottaiano. The funicular railway constructed by Thomas Cook & Sons, along with its stations, had disappeared from the face of the earth. (In 1841 in Bourbon times an observatory had been established at the same point.) From that time the mountain has remained active. It daily and hourly pushes out clouds of smoke, now more, now less, mixed with stones, and in the heart of the mountain the masses of lava rise up to the mouth of the crater, spilling over the edge and flowing over the immediate neighbourhood, which has become quite bare. The presence of this safety-valve very likely postpones violent eruptions, but does not mean that they are not still to be reckoned with.

In the uncovering of Pompeii, besides the professional Italian participants, German scholars have played a great part and have won great credit. In Fiorelli's time J. Overbeck worked very closely with him and set down the results of his studies in his famous book on Pompeii, which appeared in 1875.[2] Later August Mau gave his whole life, until the turn

[1] Alfano and Friedlaender, *op. cit.*, p. 61 f.
[2] *Pompeji in seinen Gebäuden, Altertümern und Kunstwerken.* Leipzig, 1875.

of the century, to the service of the excavations, and in close co-operation with the German Archaeological Academy in Rome, which supported him loyally, he achieved great successes. He too has given us an unforgettable memorial of himself and his work in his book, *Pompeii in Life and Art*.

With the increasing precision of scientific knowledge of the life and activities of the ancient Romans and of the appearance and style of their houses and temples, the desire also increased to enter by an effort of the imagination into the spirit of that time when all the buildings, the temples and villas which today lie in sad ruins, towered in proud splendour to heaven. The archaeological findings can give solid support to this exercise of the imagination, although there is always the danger that it may go beyond scientific conjecture, conjuring up more before the mind's eye than was ever there in reality. This was what happened in the case of C. Weichardt, another German with a passion for classical antiquity, who in his book *Pompeii before its Destruction* tried to represent the town as it once was. With the qualification just made, the book is nevertheless a thoroughly serviceable work, contributing no little to the general understanding and the total picture of the town. The Italian Aloisius Fischetti undertook a similar task, reproducing, side by side with his experimental restorations, pictures of the ruins as they are today.

The method of excavation was greatly improved in the years before the First World War. A. Sogliano, that indefatigable scholar, who is still at work on the problems of Pompeian history, was head of the operations from 1905 to 1910.[1] Under him and Spinazzola, who conducted the excavations for twelve years up to 1924, His Excellency Professor Amedeo Maiuri, the present leader of the work, won his spurs. This man and his team of fellow-workers slowly developed a quite novel procedure by giving a genuine impression not only of the contents of the houses which were exposed, but also of their former outward appearance. Each part of a broken-down or damaged building is restored in the very place where it once stood. The frescoes on the walls and the mosaics on the floors are left where they are, with appropriate

---

[1] In his latest work, *Pompei nel suo sviluppo storico. Pompei Preromana* — 80 *av. Chr* (Rome, 1937) he specially defends the much disputed theory of the Etruscan rule of Pompeii.

measures for their protection; and likewise those artistic and household objects which are characteristic of the life and activity in the house concerned. The aim is to give the illusion that the people are still living there, in every building and every shop, as though the customers were coming with their silver coins of Nero's reign to buy bread at the baker's or in winter to take a warm drink at the inn.

In the years just before and after the First World War, work was being carried on in the Street of Abundance — that other great street which runs through Pompeii from west to east, from the forum to the Porta Urbulana — in the district east of the great road from north to south, the Stabian Way. A *thermopolium* opened on to the street, with bronze vessels let into the counter containing warm and cold drinks for the Pompeians, who could take quick refreshment as they passed by. The bronze containers are still there, the lantern is hanging above them, and on the table lies the money paid by the last customer. It was even said that some ancient liquid was found in the sealed, airtight bronze vessel. Outside, on the wall of the *thermopolium*, bright-coloured frescoes of gods and elephants and the like, indicating the name of the business, were intended to attract the customers. The same purpose was served by inscriptions giving the names of the barmaids, whose favours could perhaps be enjoyed in the upper storey of the inn.

On the outbreak of the world war in July 1914 Italy was at first neutral. The excavations in the Street of Abundance could therefore be continued, and these yielded among other things a very well-preserved fuller's works, with a press for clothes and the tank for washing the cloth. The kitchen in particular, with much household equipment, and the closet, were quite undamaged and well preserved; this latter was, as in almost all houses in Pompeii, placed in remarkable and distasteful proximity to the kitchen. At that time, too, the workshop of a bronze-caster called Verus was unearthed; he lit his house by means of a great bronze lamp in the shape of a phallus. In his house there was also found an instrument for land surveying, first recognised for what it was by professors Matteo della Corte and L. Jacono. By adding new parts of wood they have completely restored it.

Not far off from this house was one built above a great

vault, a so-called *cryptoporticus*. This subterranean place was decorated with many frescoes, scenes from the Trojan war; but these were seriously damaged. It was that underground crypt into which many people of the house had fled, leaving it only when they were threatened with suffocation, and attempting to escape across the garden. But there fate had overtaken them. The excavating party were deeply moved when they looked at the eight victims, whom they found lying there with every sign of torment and anguish upon them, in cramped positions, huddled together as though seeking help from one another. Plaster casts were taken of some of these, especially of an elderly woman and a girl, who in her despair had pressed her head to the body of her older companion, perhaps her mother.

In general, however, the excavations slowed down as the political tension increased; and they practically came to a stop when Italy entered the war in May 1915. All that could be done was to preserve what had been laid bare, and to do a little work on the Street of Abundance. Circumstances did not alter much after the war had ended favourably for Italy. The inevitable social and economic convulsions in the post-war years were experienced by Italy as they were by the other belligerents. Activity in the excavations was therefore limited despite all the efforts made by the royal family, especially by the King, with his knowledge of coins, and through the enthusiasm of the Crown Prince, who possesses the happiest understanding of everything historical.

In 1919 the old soldiers' alliance, the *Fascio di combatti-mento*, founded by the thirty-six-year-old Benito Mussolini, appeared on the scene. The duce marched his Blackshirts from Naples to Rome, attained power, and in 1925 reached the head of the government. A renewal of national, political and economic vigour in Italy followed, and this gave fresh impulse to the excavations. Some fortunate finds quickened the general interest. In particular there was discovered the bronze statue of an Ephebus, which Cornelius Tegete had tried to save at the time of catastrophe by taking it from his garden into his house. This splendid piece was rescued undamaged from the lapilli. The remnants of the protecting cloth which Tegete had thrown over it were still clinging to it. In the same building were discovered four grotesques of an old cake-seller, obscene and repulsive nudes, yet incredibly realistic works of art. One can almost hear how the old man became quite hoarse with crying out his wares, and see how his whole body gradually became decrepit and ugly under the constant strain of his existence. In comparison with some noble ideal figure from the heyday of Greek art this is a repulsive work, but magnificent evidence of the versatility of classical artists.

Two years later Professor Maiuri laid bare a house which is now called after the large fresco of the comic poet Menander which was found there.[1] This was the richly furnished home of some outstanding person, who had exceptional good taste and culture in literature and the plastic arts, as can be clearly seen from the frescoes in the house. In one room, obviously the library, the wooden shelves and the rolls of papyri had not merely been carbonised, as in Herculaneum, but had unfortunately quite disappeared.

The owner does not appear to have been at home at the time of the catastrophe, although the faithful housekeeper had at the last moment lowered a chest containing precious silver plate into a subterranean cellar, and thus made it safe. One evening Professor Maiuri, who had been present at the excavation, was about to go home when calling and crying were heard from a ten-year-old lad who had crept through a small hole into an underground room. There he saw a dilapidated iron-bound box, and he called to be pulled up again, when he excitedly told what he had seen. Professor Maiuri at once had the hole enlarged sufficiently for him to squeeze his way through. Then he let himself down, or rather he fell, into the underground room. In the old chest which was discovered in this way there were countless pieces of ancient Roman silver plate, most of which had been quite new at the time of the catastrophe in A.D. 79. Some of these pieces, of pure Hellenic style, however, showed signs of wear and tear which must have occurred before the year of misfortune. There is today no doubt that these precious articles had been imported from Greece, even then possessing value as antiques, and are lovely relics of ancient Greek craftsmanship. In the House of Menander the skeletons of the dead were found in the places

[1] See his splendid publication, *La casa del Menandro e il suo tesoro di argentaria*. Pompeii, 1932. ("The House of Menander and its Silver Treasure.")

where they had sunk down as the house was overwhelmed. Huddled together and entangled with one another, they lay round the great cylindrical bronze lamp which had fallen from the hand of the slave who carried it.

Until 1927 all efforts were concentrated in Pompeii, but the new directors were anxious to carry on the work in Herculaneum. This desire was thoroughly appreciated by Mussolini, the patron of all classical treasures in his beautiful land. In May 1927 the Italian Government gave instructions that the diggings in Herculaneum should be resumed, and provided fresh resources for this purpose. The first task was to continue the work to the south of the houses of Resina, that is, from the extreme southern boundary of the ancient town as far as the probable region of the forum. Further work in this direction, however, is hindered by the town of Resina, with its 30,000 inhabitants and its thickly clustered houses. When this limit is reached, the plan is to investigate the southern, western and eastern suburbs of Herculaneum, or rather, the neighbouring countryside, which is known to be strewn with many ancient villas.

Hopes were quickened when one such country-house was discovered, the magnificent House of the Mysteries, situated towards Vesuvius, beyond the Street of Tombs.[1] It was at the beginning of April 1909 that a hotel keeper called Aurelio Item learned that there were traces of ancient walls in the district, and received permission from the Government to undertake excavations at his own expense. This was the start of the work which led to the unearthing of that fine villa with its unsurpassed frescoes. Whereas the depth of the lapilli, ashes and earth which had accumulated on the classical sites in Pompeii was somewhat over fifteen feet, the House of the Mysteries lay beneath twenty-four feet, the layer of lapilli being especially thick. The house lay beside a rise in the ground, against which the little pebbles had been heaped up to this height. When the first rooms were laid bare, and the underground room, the *cryptoporticus*, which was quite free of lapilli, was reached, the diggings had to be temporarily suspended, for in this room lurked the same poisonous gases which had killed the fugitives who sought refuge there about 1,850 years before.

[1] See Maiuri's *La villa dei misteri*. Rome, 1931.

The frescoes in the salon were as splendid as though they had been finished the day before. They depicted the secret ceremonies of the initiation of a woman into the Dionysian sect. Perhaps they represent the consecration of the former mistress of this wonderful house, so that the novice who plays the chief part in the pictures may be the mistress herself. The scenes which are depicted reach their climax in the uncovering of the symbol of the male generative power before the maiden who is being initiated. The precise significance of the pictures has been much discussed, but opinions are very different, and the last word about the matter has not yet been spoken. We are confronted by an original late Hellenistic work, painted about the middle of the first century B.C., a proof of the extent to which the Roman world was hellenised in art as well as in religion.

At the time of the catastrophe great changes were being made in the villa. A statue of the Empress Livia was being set up, and it is still leaning against a wall. The workers never finished their task, and the few people living in the house at the time, who did not take to flight, all perished. The cast taken of the porter's form is very moving, showing how he sinks to the ground, suffocated, true to the last in the fulfilment of his duty to guard the house.

Along with such outstanding finds there were also small isolated finds, which are no less interesting, for they often illuminate important questions in a striking way or, it may be, throw up new problems. One find of this kind took place in October 1938 in a building next to the lovely house that showed examples of all four styles of frescoes. In the corner of one room there was found the impression in the ashes of a wooden chest which had once stood there, but in the course of time had completely decayed and disappeared. Professor Maiuri had given orders that the immediate surroundings of such an impression should be sifted, since things were often to be found which had formerly been kept in the chest. In such boxes — as in our glass show-cases — the most valuable and the prettiest of the small articles of the house were gathered. So it happened in this case, and among other things there was found an ivory statue of the Indian Venus,[1] which

[1] Maiuri, "Statuetta eburnea di arte indiana a Pompei", *Le arti*, anno I, fasc. II. Florence, 1939.

had broken into several pieces which could easily be restored; it is in the form of a fat woman with great breasts and spreading rear, all in all a picture of superfluous and provocative fleshliness. It was a classical reproduction of Laksmis, the oriental goddess of beauty, mistress of happiness and wife of the god Vischnu; and the statue was found in that town of lower Italy whose great patron goddess was Venus, related to this Laksmis. This is the first occasion on which anything of the kind has been dug up on the coasts of the Mediterranean, and in its age too it is a unique piece, for Indian ivory art has hitherto been known only in a few very defective pieces of the late Middle Ages. This discovery also permits the conclusion that the classical Roman world traded across the Red Sea and through the Persian Gulf as far as India, thanks to the efforts of Tiberius and Nero.

If this find allows of a clear and indisputable conclusion, another was much more adapted to stirring up a lively difference of opinion. Professor della Corte, that indefatigable worker, who has discussed important Pompeian finds and questions in the *Notizie degli scavi* as well as in innumerable other writings,[1] noticed during the work on the uncovering of the *palaestra*, or gymnastic hall next to the amphitheatre, the following inscription in white stucco on one of the pillars:

```
R   O   T   A   S
O   P   E   R   A
T   E   N   E   T
A   R   E   P   O
S   A   T   O   R
```

At first no one knew what the words could mean, for the four words which were in Latin seemed to yield no meaning, while "AREPO" is not to be found in any dictionary. The remarkable thing is that these twenty-five letters always give the same five words, no matter from which side they are read,

[1] See a list of his works, "Studi e publicazioni del Dr M. Della Corte dal 1908 *al* 1933." *Indice generale*. Pompei, 1933.

and that if the word "TENET" is framed, as shown, a clear Christian cross is obtained.

The words have been variously interpreted, one interpretation being that the unknown writer wanted to warn men that God (Sator), that is, the sower and creator, holds their actions (opera) as well as the movements of the stars (rotas) in his hand. The word "arepo" remains, it is true, unexplained. Matteo della Corte and Felix Grosser pointed out that the letters could also be arranged in such a way that the first words of the Lord's prayer, the Pater Noster, appear in the form of a cross. Della Corte concluded from this that the anagram is a secret sign of the Christians, proving the presence of Christian adherents in Pompeii.

In recent times Ludwig Diehl has maintained, as against many other interpretations, the attractive view that the riddle is to be read "in the way the Plough turns, which is much used in the most ancient writings, especially the German Runic writings." That is, one has to read the first line from right to left, the second from left to right, and the third again from right to left. This would yield: "Sator opera tenet; tenet opera sator": "The sower holds the works (in his hand), the works holds (in his hand) the sower." Only the sense is not quite satisfactory.

In 1939 an indentation in the form of a cross was found in the first storey of a house in Herculaneum, impressed in the stucco of a wall. It was all the more interesting in that the earliest crosses hitherto known, which are in the catacombs, go back only to the second or third century, while those of Herculaneum and Pompeii are dated, of course, before the year 79. It is not impossible that there were Christians by that time in Pompeii; a Jewish community was certainly in existence there. We know from St Paul's Epistles, which tell of St Paul's first journey to Rome, that his journey took him from Syracuse to Rome via Reggio and Pozzuoli, which is only eight miles from Naples; and we know that this occurred at latest about A.D. 60. We cannot deduce with absolute certainty, from the mysterious square of letters found in the palaestra, the presence of Christians in Pompeii. But we may do so from this impression of the cross in the modest servant's room of a house which is extravagantly decorated with heathen frescoes. The riddle of the square of letters could just as well be something connected with the Jewish religion; but the cross hidden in the little oratory in Herculaneum points to the presence of secret adherents of the Christian teaching. Let us hope that future excavations will offer more valuable and clearer proofs of this.[1]

The most recent work in the Street of Abundance will soon reach the Gate looking towards the Sarno; this is one of the gates on the eastern side of the town which has not yet been excavated. For the rest, work is also being pushed southwards, and the palaestra next to the amphitheatre is being uncovered,[2] on the running-track and in the great swimming-pool of which many Pompeians were taking exercise at the time of the catastrophe. When the rain of lapilli began to fall they first fled to the surrounding arcades and stairways, then even to the latrines. Only when these began to collapse did they make for the only safe place, the open country. But many never reached it, having lost too much precious time by seeking shelter under the arcadings: skeletons were found heaped up everywhere, among them one huddled up under a stairway.

In Herculaneum the work goes on with the laying bare of charmingly furnished houses, which are often adorned with precious statues, for example one of a deer being brought down by dogs. Again and again one can see that there was greater wealth and a more brilliant development of culture in Herculaneum than existed in Pompeii.

Both scholars and workers have a passionate interest in those evidences of classical life, and this is the finest impulse to future success. It is not surprising, then, that the hope remains fresh that further treasures, perhaps of unheard-of splendour, will be found resting in the earth.

[1] On this point see Amedeo Maiuri's official reports on such discoveries in the *Atti dell'accademia Pontificia*, Matteo della Corte's essay on the "Lettered Cross", and the article by Guido della Valle in "L'enigma dei cristiani a Pompei, svelato da un criptogramma", in *L'Eco di Bergamo*, 29th September, 1937.

[2] In this connexion see Amedeo Maiuri's account of the sports grounds of Pompeii in the latest *Notizie degli Scavi*, 1939–40, and in "Campo sportivo a Pompeji" in *Sport fascista*, Milan, 1939.

SURVEY AND CONCLUSION

So in tracing the story of the resurrection of the towns once overwhelmed by Vesuvius we have reached our own time. Modern archaeology and the art of excavation have gained a powerful ally in the fantastic technical achievements of modern times. Air photographs taken from a great height enable the sites to be detected on which the most promising work can be done; powerful electric boring machines lighten the task of excavating even the hardest lava, and modern transport makes it possible for masses of earth to be quickly moved from one place to another.

If you fly over Pompeii today you can clearly see that about three-fifths of the town have now been exposed. The rest, and especially the district towards the sea, west[1] and north-west[2] of the amphitheatre, as well as a narrow section to the north just beside the line of wall connecting the Gate of Vesuvius with the Nolan Gate, still await excavation. In the course of the diggings there are constant surprises, which illumine the darkness of history and provide us with the most valuable information. We may continue to expect such surprises in the future, though somewhat less in Pompeii, for the unexcavated south-eastern part of the town, in the direction of the amphitheatre, does not seem to have been built up even inside the town wall, but seems to contain open spaces for sports and the like, which naturally promise a slenderer yield. The most important buildings have probably now been brought to light, only private houses and shops and the like await discovery in the part which has still to be investigated. And in general it must be remembered that expectations regarding the work in Pompeii must be moderated, because it was comparatively easy to salvage things there after the catastrophe, and we know that the inhabitants returned at once and carried away what their limited resources enabled them to move, which was nevertheless a great deal, including naturally the most valuable things.

[1] Regio II and I.   [2] Regio III and IX.

The site of everything in Pompeii which has not yet been excavated is now precisely established. Of the eight gates of the town three are still buried. The line of the walls between them is known. The precise line of the streets, even where they are not yet laid bare, is also established. The modern procedure of preserving all the buildings in the best way possible, and of carefully excavating from above, certainly makes the work advance more slowly, but it ensures that everything is brought to light in a less damaged condition than before.

The resurrection of the last two-fifths of Pompeii is therefore a matter of time and means, and it is certain that Italy will not rest satisfied until the whole town has been brought to light and one of the greatest of scientific achievements has thus been safely ended. Yet even when this work has been brought to a happy conclusion, there will still be a great deal left to do. For the suburbs and scattered villas and farms lying beyond the walls of Pompeii will still have to be investigated and excavated; they too were completely overwhelmed, and their position is naturally neither so clearly given nor so clearly visible as that of the buildings within the walls. This effort will certainly yield great surprises, and will provide inexhaustible material for the most interesting work by many future generations of archaeologists and excavators.

So much for Pompeii. In Herculaneum things are different. Here the electric boring-machines and the mechanical shovels, first used by Professor Maiuri, are of the greatest service, since they can attack the deep layer of petrified mud more easily than the simple pickaxe. The township of Resina, however, which lies above it, thickly populated as it is, is a serious obstacle. On the other hand we must remember that Resina consists mostly of poor houses and dwelling-places, which in due course will yield to social progress and the State's zealous care for the people's health. There is no doubt that the Italian Government, which has been able to solve quite different problems of opening up famous districts and of raising the standard of health in backward places, will also master this problem in a handsome way and so make it possible for Herculaneum to be uncovered. A quite exceptional prize is promised, for what the fleeing inhabitant was not able to snatch up hastily during the catastrophe and carry off with him, has remained where it was, firmly anchored by the hardening mud. Here, where the town lies beneath forty-five to sixty feet of strong, solid covering, no fugitive returning after the catastrophe was able to save anything. Everything remained in Herculaneum more or less untouched, and is lying in the unexplored sections of the town as it has always lain. It is therefore no accident that all the treasures of the Villa of the Papyri, for example, were found undisturbed and undamaged. If they had been buried under lapilli and ashes, as in Pompeii, the splendid bronzes and marbles, which have been found in such rich quantity and which today adorn the museum in Naples, would have been carried off and in the course of time would have disappeared.

On the other hand, the layer of stone is so hard that even that splendid villa, discovered in 1752, has not been completely investigated. A part of its dwelling-rooms has not been explored, for the building has not been wholly freed from its stone covering, but has been opened up beneath the present level of the ground. What has so far been excavated of Herculaneum is a much smaller part of the town than in the case of Pompeii. There is therefore an enormous area of work for the future, once a solution has been energetically sought for providing the inhabitants of Resina with some other accommodation, which will permit of free and unencumbered work.

But once Pompeii and Herculaneum, in their narrow limits, have been fully excavated, attention will have to be turned to other places. Then it will be essential to make a thorough examination of the many other villages and settlements which were swallowed up in A.D. 79 or during later eruptions of Vesuvius. The diggings already carried out have had significant results, especially from a scientific point of view. It is to these excavations, for instance, that we owe, beside other things, the knowledge of the close assimilation of the Roman to the Hellenistic way of life, and of the way in which the two cultures were complementary to one another. Many other goals are set for our investigation.

In earlier times people were content to study the works of art and the separate articles which came to light, but today a study is made of the whole economic and social life and

37. Group of dead in the house with the underground vault (cryptoporticus). In the foreground two women, the younger nestling in her death agony in the breast of the other, perhaps her mother. Plaster casts round skeletons. Reg. I, Ins. VI, No. 2.

(See page 203)

Photo: Anderson

38. Fresco in the House of the Mysteries. The Novice's Fear of Initiation.

(See pages 31, 52, 206)

activity of the two towns, which can be conjured up by means of the discoveries.

But it is not only artistic, historical and cultural knowledge which can be gained from these excavations. When all is said, it is man and his fate which is the most important and most interesting study. The particular attraction of Pompeii and Herculaneum is that they make it possible for us, almost two thousand years after the disaster, to see so vividly and movingly both the disaster itself and the terrible fate of the inhabitants, that we are moved to real sympathy with these people. In Pompeii especially those silent yet speaking traces of human destruction, the skeletons, are found scattered wherever digging has been carried out. About two thousand people in Pompeii succumbed, sinking down in the houses, in the vaults, on the streets and in the open spaces. Countless other fugitives must have met their death outside the town, on the roads leading towards the sea or to Naples, perishing in the rain of ashes.

In Herculaneum only very few skeletons have been found, at most twenty or thirty, most of the inhabitants having got safely away.

The remains of those who died in both towns, however, bring vividly before the visitor both the people who lived there and their terrible end. They give an impressive warning of the transitoriness of all earthly life and the equality of all living creatures in face of the power of nature.

But towering above everything is that mountain in its eternal majesty which has sown so much misfortune in the countryside around it, and is still a threat today. And when one faces the question whether all the wonderful evidence of classical culture should be left where it is found, or whether it would be advisable to remove it from the dangerous neighbourhood of the volcano, it is not possible to dismiss the thought that the day might come, as it came to earlier times, when an even more terrible eruption than that of A.D. 79 might once more bury everything that in centuries of toil and trouble has been wrested from the earth.

A SHORT LIST OF BOOKS

It is beyond the scope of this book to provide an exhaustive bibliography concerning the towns of Pompeii and Herculaneum. The following suggestions are intended only to help those who are specially interested to find the data they desire.

The book by Friedrich Furchheim, *Bibliografia di Pompei, Ercolano e Stabia* (Naples, 1891), contains a fairly complete list of the relevant works up to the date of its publication. The second edition of Mau's *Pompeji* (1913) in an appendix by F. Drexel, as well as Pauly's *Realenzyklopaedie*, article "Herculaneum" (the article "Pompeii" is in preparation), give full references.

Of modern literature the works of Amedeo Maiuri, the one-time leader of the excavations, must be mentioned, although there is no comprehensive bibliography of his writings. The studies and other publications of Matteo Della Corte are listed in an *Indice Generale* which appeared in Pompeii in 1933.

Further, mention must be made of the *Notizie degli scavi*, published in Naples and still appearing; of the reports of the German Archaeological Institute in Rome; and of the accounts of discoveries given in the *Archaeologischer Anzeiger*, a supplement to the *Jahrbuch des archaeologischen Instituts des Deutschen Reiches*.

The works of A. W. van Burens of the American Academy in Rome are very valuable, especially his *Companion to the Study of Pompeii and Herculaneum* (1938), which gives, along with a full and up-to-date bibliography, a very handy and valuable list of the references to the two towns in various classical texts, quoting the passages in the original. Finally, there are the excellent short guides by Maiuri, Ippel, Mau and Engelmann.

INDEX OF NAMES

INDEX OF SUBJECTS